Sports Law in Poland

Sports Law in Poland

Third Edition

Eligiusz Jerzy Krześniak

This book was originally published as a monograph in the International Encyclopaedia of Laws/Sports Law.

Founding Editor: Roger Blanpain
General Editor: Frank Hendrickx
Volume Editor: Michele Colucci

Wolters Kluwer

Published by:
Kluwer Law International B.V.
PO Box 316
2400 AH Alphen aan den Rijn
The Netherlands
E-mail: lrs-sales@wolterskluwer.com
Website: www.wolterskluwer.com/en/solutions/kluwerlawinternational

Sold and distributed by:
Wolters Kluwer Legal & Regulatory U.S.
920 Links Avenue
Landisville, PA 17538
United States of America
E-mail: customer.service@wolterskluwer.com

Printed on acid-free paper

ISBN 978-94-035-0637-1

e-Book: ISBN 978-94-035-0647-0
web-PDF: ISBN 978-94-035-0657-9

The Author

Eligiusz Jerzy Krześniak is a Professor of the Faculty of Law and Administration at Łazarski University in Warsaw, Poland where he holds the chair of Commercial Law Department, attorney-at-law, managing partner of the Polish Office of the global law firm, Squire Patton Boggs, arbitrator at the Court of Arbitration for Sport (CAS) in Lausanne, Switzerland and Qatar Sports Arbitration Tribunal in Doha, Qatar. A graduate of the University of Wrocław, Poland, he also studied at universities in Germany (Philipps-Universität in Marburg and Rheinische Friedrich-Wilhelms-Universität in Bonn) and the United States (the University of North Carolina at Charlotte).

Many of his papers on Polish, German and American commercial and sports law have been published in recognized journals, and he is the author and co-author of several legal monographs and books.

His experience includes acting in proceedings under the UNCITRAL, ICC, SCC, CAS, KIG and Lewiatan Rules, as well as in ad hoc arbitrations.

The author chairs the committee on discipline and rules at the Polish Golf Union and, until recently, was the chairman of the supervisory board of Alior Bank S.A., one of Poland's top ten banks listed on the stock exchange; in the past, he has also been deputy chairman of the supervisory board of Poland's largest bank, PKO BP and a member of the supervisory board of Poland's largest insurance company, PZU S.A. He has been recommended for years as a leading lawyer in Poland, including in the Chambers Europe and Legal 500 rankings.

He started his career as a radio journalist in Wrocław, Poland and a foreign correspondent in the United States and Germany.

The Author

Table of Contents

List of Abbreviations

Sources of Law

Act on Physical Culture of 1996	Act on Physical Culture of 29 September 1995 (Consolidated Text: Journal of Laws of 2007, No. 226, item 1675, as amended) – not applicable
AoQS	Act on Qualified Sport of 29 July 2005 (Journal of Laws, No. 155, item 1298, as amended)
AoS	Act on Sport of 25 June 2010 (Consolidated Text: Journal of Laws of 20220, item 11331599, as amended)
AoSSS	Act on the Social Security System of 13 October 1998 (Journal of Laws of 20221, item 4231009, as amended)
Constitution of the Republic of Poland	Constitution of the Republic of Poland of 2 April 1997 (Journal of Laws No. 78, item 483, as amended, corr. Journal of Laws of 2001, No. 28, item 319)
Copyright Law	Act on Copyright and Related Rights of 4 February 1994 (Consolidated Text: Journal of Laws of 202219, item 12312509, as amended)
CPC	Civil Procedures Code of 17 November 1964 (Consolidated Text: Journal of Laws of 20210, item 12751805, as amended)
Law on Associations	Law on Associations of 7 April 1989 (Consolidated Text: Journal of Laws of 2020, item 2261, as amended)
LC	Labour Code of 26 June 1974 (Consolidated Text: Journal of Laws of 20220, item 13201510, as amended)

List of Abbreviations

PCC	Polish Civil Code of 23 April 1964 (Consolidated Text: Journal of Laws of 20220, item 17401360, as amended)
TFEU	Treaty on the Functioning of the European Union (consolidated version OJ C 326 of 26/10/2012, p. 47)
Treaty of Lisbon	Treaty of Lisbon Amending the Treaty on European Union and the Treaty Establishing the European Community, signed at Lisbon on 13 December 2007 (Journal of Laws of 2009, No. 203, item 1569)
White Paper	White Paper on Sport of 11 July 2007, presented by the European Commission to the Council, the European Parliament, the Committee of the Regions and the European Economic and Social Committee, COM(2007) 391

Adjudicating Bodies

CAS	Court of Arbitration for Sport based in Lausanne
ECJ	European Court of Justice
IPC	International Paralympic Committee
OCCP	Urząd Ochrony Konkurencji i Konsumentów (Office of Competition and Consumer Protection)

FIFA	Fédération Internationale de Football Association (International Federation of Association Football)
IAAF	International Association of Athletics Federations
IOC	International Olympic Committee
NCAA	National Collegiate Athletic Association
POC	Polish Olympic Committee
PZHL	Polski Związek Hokeja na Lodzie (Polish Ice Hockey Association)
PZKosz	Polski Związek Koszykówki (Polish Basketball Association)
PZPN	Polski Związek Piłki Nożnej (Polish Football Association)

PZPS	Polski Związek Piłki Siatkowej (Polish Volleyball Association)
UEFA	Union of European Football Associations
WADA	World Anti-Doping Agency
WADC	World Anti-Doping Code

Legalis	System informacji prawnej Wydawnictwa C.H. Beck (C.H. Beck legal information system)
LEX	System informacji prawnej LEX (LEX legal information system)
NGB/NF	National Governing Body/National Federation (the organization considered to be the leading organization in the given sport in the spirit of the Olympic regulations)
OSA	Orzecznictwo Sądów Administracyjnych (Case Law of the Administrative Courts)
PiP	Państwo i Prawo
PPH	Przegląd Prawa Handlowego
PS	Przegląd Sądowy

List of Abbreviations

Acknowledgements

This work reflects the contributions of the legal academics based in Poland, who have contributed to all the published work I reviewed when preparing this monograph. I am grateful for their work.

I would like to thank Professor Józef Frąckowiak, Supreme Court Justice and Director of the Department of the Commercial and Business Law at the Faculty of Law, Administration and Economics of Wrocław University for his kind mentoring and academic support over the past twenty years. I would not have been a part of the academia any longer if not for his continuous encouragement.

I would also like to thank Wojciech Dmoch, Małgorzata Karbowiak and Hubert Bińkiewicz for their kind research support for parts of this monograph.

And, finally, many thanks to my beloved Joanna Bistram, whose love and support make everything I do possible and worth doing.

General Introduction

Chapter 1. General Background

1. The history of the development of the European legal doctrine and the legislation of the individual European countries with respect to sport is a history of difficult compromises. The need to maintain a balance between the typical features of sport, which include far-reaching autonomy and the actual (and sometimes legal) monopoly of a single organization in organizing sports matches and events and the need to ensure conditions allowing for competition without interference is very difficult. Various countries have coped with this in different ways. Given that sports issues are common, no country can escape from them – even the Vatican has established a special sports department.[1]

2. The models of sports governance appearing around the world have many common features. However, there are many differences in the details. Every country builds its structure of sports governance and organizes meetings in its own way. There are many reasons for the differences – legal tradition and local legal solutions, different visions of the development of sport, differences in views on such issues as the financing of sport, combating doping or the supervision of entities involved in sport. However, in principle, each of the models of sport regulation around the world can be assigned to one of the two groups – an interventionist model and a non-interventionist model.

3. The difference between these models of regulating sport lies in the level of intervention on the part of the State and the State authorities in sports activities. Some countries are of the opinion that far-reaching freedom and autonomy of sports associations (non-interventionist model) should be admissible. However, some believe that far-reaching State intervention is important and necessary, while the development and the administration of sport are regarded as remaining within the responsibilities of State administration (interventionist model). Therefore, the main dividing line lies in the legal method of regulating sport. However, the term 'interventionist' should not be construed as suggesting that this is about some regimes that resort to unethical methods, treating sport as a plane for demonstrating their political advantage. When some foreign authors write about the interventionist model of regulating sport, they still indicate that it is 'typical of totalitarian States

1. *See* B. Mielnik, 'Międzynarodowy Komitet Olimpijski' (in:) Sport w prawie europejskim współczesne wyzwania dla teorii i praktyki, ed. D. Kornobis-Romanowska, p. 229.

and those in which civil liberties are restricted',[2] which can be considered to be somewhat of an abuse. This is rather about the philosophy of action – whether we perceive sport to be an element of civic freedoms or rather as the role of the State.

4. The countries that apply an interventionist model are primarily the countries of Southern and Eastern Europe. In this model, sports organizations are licensed and largely financed from the State budget. It is assumed in the 'classic' interventionist model that the State has the right to regulate sport and apply disciplinary sanctions. This does not change the fact that all or some of these activities are actually performed by private entities – most frequently national or regional sports associations. However, the authority to act and the powers conferred on such entities depend on the State's consent (expressed, for instance, by the consent of the responsible minister for the given sports association) and can, under certain conditions, be withdrawn.[3]

5. Countries which apply the interventionist model take the view that it is possible to achieve uniform regulation, better supervision and a greater level of association of sports life with public opinion and the public in this kind of model. Such a system also prevents individual sports federations or bodies of these federations fighting among themselves, if only because consent cannot be obtained for the establishment of a new, competitive entity if a national association already exists in the given sports discipline. In this model, the State most frequently has an important element of control, namely financial support, which can only be withdrawn if the organization fails to meet certain requirements.[4]

6. A prime example of a country that has implemented an interventionist model of regulating sport is France.

7. In countries applying a non-interventionist approach, the rights of sports organizations do not arise from a mandate granted by the State and are not directly supported by the regulations. Their powers are based on voluntary compliance and a contract between them and their members. The uniform application of the sports rules and the assurance of compliance with them is achieved by actually bringing about the situation in which the members of the organizations and people related to them (sportspeople who are members of sports clubs, which are members of the given sports association) only participate in such competitions as are sanctioned by the given organization.

---

2. As in M. Schneider, *Sponsoring von Hochleistungssportlern unter rechtshistorischen und verfassungsrechtlichen Gesichtspunkten*, Frankfurt am Main 1998, pp. 43–44. The author also refers to an extensive study of legal issues of sport in Germany before the Second World War, including numerous dissertations on this subject in 1934–1939.
3. More in E.J. Krześniak, *Kluby i organizacje sportowe w prawie polskim na tle rozwiązań zagranicznych*, Warsaw 2016, pp. 72–78.
4. J. Taylor & J. Herbert, *Government Intervention in the Sports Sector*, in *Sport: Law and Practice* Ch. A1, 4–5 (Bloomsbury Professional, 2014).

8. Countries which have implemented this kind of model of regulating sport are most frequently lacking a separate legal act, which comprehensively regulates issues related to sport.

9. In turn, the countries that have implemented a non-interventionist model of regulating sport include the United Kingdom, Germany and Switzerland.

10. The Polish model of regulating sport is roughly halfway between the classical interventionist model of regulating sport and the non-interventionist model. In other words, the Polish model has a number of features that are typical of the interventionist model, but with strongly emphasized autonomy of sports organizations.

11. This monograph describes both the issues on how sport is organized in Poland and practical issues related to playing sports. The structure of this monograph itself is consistent with studies published earlier on sports law in other countries. It has been divided into four main thematic blocks (parts), in addition to the introduction, which are then divided into chapters.

12. The first is the introduction to the matter of sports law in Poland (General Introduction), which describes the sources of sports law and the specificity of sport.

13. The next part (Part I) has been devoted to a description of the organization of sport in Poland, broken down into issues related to the functioning of private and public sports-related institutions (Sports Governance), as well as regulations on sport as such (Public Regulation).

14. The next part (Part II) of the study has been devoted to a description of the issues related to labour regulations in sport (Sport and Employment).

15. The third part (Part III) addresses issues of doping in sport and the means that Poland uses to combat this doping.

16. Meanwhile, the last, fourth part (Part IV) addresses issues related to the broadly understood relationship between sports and commercial life (Sport and Commerce). This section describes, *inter alia*, issues related to the management of radio and television broadcasting rights to sporting events, sponsorship, sales of sports memorabilia (merchandising) and ownership of sports clubs.

17. The monograph ends with a bibliography and index.

Chapter 2. Sources of Sports Law

§1. Introduction

18. Poland is a country in which belief is the driving force of a statute or an act that changes public reality, despite the existence of a great deal of evidence that this argument is wrong, is still strong. It is no different in the case of sports. Therefore, the solution to the challenges arising in this area – and there were many, if only to mention the issues of doping or stadium security – is very often a change in the laws in the naïve belief that it is sufficient to change the laws to change the world. Obviously, this has not happened. As a result, further amendments were enacted after several years. Such an approach, combined with the conviction that the State has a dominant role in the process of organizing and managing sports, had to result in extensive legislation regulating the vast majority of sports-related issues.

19. At the same time, we all probably realize that European integration has left new tasks through contemporary civil law and, one of these is the introduction of private law from the national locality to universality.[5] While the final objective in the form of the full standardization of the supranational legal order and the modernization of national regulations in this spirit[6] appears to be too ambitious, at least for the time being, some form of standardization of national regulations and their approximation to each other in certain areas is a fact of life. The area of sport is certainly one of these. In practice, international sports federations, such as Fédération Internationale de Football Association (FIFA) and Fédération Internationale de Basketball (FIBA), operate as supranational organizations and are effectively seeking such supranationality.[7]

20. The role of international federations and the role of Polish sports associations, as well as the role played by the State administration in Poland are also undergoing an evolution.

21. A brief introduction should be presented before discussing the current state of Polish legislation in the area of sport.

5. P. Łochowski, *Uwagi o stosowaniu metody prawnoporównawczej w nauce prawa prywatnego na marginesie transmisji spadku w prawie polskim*, Palestra 2016, Nos 1–2, p. 93.
6. W. Dajczak, *Kodeks zobowiązań jako lekcja metody prawnoporównawczej*, KPP 2014, book 4, p. 846 quoted from P. Łochowski, *Uwagi o stosowaniu metody prawnoporównawczej ...* , p. 94.
7. G. Manssen talks about this, using the term 'anationality' (*Anationalität*). *See* G. Manssen, *Buchbesprechung von: Klaus Vieweg, Normsetzung und -anwendung deutscher und internationaler Verbände – Eine rechtstatsächliche und rechtliche Untersuchung unter besonderer Berücksichtigung der Sportverbände*, p. 121, http://epub.uni-regensburg.de/9349/1/ubr04075_ocr.pdf, accessed on 26 Sep. 2017. *See also* E.J. Krześniak, *Prawne mechanizmy zabezpieczenia realizacji zasady autonomii sportu na przykładzie struktury i sposobu funkcjonowania Międzynarodowej Federacji Piłki Nożnej (FIFA)*, PPH 2016, No. 2, pp. 12–21.

I. Until 1989

22. From the end of the Second World War until 1989, sport was seen as a tool for demonstrating a political advantage, and all legal regulations were subordinated to this objective.[8] A good example of this is that of sports grants under the Act on Physical Culture of 3 July 1984,[9] enabling the fiction that amateur sports are played universally to be upheld. Competition sports were treated by the political authorities as non-profit activities, as the existence of professional sport would stand in conflict with the socialist ideals. This led to the legal sanctioning of all sorts of fictional solutions, the most glaring manifestations of which were fictitious jobs of sportspeople allegedly working for enterprises. Professional sportspeople were treated as amateurs, and their salaries were not paid as salaries for sports, but, for example, for working in a coal mine, while their only contact with this 'place of work' was their monthly visit to the cash desk to collect their salaries.

23. Sports grants, which operated from 1981, were of a similar nature, de facto being compensation for playing sports, but not formally being of such a nature. This latter solution was even formally sanctioned by appropriate regulations. According to the regulations in force at that time, it was the sports clubs themselves that awarded the grants. The player was required to represent the club in exchange for a grant. After some resistance and hesitation, the contract itself on the representation of the club was accepted in the legal doctrine as a specific type of employment contract,[10] simultaneously indicating that it was not actually possible at all to strictly differentiate club membership from employment by the club. It was only after 1989, when Polish researchers were able to express themselves freely, that it was unequivocally acknowledged that the whole regulatory concept of acts on sports before 1989 was, in fact, a deception.[11]

24. Sport, just like any other area of social life, was also subject to far-reaching control by the authorities – hence the prohibition on making permanent transfers of football players abroad[12] or restrictions on the establishment of associations.

25. Nevertheless, this enactment of the Act on Physical Culture (3 July 1984) – even before the peaceful revolution and the transformation of the economic and political system in Poland in 1989 – gave rise to the modern regulations on organizing and playing sports. This act was based on two fundamental assumptions. First, sports were supposed to be played in physical culture associations and unions or other organizational units conducting sports activity. Second, the act accepted

---

8. More on the history of Polish legislation in sport in E.J. Krześniak, *Kluby i organizacje sportowe* ..., Warsaw 2016, pp. 247–287.
9. Journal of Laws No. 34, item 181, as amended.
10. *See* A. Kijowski, *Transfer w piłce nożnej w świetle polskiego prawa cywilnego i prawa pracy* (in:) A.J. Szwarc (ed.), *Prawne problemy transferu w piłce nożnej w Polsce i Republice Federalnej Niemiec*, Poznań 1991, p. 70.
11. A. Kijowski, *Status prawny sportowca zawodowego* (in:) A. Kijowski (ed.), *Problemy prawne sportu zawodowego*, Poznań 1995, pp. 29.
12. *See* A. Kijowski, *Transfer w piłce nożnej* ..., pp. 65–66.

that, in addition to regulating the organizational forms in which the sports are played, sportspeople should also be regulated, imposing certain obligations on them, including the prohibition to represent more than one club in one sport, the prohibition on the use drugs for doping or the obligation to wear the national colours.[13]

26. However, the Act on Physical Culture of 1984 did not define physical culture itself, and did not, in principle, differentiate between competitive sport, professional sport and amateur sport, accepting that professional sport does not exist in Poland.[14]

27. Therefore, the Act on Physical Culture of 1984 sanctioned the State monopoly and the few official associations accepted by the State in creating an organizational model of physical culture and sport.[15]

28. Sport became rapidly professionalized after the sociopolitical changes of 1989. Initially, this de facto happened outside the Act on Physical Culture of 1984.[16] Paradoxically, the mismatch between this legal act and the realities of professional sports helped the development of sport, because the provisions of this Act did not interfere.

29. Given that the Act on Physical Culture of 1984 did not reflect the realities of sport after the political and economic transformations, while developing professional sport was introduced into the framework provided for in the previous legal regime for amateur sport, work started on a new legal act comprehensively regulating sports-related matters.[17]

30. The first comprehensive Act regulating sports-related issues after the systemic transformations was the Act on Physical Culture enacted on 18 January 1996. This Act was much more complex than its predecessor. A clear demarcation was made for the first time between the rights and duties of State (government and local authority) administration, physical culture associations and other institutions operating in the area of sports. Regulations were introduced on professional sport, doping and the settlement of disputes in the area of sport. Matters related to the organizational structure of sport were regulated, as were the rights and duties of sportspeople, while rules were also added on sports safety. A new type of company was introduced, namely a joint-stock sports company, and new regulations were

13. *See also* A. Kijowski, *Transfer w piłce nożnej* ..., pp. 67–68.
14. Meanwhile, A. Wach, for instance, accepted that the Act on Physical Culture of 1984 was formulated so generally that it did not prevent professional sports from being played by Polish players (A. Wach, '*Transfer piłkarski w Polsce i jego regulacje w przepisach sportowych*' (in:) Prawne problemy transferu w piłce nożnej ..., ed. A.J. Szwarc, p. 16).
15. *See* A. Nowakowski, *Propozycje zmian modelu organizacyjnego kultury fizycznej w Polsce z 1981 roku. Kartka z najnowszych dziejów kultury fizycznej*, Prace Naukowe Wyższej Szkoły Pedagogicznej w Częstochowie. Kultura Fizyczna 2000, z. 3, p. 88.
16. The issue of professional sports also started to be widely discussed in the legal literature at that time. *See*, among others, A. Wach, *Transfer piłkarski w Polsce* ..., pp. 15–29 and A. Kijowski, *Transfer w piłce nożnej* ..., pp. 65–84.
17. *Prawne problemy sportu zawodowego*, Poznań 1995, ed. A. Kijowski, p. 9.

introduced in professional leagues. A new feature was the principle of requiring sports clubs taking part in professional competitions to obtain a concession to conduct activities; a similar concession was required for Polish Sports Federations (PSFs) to conduct business. The concessions were granted by the President of the Office of Physical Culture and Tourism (Articles 29 and 30 of the Act on Physical Culture of 1996).

31. A new institution was introduced into the Polish legal order during the validity of the Act on Physical Culture of 1996 – the Polish Sports Confederation (in 2002).[18] The Polish Sports Confederation was responsible for coordinating and co-funding the Olympic squad's preparations for its participation in the Olympic Games, as well as world and European Championships, financing sports grants for members of the Olympic squad and the national squad, participating in various programmes intended to combat doping and to ensure safety during sports events, initiating actions in support of international sports cooperation and preparing modernization and repair programmes for certain key sports facilities (Article 4 of the Act on the Polish Sports Confederation). The idea turned out to be a complete flop and the Polish Sports Confederation disappeared from the Polish legal order after just three years from its inception.

32. The Act on Physical Culture of 1996 consolidated the interventionist model of sports management for many years. Of the solutions that existed in France, Spain and Italy,[19] in principle, only those solutions which restricted the freedom of sports clubs to operate and simultaneously safeguarded the interests of sports associations and the public administration were accepted. However, solutions dominated by a liberal approach to sports matters from Germany and the UK were ignored.

33. Almost ten further years were needed to move away from a fully interventionist model of management and supervision of sports and to give sports clubs, associations and sportspeople greater freedom. This was done in 2005 by passing the Act on Qualified Sport (AoQS), whereby the concept of 'qualified sport' in principle encompassed sports activity organized and conducted by the PSFs.

34. The approach of the Polish lawmakers to sports matters was most fully expressed in the provision of Article 1, paragraph 2 of this Act, according to which sports organized under the aegis of the PSFs (which required the consent of the respective minister to be established) could be played in accordance with the provisions of the AoQS, the provisions of the statutes and regulations of the sports associations, PSFs and international sports organizations. This is not even about the rule itself, which is obvious, but the fact that the lawmakers considered it appropriate to raise it to the rank of a law. The principle of binding people and entities involved in organized sports with the rules and statutes of sports unions and international federations in countries with a non-interventionist model of sport (e.g., in Germany or the United Kingdom) arises from the autonomous, individual decision of these

18. Journal of Laws, No. 93, item 820, as amended.
19. *See* W. Sawicki et al., *Ustawa o kulturze fizycznej z komentarzem*, Kraków 1996, p. 7.

people and entities. Even if their choice is illusory – those who do not respect these regulations and statutes are not admitted to organized sports competitions – this is always the decision of these people and entities. Under the AoQS, the autonomy of the interested parties was replaced by an appropriate order of the Act.

35. The AoQS was in force for five years, from 1 September 2005 to 15 October 2010.

II. Current Legal Situation

36. Today, the legal act comprehensively governing matters of sport is the Act on Sport of 25 June 2010 (AoS).[20]

37. The provisions of the AoS are based on the assumption that sport is an area of civic rights and liberties. Since this is the case, the State should not, in principle, interfere at all in sports organized by entities other than the PSFs or entities acting under their authority. However, in the case of sports organized by the latter entities, the State should interfere only to the extent necessary, whereby, obviously, the views as to what is necessary and what is excessive can differ according to who is asked.[21] Even so, the number of provisions governing sport has been significantly reduced, which, in practice, has meant the liberalization and the release of the area of sport from the onus of excessively restrictive and detailed regulation.

38. Many further changes were also of a liberalizing nature. For example, the withdrawal by the appropriate minister from defining the list of disciplines in which PSFs can operate[22] and the withdrawal from the introduction of a legal division into amateur and professional sports can be mentioned here.

39. The generally liberalizing direction of statutory changes was not preserved in the subsequent years. The revisions of 2015 and 2017 rather headed in the opposite direction, increasing the range of matters that are subject to statutory regulation and increasing the supervision of the Minister of Sport over Polish sports and the organizations that are active in it.

40. The AoS obviously does not exhaust the statutory matter that is applicable to sport, to which many other regulations apply. In sport, probably as in no other

20. Consolidated text: Journal of Laws of 20220, item 1599133, as amended.
21. A. Giersz, *Cele i założenia* ..., pp. 13–14.
22. As A. Giersz wrote, this generated problems with the creation of new associations (A. Giersz, *Cele i założenia ustawy o sporcie* (in:) A.J. Szwarc (ed.), *Ustawa o sporcie* ..., p. 15). However, I would raise a major objection to this regulation – in my opinion the principle, which was introduced, that Polish sports federations can only operate in sports in which international organizations are recognized by the International Olympic Committee (IOC), can give rise to concerns of a constitutional nature. I shall discuss this further later in this monograph.

area of life, the matter of civil law, including company law, regulations on associations and the matter of administrative law and criminal law are constantly intermingling. The AoS itself refers to parts of other regulations. Some of them must be applicable because of the subject matter itself that is subject to regulation. A few examples:

(1) the organizational structure and the method of functioning of sports associations is determined by the provisions of the Law on Associations;
(2) the organizational structure of many clubs is subject to the Code of Commercial Companies of 15 September 2000;[23]
(3) relationships between the sports club and the players are based on the Labour Code of 26 June 1974[24] (LC) (if there was an employee relationship) or the Civil Code of 23 April 1964[25] (reference to the application of the provisions of the personal service contracts in the case of contracts on the provision of services, Article 750 PCC);
(4) the liability of the organizer of the sporting event for damage caused during the course of that event may be subject to the Act on the Safety and Security of mass events of 20 March 2009;[26]
(5) water sports may be played with the observance of the provisions of the Act on the Safety of People in Aquatic Areas of 18 August 2011;[27]
(6) while playing and organizing winter sports, the provisions of the Act on Safety and Rescue in the Mountains and on Organized Ski Areas of 15 July 2011[28] must be observed;
(7) control over PSFs by the Minister of Sport in the procedure of Articles 16 AoS et seq., is subject to the framework laid down in the Act on Control by the Government Administration of 15 July 2011.[29]

41. A very important piece of legislation is also the Act on Combating Doping in Sport of 21 April 2017 (Consolidated text: Journal of Laws of 202219, item 18721258, as amended).

42. Attention should also be drawn to the Sports Development Programme up to 2020 that was adopted by the Polish Government.[30]

43. The regulations of European law obviously constitute a part of the Polish legal order.

44. In the case of sports, the analysis of only the generally applicable legal regulations is insufficient – this area of life is largely subject to self-regulation. In the

23. Consolidated text: Journal of Laws of 20220, item 15261467, as amended.
24. Consolidated text: Journal of Laws of 20220, item 13201510, as amended.
25. Consolidated text: Journal of Laws of 20220, item 17401360, as amended.
26. Consolidated text: Journal of Laws of 202219, item 21711466, as amended.
27. Consolidated text: Journal of Laws of 20220, item 350147, as amended.
28. Consolidated text: Journal of Laws of 202219, item 10841425, as amended.
29. Consolidated text: Journal of Laws of 202219, item 18721258, as amended.
30. Regulation of the Council of Ministers of 31 Aug. 2015 (M.P. item 989).

justification of one of the bills on sport, the Polish lawmakers even use the term that 'a significant proportion of activity in … sport takes place outside the sphere of legal regulation'.[31] However, this term itself can be considered to be wrong, as every sphere of human activity remains within the sphere of legal regulation in one way or another. However, this quote shows the essence of things: the sports world is trying to govern on its own and, de facto, ignore the existence of separate national legal orders. The author, who does not accept this, will move around in the ideal and not the real world, and this should not be the objective of any research and studies.

45. Therefore, the list of sources of laws governing sports issues will not be complete without indicating the statutes and rules of the PSFs, international sports federations and arbitration courts that are active in the settlement of disputes in sport. None of these regulations are, of course, the law in the strict sense of this word, although, this does not change the fact that the resolution of all situations in which there is or could be a conflict between the sports rules adopted by the sports associations and unions, as well as by international private organizations, and the generally applicable provisions of the law are not as obvious as would appear to lawyers who do not deal with sports law day to day. The simple answer is that the appropriate law always takes precedence, but while it may be legally correct it may be actually incorrect.

31. Such a formulation appears in the justification to the bill on sport, Sejm of the sixth term of office, parliamentary form No. 2374. I consider this to be a logical error. No sphere of life, including sport, remains outside the sphere of legal regulation. The German legal doctrine considers it completely obvious that sport never happens 'outside the sphere of legal regulation'. K. Vieweg specifies directly – 'Sport today is not an area that is free of the law' ('*Der Sport ist heute kein reschtsfreier mehr Raum*') (K. Vieweg, Faszination *Sportrecht*, p. 79, university study (legal status as at 1 Sep. 2015) only available online via the website of the Institute of Law and Technology at the University of Erlangen-Nuremberg (*Institut für Recht und Technik, Friedrich-Alexander Universität Erlangen-Nürnberg*), http://www.irut.de/Forschung/Veroeffentlichungen/OnlineVersionFaszinationSportrecht/FaszinationSportrecht.pdf, accessed on 30 May 2016).

Chapter 3. Specificity of Sport

§1. Statutory Definition of Sport

46. The Polish lawmakers consistently stick to the statutory definition of the notion of sport. According to Article 2 AoS, sport is all forms of physical activity which, through ad hoc participation or organization, contribute to the development or improvement of the physical and mental conditions, the development of social relations or the achievement of sports results at all levels. With such a definition, it is difficult to find any physical activity, which would not meet the statutory qualification of sport.[32] Theoretically, jointly picking fruit from a tree could also be classified as sport – because there is an element of ad hoc participation, while the requirement of contributing to an improvement of the condition is also satisfied. In short, Polish law has a definition of sport, although it is completely unnecessary.

§2. Contradiction of the Non-legal Sports Regulations with the Legal Regulations as an Example of a Specificity of Sport

47. Of the many different aspects that could indicate the specificity of sport, one should be mentioned as a key issue.

48. In every situation where a complex set of norms exist, having been laid down by various authorities and encompassing different circumstances, but simultaneously related to each other, this may lead to non-compliance of certain norms with others. This is all the more likely when some norms are from private entities, some from international treaties (supported most frequently then by extensive case law), and the remainder are a part of the legal order of the given State. There are too many different interests and too many different points of view, to ensure full consistency between all these norms.

49. Sport is the best illustration of this argument. Equally, the Polish lawmakers, the world sports federations, PSFs, as well as the European lawmakers have their own ideas on how the management and organization of sport should look. The Polish lawmakers expressed this by enacting the AoS and the earlier acts regulating sports issues. The European Union (EU) regulations on sports are far more frugal and fundamentally limited to Article 165 TFEU, which contains the principle of the promotion of sport by the EU. However, the case law of the European Court of Justice (ECJ) contains many groundbreaking judgments, which have left their mark on the face of contemporary sport. The 'lawmaking' activity of the world sports federations is even greater than that of the Polish lawmakers. Likewise, PSFs, which specify the manner of conduct under the norms of international sports federations, are the actual lawmakers in the area of sport, under the same law that grants PSFs

32. S. Fundowicz, *Prawo sportowe*, p. 19.

the exclusive right to establish and implement sports, organizational and disciplinary rules in sporting competitions organized by the association.

50. The legal doctrine has developed many methods of dealing with possible inconsistencies of the standards within the wider system. Every student of law knows the rules of *lex posterior derogat legi priori, lex specialis derogat legi generali* and several others. The principle appears to be so obvious that the provisions of the universally binding law take precedence over non-legal norms, for instance, the provisions of the secondary regulations, which are applicable in a specific organization or environment. However, in the realities of contemporary sport, these rules are proving to be insufficient.

51. The specificity of sports law involves, *inter alia*, the fact that, such conflicts are almost par for the course, as perhaps in no other discipline of law. In addition, the actual power and driving force of international sports federations means that the settlement of conflicts of this kind is much more difficult than it might seem at first glance.

§3. Is Sports Law an Independent Legal Discipline, a Branch or Division of Law?

52. Opinions on the distinctness of sports law are divided in Poland. Some authors consider sports law to be a separate field of law.[33] In turn, others believe that such a separation is unreasonable.[34]

53. Unlike in such countries as Germany, the United Kingdom or the United States, Poland has a comprehensive legal act regulating issues related to sport. However, the lack of comprehensive legislation has not become an obstacle to recognizing the distinctness of sports law in studies of the laws in the countries mentioned above. In Germany, the independence of sports law (*Sportrecht*) has been widely accepted since the 1970s.[35] Likewise, in the United States and the United Kingdom, sports law is treated as being fully independent.

---

33. K. Sondel, *Prawo o stowarzyszeniach i związkach sportowych w Drugiej Rzeczpospolitej, Czasopismo Praw-no-Historyczne 2004*, nr 2, p. 66; H. Radke, '*Sport i prawo – jakie regulacje, jaki zakres*?', *Sport Wyczynowy* 2007, Nos 7–8, pp. 511–513; Z. Brodecki, B. Rischka-Słowik, *Jaki świat, takie igrzyska*, GSP 2011, vol. 26, pp. 79–92.
34. *See* F. Zedler, *Postępowanie polubowne polubowne w sporcie* (in:) A.J. Szwarc (ed.) *Ustawa o sporcie*, p. 47. Similarly, A. Kijowski, *Stosunki prawne sportowców ...*, p. 53.
35. Such a moment is given by N. Korff, *Sportrecht*, p. 1. Likewise, K. Vieweg states that the beginning of the 'successive coverage of sport with legal regulations' and its related independence of sports law (*Sportrecht*) is the moment of the outbreak of the scandal related to buying matches by players from the football Bundesliga, the so-called *Bundesligaskandal* from the early 1970s. *See* K. Vieweg, '*Teilnahmerechte und -pflichten der Vereine und Verbände*' (in:) Teilnahme am Sport als Rechtsproblem. Teilnahme am Sport als Rechtsproblem. Verbands-, vereins- und deliktsrechtlichen Probleme ed. E. Deutsch, Heidelberg 1993, pp. 23–49. This period of the evolution of sports law in Germany is also presented more extensively by H. Hilpert, *Sportrecht und Sportrechtsprechung im In- und Ausland*, Berlin 2007, pp. 209–220.

54. There are strong arguments in favour of treating sports law as a separate branch of the law, all the more so in the Polish legal order.

§4. EU Principle of Free Movement and Sport

55. One of the tasks of the EU is to create a common market. The ECJ[36] defines this requirement as removing all obstacles preventing common business trading, so that one common European market arises in place of individual national markets. The requirement to ensure the free movement of people, goods and services within the common economic area arises from such an accepted policy.[37]

56. The achievement of this objective is not only possible through legal means, but also through internal, 'private' rules. In this context, the activities of international sports federations frequently seem to implement this idea to a fuller extent than the European lawmakers manage to do. The objectives of the international sports federations are consistent with what the European lawmakers want to achieve. The objective of sports norms is for a certain number of people and other entities from various countries to respect the same rules thereby allowing sports competition. Therefore, for example, the rules laid down by sports associations have the objective of enabling players from various countries to change clubs or cause all sportspeople, regardless of their country, to observe the same anti-doping rules.[38]

57. At the same time, however, in the past, the international sports federations have sought to provide a 'national' character if only to league matches in the individual countries through the introduction of restrictions on the number of foreigners who can be employed by the sports clubs. This principle, if read literally, seemed to breach the principle of the free movement of people and services within the framework of the common economic area. However, while there is no doubt that all national lawmakers in this area are obliged to respect the fundamental rights and freedoms to which all citizens of countries within the European area are entitled, it was appropriate to ask whether the same requirement can be formulated with respect to the private 'legislators', namely sports associations and international sports federations. In other words, whether the same requirement applies in the relationship between the sportsperson and the sports associations.[39]

58. In the judgment of the Court of Justice of 12 December 1974 in *B.N.O. Walrave and L.J.N. Koch v. Association Union cycliste internationale*, Koninklijke

36. In the legal situation before the Lisbon Treaty entered into force, it was colloquially called the European Court of Justice. Hereafter in this monograph, I shall use the term ECJ (with respect to judgments issued before the Treaty of Lisbon entered into force) and the Court of Justice of the European Union (in the post-Lisbon context).
37. Cf. E.J. Krześniak, *Kluby i organizacje sportowe* ... ., Warsaw 2016, p. 58.
38. Haas, Martens, *Sportrecht*, p. 84.
39. Cf. E.J. Krześniak, *Kluby i organizacje sportowe* ... , Warsaw 2016, pp. 58–59.

Nederlandsche Wielren Unie et Federación Española Ciclismo[40] and in the judgments of 14 July 1976 in *Gaetano Donà v. Mario Mantero*[41] and, primarily, in *Union royale belge des sociétés de football association ASBL v. Jean-Marc Bosman* of 15 December 1995[42] and several other judgments (*Christelle Deliège v. Ligue Francophone de Judo et Disciplines Associées ASBL*, Ligue Belge de Judo ASBL, Union Européenne de Judo (C-51/96) and François Pacquée (C-191/97) of 11 April 2000,[43] in *Jyri Lehtonen and Castors Canada Dry Namur-Braine ASBL v. Federation Royale Belge des Societes de Basket-Ball ASBL* of 13 April 2000[44] and in *Igor Simutenkov v. Ministerio de Educación y Cultura and Real Federación Española de Fútbol* of 12 April 2005),[45] the ECJ accepted that the principles arising from the European treaties must also be implemented by the norms established by the sports associations. Therefore, the ECJ held that the scope of application of Treaty freedoms in the world of sports is not only restricted to the activities of public authority, but also includes the activities of sports federations (namely private organizations). Based on all these judgments, it can be unequivocally concluded that the principles of European law on free trade also apply to all domestic and international federations within the EU.[46]

59. From the practical side, the requirement to ensure freedom of movement affects the whole spectrum of issues of importance in sport. Here, such issues can be mentioned as, for example, the rules on the transfer of players, the principles of applying so-called transfer windows, the rules on the prohibition of one person or one entity from holding shares in more than one club,[47] the prohibition of third-party ownership and the principles of selecting players for national teams.

60. However, it should be remembered that an attempt to introduce the principles of a free market as a whole into European sports could lead to bad results. The autonomy of sports associations and federations is protected in different ways by the legislature of the different countries, but, in principle, this is universal protection throughout Europe. For this reason, account should always be taken of both sides of the same coin – on the one hand, the rights protected by European norms and, on the other, the rights of sports associations and the sportspeople themselves. However, the difference between control of compliance of the norms of international sports federations, with a general 'European legal order', and control of the

40. C 36/74, ECR 1974, p. 1405.
41. C 13/76, ECR 1976, p. 1333.
42. C-415/93, ECR 1995, p. I-04921.
43. ECR 2000, p. I-02549.
44. C-176/96, ECR 2000, p. I-02681.
45. C-265/03, ECR 2005, p. I-02579.
46. The doctrine of European law also devotes some space to the possibility of enjoying the benefits arising from the treaties by people from third countries (which are not members of the European Union) in the context of sport: B. Kennelly & R. Richards, *EU Free Movement Rules and Sport*, in *Sport: Law and Practice* Ch. F3, 1257–1260 (Bloomsbury Professional, 2014).
47. This is important from the point of view of fair sports competition (two clubs controlled by one owner could, for example, arrange the result of meetings between them and, therefore, interfere with league matches). Consequently, this principle has a fundamental sports justification, but, from the point of view of the principles of competition law, it can give rise to doubt.

compliance of these norms with the national legal order is that the main motive of the ECJ, when analysing these sometimes conflicting interests, is not so much the structural disequilibrium between the sports associations and the sportsperson, but rather the fact that sports associations and international sports federations operate as 'substitutes of the lawmakers', and therefore may be subject, in principle, to similar controls as national lawmakers.[48]

61. The Treaty of Lisbon (TE)[49] introduced Article 165 into the Treaty on the Functioning of the European Union[50] (TFEU) stating that 'The Union shall contribute to the promotion of European sporting issues, while taking account of the specific nature of sport, its structures based on voluntary activity and its social and educational function.' However, in accordance with Article 165(2) and (3) TFEU, Union action shall be aimed at developing the European dimension in sports, by promoting fairness and openness in sporting competitions and cooperation between bodies responsible for sports, and by protecting the physical and moral integrity of sportsmen and sportswomen, especially the youngest sportsmen and sportswomen.

62. Therefore, sport was listed as one of the areas in which the EU has supporting, coordinating and supplementing powers.

63. Given the laconic nature of the Treaty regulation cited above, a key document, in which the position of the EU and its bodies with respect to sport is expressed, is, to this day, the White Paper on Sport of 11 July 2007, presented by the European Commission to the Council, the European Parliament, the Committee of the Regions and the European Economic and Social Committee.[51]

64. In addition, on 12 December 2008, the European Council adopted a Declaration on Sport, which acknowledged both the values that sport brings and the specificity of sport.

65. All the above legal acts either directly constitute a part of the Polish legal order or have an influence on that legal order.

66. In the White Paper, the European Commission acknowledged that any attempts to define a unified model of sports organization in Europe have no chance of success. The European Commission also acknowledged that the organization of sport is primarily a responsibility of the authorities of the federations and sports

---

48. Cf. under the German legal doctrine, Haas, Martens, *Sportrecht*, pp. 86–87. *See also* E.J. Krześniak, *Kluby i organizacje sportowe ...* , Warsaw 2016, pp. 64–65.
49. The Treaty of Lisbon amending the Treaty on European Union and the Treaty establishing the European Community, signed on 13 Dec. 2007, which entered into force on 1 Dec. 2009 (Journal of laws of 2009, No. 203, item 1569).
50. Consolidated version, Official Journal of the EC C 326 of 26/10/2012, p. 47.
51. COM (2007) 391, https://d1dmfej9n5lgmh.cloudfront.net/msport/files/Downloads/20130103151557/BIALA_KSIEGA_NA_TEMAT_SPORTU.pdf?1357226159, accessed on 3 Jun. 2016. For more on the White Paper in the Polish literature, *see Sport w prawie europejskim. Współczesne wyzwania dla teorii i praktyki*, ed. D. Kornobis-Romanowska.

associations and, to some extent, Member States and other entities.[52] The European Commission also concluded that the most contentious and difficult issues related to the organization of sport and sports competitions may be appropriately resolved in the internal regulations of the sports federations and associations, assuming that the provisions of European law are respected, and the fact that the European Commission itself is ready to intervene, if necessary, is taken into account.

§5. European Regulatory Model of Sport

67. The principle referred to as the 'European regulatory model of sport' is applicable in many countries of the world in sport.

68. The term 'European model of sport' means a system of organization in sport, which is based on the model of a pyramid, on the basis of which sport is organized in the EU Member States.[53] The base of the pyramid is made up of the clubs offering membership to all potentially interested parties. At the next level, there are regional associations, the members of which are mostly clubs. The next level contains the national federations (NFs), one for each discipline. Most frequently, all regional associations are members of a NF. National federations govern all general issues that apply to the given sport, and simultaneously represent the given country in the European or international structures. They also organize national championships and are regulatory bodies. The European federations, which are organized along similar lines to the NFs, are at the peak of the pyramid. Every European federation allows for membership of only one NF of the given country. International organizations guard their position through rules prohibiting, among others, involvement in championships organized by unrecognized organizations, as well as imposing sanctions for a breach of this prohibition.

69. The above description is, in principle, correct and still current, with one correction – in contrast with the European Commission's assumptions, the peak of the pyramid has not so much European federations, but international federations. This is because each of these European federations is a member of an international federation that governs the given sport.

70. Therefore, the principle of 'one sport, one organization' is about the rule that every sport in a given country is represented by only one organization. Such an organization most frequently operates in the form of an entity with legal personality. This structure is also based on one international federation governing and overseeing the given sport at an international level. Without these two organizational

52. *See* B. Kennelly & T. Richards, *European Union Sports Policy,* in *Sport: Law and Practice* Ch. F1, 1117 (Bloomsbury Professional, 2014).
53. *The European Model of Sport*, November 1998, consultation document of the European Commission (DG10).

principles, the whole system would have no raison d'être. Therefore, the statutes of international sports federations contain rules that assure compliance with this policy.[54]

71. The integrity of this system can only be assured when the contestants (sportspeople) of matches only appear in such sports events that are sanctioned by the NFs and played according to the rules accepted by that organization. Sportspeople have the opportunity to participate in international and national sports competitions, only when they accept the principle described above.

72. This structure has a clear statutory legitimacy in Poland. Therefore, in contrast with certain other countries, the admissibility of this kind of monopolistic structure does not give rise to doubt and has not been assessed by the courts.

73. Another rule enabling the functioning of the pyramid system is also the principle that the disciplinary sanctions imposed by one national organization automatically apply to all other organizations in the world, or that the international federation will have the right to extend the sanctions to encompass the whole world. This applies to the avoidance of the situation in which, for example, a sportsperson receives a penalty of disqualification for doping and is able to circumvent this penalty by entering tournaments organized by other national organizations. A situation in which an international organization may extend a ban to encompass other countries may, in practice, give rise to problems of interpretation in all situations where sanctions imposed by the given national organization do not satisfy the requirements to be met by such sanctions in another country, if these requirements in that other country arise directly from the provisions of national law.

74. This fundamental structure, which is based on the principle of a pyramid, coexists with a flat structure, in which the Olympic movement is organized. A key role in this structure is played by the International Olympic Committee (IOC). However, the IOC itself plays an important role in assuring the durability of the European regulatory model of sport. It does this through the recognition of only one international federation for each sport and the acceptance that only this one international federation has the exclusive powers and responsibility to manage that sport.[55] The Olympic Charter and the secondary regulations to the Olympic Charter also prejudge that national Olympic committees (in Poland, this will be the Polish Olympic Committee (POC)) recognize only one NF for each sport (the NF that is a member of the international federation recognized by the IOC) and choose the participants of the Olympic Games only from the sportspeople who are nominated by precisely that NF.[56]

---

54. Examples of the statutes of various organizations are given by J. Taylor & J. Herbert, *Government Intervention in the Sports Sector,* in *Sport: Law and Practice* Ch. A1, 5–6 (Bloomsbury Professional, 2014).
55. Rule 26.1 of the Olympic Charter.
56. Paragraph 1.2 of the rules of the Olympic Charter, rules 27 and 28 of the Olympic Charter.

75. Of course the system described above is not the only one. Even in Europe, in some sports, the system admitting entry into competitions is just as closed as that which applies to professional leagues in the United States and differs from the system in force in other sports. An example would even be cycling.

§6. Introductory Comments on the Polish Regulatory Model of Sport

76. The Polish system of managing and organizing sports in Poland is described in the professional literature as interventionist, centralized, unconsolidated and bureaucratic.[57] At the statutory level, this model is a complex regulation of sports-related issues and extensive supervisory and control powers of the bodies of public administration. Another characteristic feature of the Polish regulatory model of sport is the statutorily guaranteed monopoly (in specified areas) for PSFs and the actual transfer of some of the key responsibilities in the area of sport to the hands of private foreign entities – international sports federations, without the approval of which no PSF can be established.[58]

77. The premises for choosing such a regulatory model of sport are not entirely clear. Numerous changes in the laws indicate some inconsistency of the legislature. Basing the system of financing sports activities on funding from the public sector is a factor that largely determines the shape of the Polish model of sports.

78. The Polish sports system is also described as unconsolidated, because Poland has no single non-governmental organization consolidating the sports movement. The power is actually concentrated in the hands of the State because the main decision-maker is the minister for issues of physical education (currently the Minister of Culture, National Heritage and Sport, hereinafter: the Minister of Sport).

57. J. Żyśko, *Zmiany we współczesnych systemach zarządzania sportem wyczynowym w wybranych krajach europejskich*, Warsaw 2008, p. 115.
58. Cf. E.J. Krześniak, *Kluby i organizacje sportowe ...*, p. 102.

Part I. Organization of Sport

Chapter 1. Sports Governance

§1. Governmental Institutions and Bodies

79. The structure of Polish sport is based on the so-called State/social model, which means that two main sectors coexist and cooperate in it: the public sector (sector of public organizations) and the non-governmental sector (sector of non-governmental organizations, the so-called non-profit organizations). Both these sectors are based on a three-tier structure in which individual entities operate at national, regional and local levels. The interdependencies between them are based on statutory, hierarchical and functional ties.[59]

80. Therefore, Polish sport has many entities in a variety of forms. However, there is no single criterion that would enable a clear and transparent division of these entities into categories. A division into two very basic subgroups is possible. One is that of public law entities. The following entities can be mentioned:

(1) the minister responsible for physical culture;
(2) the minister responsible for national defence and the minister responsible for internal affairs (regarding sport in the organizational units of the services for which these ministers are responsible or which are supervised by them);
(3) the minister responsible for health matters (regarding the problem of financing the costs of medical care for players who qualify for the national squad in Olympic and Paralympic sports);
(4) the heads of counties (starosts);[60]
(5) the Polish Anti-Doping Agency;

59. Cf. E.J. Krześniak, *Kluby i organizacje sportowe* …, pp. 102–103.
60. Because of the supervision over associations (Art. 8, para. 5, item 2 of the Act on Associations). *See also* Art. 4, para. 4 in connection with Art. 4, para. 7 of the AoS. In practice, the people directly supervising sports clubs in the major cities are the directors of units most frequently referred to as the office of sport and recreation. *See, inter alia*, the information available at the website of the Office of the City of Warsaw: http://sportowa.warszawa.pl/kontakt.

(6) the Institute of Sport in Warsaw, which is an independent scientific institution;[61]
(7) the Foundation for the Development of the Education System established by the State Treasury (to the extent to which the minister responsible for physical fitness commissions tasks to it on physical culture within the framework of EU programmes);[62]
(8) the Central Sports Medicine Centre;
(9) PL.2012+ sp. z o.o. which manages the National Stadium in Warsaw;
(10) a special State budget institution, namely the Central Sports Centre;[63]
(11) sports councils operating within local authorities.[64]

81. Put briefly, it can be concluded that the public sector in Polish sport is divided into two subsectors. The first includes the central State administration and its field bodies, including the central government authority for sport (the Minister of Sport), together with his subordinate and supervised units. The second is the local authority subsector, consisting of local authorities and their subordinated regional sports and recreation centres, as well as the sports and recreational centres which are frequently under their municipal management.

82. In certain cases, public higher physical education institutions and the Sports and Tourism Museum are also included in this sector.[65]

83. The tasks of the organization representing this sector have been defined directly in the AoS. In turn, the objectives that these units pursue are set in strategies and operational programmes, while the priorities include the development of competition sports, as well as youth, disabled and universal sports, and the development of the sports infrastructure.

84. However, the local authority structures are responsible for creating the conditions for playing universal sports (as a part of their own tasks); local authorities are actually responsible for financing youth sports at regional and club levels. Affluent local authorities can afford to build and maintain a sports infrastructure and support professional sport.

---

61. The Institute of Sport was established by order of the Chairman of the Council of Ministers No. 60 of 4 Nov. 1977 and operates as a research and development unit, which has been entered into the National Court Register. For more about the Institute, *see* W. Cajsel, *Ustawa o sporcie*. Komentarz, Warsaw 2011, pp. 367–369.
62. *See* Art. 29a AoS.
63. *See* Art. 29, para. 1a AoS.
64. They mainly have an advisory role. Postulates have been reported in the legal doctrine to withdraw from the sports councils as they do not have authoritative powers and, for this reason, are unnecessary. Ultimately, for pragmatic reasons, it was accepted that the existence of the sports councils at the local authorities are harmless and can contribute to a greater interest of local communities in matters of local sports. *See* Art. 30 AoS.
65. J. Żyśko, *Zmiany we współczesnych systemach* … , pp. 119–120; B. Chełmecki, *Rola menadżera Rola menadżera w polskim związku sportowym a jego przygotowanie zawodowe*, pp. 50–51.

85. This second group consists of private law entities. These include:

(1) sports clubs;
(2) sports associations;
(3) PSFs;
(4) POC; and
(5) the Polish Paralympic Committee.

86. They will be discussed further in the following points.

87. At this point, it should be mentioned that sport is one of the few areas of life in which it has been possible to achieve far-reaching harmonization of the solutions that have been adopted. Sport is inherently related to international rivalry. Many clubs and all PSFs participate in one way or another in this rivalry and operate within a broader international system of modern sport, in which a leading role is played by international sports federations. In practice, the latter, working most frequently as registered Swiss law associations, control a large proportion of modern sport. They also impose specific legal solutions that are then implemented in practice on the basis of the legislation of individual countries, as well as applying their own internal standards, which, despite not being the law in the strict sense, have a similar role.

88. Sports organizations have a role that is not only quasi-legislative but also purely executive – they administer the acceptance and application of, as well as compliance with, the rules and impose sanctions, as well as awarding rights to participate in sports competitions. International sports federations can sometimes be directly compared to national governments. In one of its judgments the Lausanne Court of Arbitration for Sport (CAS) referred to the analogy between the authorities of the sports federations and government authorities, indicating the similarities of the roles and functions of these bodies in regulatory, administrative and sanctioning terms (Judgment in *AEK Athens v. UEFA*, CAS 98/200, of 20 August 1998).

89. Therefore, with regard to the legal regulations on sport, norms coexist which some authors in the British legal doctrine refer to as international sports law and global sports law. Ken Foster, who makes such a distinction, uses the term 'international sports law' to describe the legal norms that can be applied by the national courts and refers to global sports law in the context of the norms from international sports federations, which may sometimes be in conflict with those norms of the generally applicable law that apply to sport.

90. Therefore, there is no way of understanding sports law by looking at it purely from the point of view of national legal solutions. Any analysis of the solutions in this area should always be conducted with account taken of the wider European and international context. It should be no different when talking about key entities involved in sport in Poland.

91. Many decisions of public authorities regarding individual cases cannot be ignored when analysing the legal issues related to sport. These are decisions of the supervisory authorities – the Minister of Sport, the registration and supervisory authorities of associations, the body supervising the POC, the Office of Competition and Consumer Protection (Urząd Ochrony Konkurencji i Konsumentów, OCCP) and the European Commission.

§2. National Olympic Committee

92. The legal grounds for the functioning of the POC are contained in Articles 24 and 25 AoS. POC was defined in the AoS as a federation. POC associates four different categories: PSFs (National Governing Bodies (NGBs)), other legal persons associated with the national Olympic movement (for instance, the Polish Olympians' Society), organizational units not having legal personality associated with the national Olympic movement and individuals related to the national Olympic movement (e.g., Polish participants of the Olympic Games).

93. The POC also includes supporting members.

94. The provision of Article 24, paragraph 2 AoS, which defines the POC as a non-governmental organization, is not unequivocal, because Polish law does not have a legal definition of a non-governmental organization.[66] We therefore accept the colloquial understanding which places non-governmental organizations outside the government and business sphere.

95. The POC has no direct influence on the management of sport and its role boils down mainly to the integration of the sports community, cultivating traditions promoting Olympism, selection of the Olympic team and the assurance of the necessary logistics related to the involvement of Polish sportspeople in the Olympic Games.[67]

96. The POC is simultaneously obliged to 'cooperate' with the minister responsible for physical culture, as referred to in Article 25, paragraph 1 AoS.[68]

97. The regulations on the fundamental powers of the POC are contained in Article 25 AoS. Among other things, the POC issues opinions on draft legislation in

66. Perhaps this unfortunate formulation found its way into the Act on Sport as a calque of the provision of Art. 3.5 from the chapter 'Olympic Movement' of the Olympic Charter: 'The IOC may recognize non-governmental organizations connected with sport, operating on an international level, the statutes and activities of which are in conformity with the Olympic Charter', although I believe this point does not apply to national Olympic committees (Art. 3.2 the Olympic Charter is devoted to them).
67. *See* B. Chełmecki, *Rola menadżera ...* , p. 47.
68. On the practical aspects of this cooperation, *see* R. Leniarski, *Igrzyska olimpijskie 2016. Czym polec ąPolacy? PKOl ma problem*, Rzeczpospolita of 19 Oct. 2015, http://www.sport.pl/rio2016/1,130063,19049778,igrzyska-olimpijskie-2016-czy-leci-z-nimi-pilot.html, accessed on 6 Jun. 2016.

the area of sports. It is exclusively entitled to use the Olympic symbol, as well as the names of the Olympic Games, the Olympic Committee, the Olympic team, the Olympic movement and Olympic Charter.

98. The authority exercising supervision over the POC is the Mayor of the City of Warsaw. However, actual supervision of the POC is exercised by the Administration and Civic Affairs Office of the Mayor of the City of Warsaw. It is this unit, which handles cases involving the Mayor exercising supervision over the activities of associations and foundations.[69]

99. Supervision of the POC is exercised on the basis of the general mandate arising from the Act on Associations and on the principles set out in those provisions. With regard to amendments of the statutes, this means that the registration court notifies the Mayor of the City of Warsaw of the registration of changes in the statutes.

100. Furthermore, if the POC's activities are found to be in conflict with the law or breach of the provisions of the statutes, the Mayor could theoretically request their elimination within a specified period, issue a warning to the POC's authorities, file a petition with the court to issue a warning to the POC, repeal the POC's resolution which is in conflict with the law or the statutes or – in theory – even dissolve the POC.

101. In addition, the Mayor of the City of Warsaw has the right to request the Management Board of the POC to provide copies of the resolutions of the general meeting of members and the authorities of the POC to provide any necessary explanations (Article 25, paragraph 2 of the Law on Associations) and if the POC were to fail to fulfil these requirements, the Mayor may file a petition with the court to impose a fine (Article 26 of the Law on Associations).

102. In addition, the Law on Associations (Article 30, paragraph 1) provides that, in the event of finding that an association does not have a management board with the capacity to conduct legal transactions, the supervisory authority may file a petition with the court to establish a trustee for it.

103. In the period from April 2015 to April 2016, the Mayor of the City of Warsaw did not take any supervisory action with respect to the POC.[70] This appears to arise from the fact that the Mayor of Warsaw simply does not have the authority to exercise such control. However, supervision over PSFs is exercised by another authority – the Minister of Sport. A postulate has been raised in the Polish literature for supervision over the POC to be transferred to the Minister of Sport in the future.[71]

---

69. *See* letter of 18 Apr. 2016, AO-I.1431.10.2016.PBO (letter in the author's possession).
70. Information from the letter of the Director of the Administration and Civic Affairs Office of the Warsaw City Hall of 18 Apr. 2016, AO-I.1431.10.2016.PBO (in the author's possession).
71. *See* M. Badura, H. Basiński, G. Kałużny, M. Wojcieszak, *Ustawa o sporcie. Komentarz*, p. 335.

104. It should be mentioned that an important role in the Polish sports model is played by the IOC. The status of a PSF (NGB), which will be referred to in more detail below, is reserved exclusively for entities that hold a certificate of membership of an international sports federation operating in an Olympic, Paralympic or other sport recognized by the IOC.[72] The lack of such membership is a factor that rules out the possibility of the given association having the status of a PSF (Article 12a paragraph 1 AoS). In accordance with the provision of Article 12b AoS, organizations of this kind become sports associations operating in the form of a federation on the basis of a decision of the minister responsible for physical culture. As has been rightly noted in the literature, this carries far-reaching negative consequences for them.[73]

105. The status of a PSF has been reserved exclusively for organizations recognized by the IOC through the introduction of the requirement for the certificate mentioned above to be attached to the application for approval to establish a PSF (Article 11, paragraph 2, item 4 AoS).

106. This requirement was introduced into Polish law in 2010. The fact that this rule entered into force resulted in new requirements for operating sports associations, which had been established earlier. Although all NGBs automatically became NGBs in the meaning of the new regulations, in accordance with the transitional regulations, they were (and still are) obliged to adjust to the requirements contained in the AoS. The deadline for such adjustment passed in October 2012 and, despite this, the list of PSFs contains organizations that should not have such a status under the applicable rules. This is because, in the case of several PSFs, it is obvious that they will never meet the requirement of belonging to the Olympic family, simply because they operate in sports that do not have the nature of Olympic sports or those which cannot expect to achieve Olympic status in the coming few years.

107. The argumentation of these 'non-Olympic' PSFs is heading towards indicating that the requirement to present a certificate of membership of an international sports federation operating in an Olympic, Paralympic or another sport recognized by the IOC is in breach of the durability of previously issued administrative decisions, breaches correctly acquired rights and infringes the prohibition of the retroactivity of the law. Such an interpretation was rejected by the administrative courts.[74] As a result, it can be expected that further 'unseating' decisions will

72. The full list is available through the IOC's website. *See,* http://www.olympic.org/content/the-ioc/governance/affiliate-organisations/all-recognised-organisations/.
73. B. Chełmecki, *Rola menadżera* ... , p. 52.
74. *See* Judgment of the Voivodship Administrative Court in Warsaw of 7 Jan. 2014 VI SA/Wa 2072/13, LEX No. 1577785. *See also* Judgments of the Voivodship Administrative Court in Warsaw of 24 Jan. 2014, VI SA/Wa 2130/13, LEX No. 1577796; of 7 Jan. 2014, VI SA/Wa 2072/13, LEX No. 1577785; of 31 Jan. 2014, VI SA/Wa 2207/13, LEX No. 1573530; of 5 Feb. 2014, VI SA/Wa 2074/13, LEX No. 1577786.

be issued for certain NGBs, such as, for example, the Polish Mountaineering Association and the Polish Underwater Sports Federation.

108. When talking about the Olympic movement, the Paralympic movement cannot be ignored.

§3. The Paralympic Movement

109. The operation of the Paralympic movement at national level is based on the Polish Paralympic Committee (Article 26 AoS), which was modelled on the POC, with some exceptions. The most important of these exceptions is the organizational form – because, although the provisions of the AoS regarding the POC do not provide for derogations from the principle that it is a federation, the Polish Paralympic Committee also has the right to operate as an association. This appears to have the purpose of preventing the need to dissolve this organization if the number of its associations drops below three. Article 26 AoS also contains a reference to Article 24, paragraph 2 and Article 25, paragraphs 1 and 2 AoS, which are applied accordingly. There is evidence of a very similar legal status of the Polish Paralympic Committee and the POC. The powers of the Polish Paralympic Committee include the use of the Paralympic symbolism and the names of Paralympic Games and the Paralympic Committee.

110. The Polish Paralympic Committee itself, having been established in 1998, is a member of the International Paralympic Committee (IPC) and the European Paralympic Committee and works with the Organizing Committee of the Paralympic Games and other national Paralympic Committees. The Committee members are currently the following organizations: the Polish Sport Association for the Disabled 'Start', the Association of Sports Associations 'Sprawni Razem', the Foundation for Active Rehabilitation, the Blind and Partially Sighted Association of Physical Culture, Sport and Tourism 'CROSS', the Physical Culture Association 'OLIMP' and the Federation 'Polska Federacja Bocci Niepełnosprawnych'.

111. The legal relationship between the national Paralympic committees and the IPC is formed differently (relationship of membership) than is the case in the relationship between the IOC (consisting of only natural persons) and the national Olympic committees. Other than the national Paralympic committees, the membership of the IPC includes international sports organizations of the disabled, international Paralympic sports federations, as well as regional and continental Paralympic organizations. Natural persons, namely persons who may be members of the IOC, cannot be members.

§4. SPORTS ASSOCIATIONS

I. Introduction

112. The key entities in the Polish model of sports regulation are sports associations and PSFs.

113. According to the AoS, the category of sports includes voivodship and regional sports associations. Sports associations often establish field representations within their organization structures, which do not have the nature of separate legal persons; they are also not separate sports associations.

114. The regulation of the AoS with regard to sports associations is laconic. It only arises from the provision of Article 6 AoS that at least three sports clubs can form sports associations and a sport association operates in the form of an association or a federation. Therefore, the AoS introduced the requirement for a minimum number of sports clubs that can establish a sport association, but, in principle, it does not regulate any other issues related to the establishment and operation of sports associations.

115. Despite the apparent simplicity, the norm that has been established suggests various interpretations, both at the stage of establishing sports associations and at the stage of their operation.

116. At the stage of establishment, it is clear that two sports clubs cannot establish a sports association, but four can. However, the question arises of whether, alongside sports clubs, natural persons or entities which are not sports clubs can appear as founding members or members. Although there are arguments confirming that this is possible, views on this subject are divided in the Polish legal doctrine.[75] This is because only the general formulation would have been left whereby 'it is admissible to establish sports associations in the form of associations or federations'.[76]

117. The procedure for establishing sports associations is subject to the Law on Associations. Therefore, sports associations, like all other associations, must be registered with the National Court Register (Article 8, paragraph 1 of the Law on Associations), while the sports association itself acquires legal personality and may start to operate at the time the entry is made into the National Court Register (Article 17, paragraph 1 of the Law on Associations). The activities of an association are supervised by the voivod with territorial jurisdiction over the association's seat. The rules governing the functioning of a sports association, including decision-making issues at the association will, therefore, be subject to the appropriate regulations of the Law on Associations.

---

75. In contrast, *inter alia*, W. Cajsel, *Ustawa o sporcie. Komentarz* ... , p. 65.
76. W. Cajsel, *Ustawa o sporcie. Komentarz* ... , p. 65.

II. Polish NFs

A. PSFs: Introduction

118. PSFs are another basic legal form in Polish sports. The legal regulations on PSFs are fundamentally a structural component of the AoS.[77] There are currently sixty-nine PSFs.[78]

119. From the point of view of international relations, PSFs are treated as so-called NFs, namely organizations controlling sport meetings in the given sport, which are responsible for the promotion and administration of that sport in the particular country. While the appropriate and actual 'authority' over the given sport is exercised by international sports federations, NFs also play an important role. Apart from several self-financing, primarily the largest NFs, such as the Polish Football Association (PZPN), in practice, Polish national sports federations depend on financing obtained from the State.

120. PSFs are private law entities. However, they sometimes appear in a role which is similar to that played by the bodies of administration.[79] This primarily arises from the award of exclusive rights to PSFs. In certain cases PSFs act as authoritative entities, having the ability to make binding decisions. This has encouraged some authors to claim that PSFs should be assigned the status of public authorities in the functional meaning,[80] which should be considered to be a far-reaching exaggeration. NFs certainly do not have the nature of bodies of administration even if they sometimes appear to forget about this.

121. PSFs are positioned at the peak of the pyramid of the organizational structure, with several possible intermediate levels, such as regional or voivodship sports associations operating in individual sports disciplines. In contrast with countries with fully liberal regulations on sports or a complete lack of such regulations (countries applying the so-called non-interventionist model of sports regulation), in the Polish legal system, Polish sports organizations, which are key sports organizations, have a number of legally protected exclusive rights.

122. The establishment of a PSF requires the consent of the Minister of Sport.

123. The PSF must be registered in the National Court Register (Article 12, paragraph 1 AoS).

---

77. M. Badura, H. Basiński, G. Kałużny, M. Wojcieszak, *Ustawa o sporcie* ..., p. 52.
78. As at 23 Sep. 2020 according to the data provided by the Ministry of Sport, National Heritage and Sport, http://www.gov.pl/web/kulturaisport/polskie-zwiazki-sportowe.
79. *Ustawa o sporcie. Komentarz*, ed. M. Gniatkowski, pp. 43–44.
80. K. Karski, '*Problematyka funkcjonowania polskich związków sportowych – zagadnienia wybrane*' (in:) Młodzi o sporcie ..., ed. K. Nessel, p. 170.

124. The approval of the statutes and any amendments to the statutes is also one of the key powers of the minister responsible for matters of physical culture with respect to the PSFs.

125. Sports clubs, sports associations and other legal persons, the statutes, articles of association or founding deeds of which provide for the pursuit of activities in a given sport, may be members of a PSF (Article 8, paragraph 1 AoS). Furthermore, the AoS, which is laconic in this respect, requires the sports club, which is a member of the PSF, to participate in sports competitions organized by that association (Article 8, paragraph 2 AoS).

126. The position of the Polish legislature regarding the potential membership of PSFs has been evolving. In the case of natural persons, this evolution is not moving from the conservative and interventionist model (strict regulation on who may be a member of a PSF) to the liberalist and non-interventionist model (freedom in this area), but vice versa. This is because the regulations in force until 2010 were more liberal. They allowed natural persons to be members of PSFs. This is currently inadmissible.

127. The legal doctrine does not give full consent for the two criteria set out in Article 8, paragraph 1 AoS (the type of entity and the intention to pursue activities in the given sport, as disclosed in the statutes, articles of association or founding deed) to be the only criteria that the potential PSF member candidate must satisfy. In other words, that each sports club pursuing activities in the given sport has a claim for admitting it as a member of the PSF or that the statutes of the PSF or any other internal deed of that PSF can make admittance of members contingent on them satisfying additional requirements. In practice the statutes of PSFs contain provisions that actually require that such additional criteria are satisfied by member candidates of PSFs.

128. An example of this could be the statutes of the PZPN, which imposes such additional requirements. One of these requirements is that, upon acceptance into the PZPN, the club declares that it undertakes to organize official matches, which it hosts, exclusively in Poland.[81] Such a declaration may require financial outlay to be incurred. Therefore, membership in PZPN is open to all sports clubs with football sections, but only on condition that they assume a number of commitments, some of which have a quantifiable financial dimension.

129. The second example is that of the statutes of the Polish Wrestling Federation. In contrast with PZPN, the statutes of this PSF do not introduce any additional requirements that sports clubs with wrestling sections have to satisfy to be accepted as members. However, full membership of a club in the Polish Wrestling Federation only arises when a licence is awarded to participate in sports events on the basis

81. Article 16 of the PZPN statutes.

of an application, together with the required attachments, confirmed by the Voivodship Wrestling Association (§ 12, clause 1, item a of the statutes of the Polish Wrestling Federation). The attachments to be submitted together with the application are specified by the Management Board of the PSF which, in principle, can define it in at its own discretion.

130. The requirements introduced into the Polish Golf Union's (PZG) statutes should also be considered far-reaching. According to this organization's statutes, a golf club which can apply for full membership must have at least fifteen people who hold a Polish Golf Union licence or an equivalent document of another national golf association; other NFs do not stipulate the minimum number of members.

B. Structure and Authorities of Polish NFs

131. Polish law does not contain any specific norms devoted to the internal management structure of PSFs. This enables their members to freely define the internal organizational framework.

132. The objectives of the PSF's statutory activities and the method of their fulfilment are defined by the provisions of the PSF's statutes. These objectives are most frequently specified as the organization, development and promotion of a specific sports discipline, as well as conducting training and competitive sport.

133. In practice, the tasks of the PSFs focus primarily on matters related to competitive sports. From the point of view of the purposes on which the funds available to PSFs are spent, amateur sport is still a marginal activity of PSFs.[82] Occasionally, only PSFs are catalysts of sporting events which have a significant economic impact on the development of the whole country, while the beneficiaries of this development are all the inhabitants of the country – this will be so in the case of large events, such as the European Football Championships held in Poland and Ukraine in 2012.

134. The Law on Associations allows registered associations to conduct business while introducing the requirement that the income is used for pursuing statutory purposes.

C. Monopoly of PSFs

135. The assurance of a statutory monopoly is a fundamental instrument that is implemented in the broadly understood sports policy.[83] The partners of the Minister of Sport in the first place are precisely the PSFs. State grants are targeted at some

82. *See* U. Starakiewicz, M. Kubów, *Przejawy przedsiębiorczości w sporcie w kontekście uwarunkowań kulturowych i organizacyjnych rozwoju branży*, Problemy Zarządzania 2014, nr 3, p. 111.
83. *See Prawo gospodarcze publiczne*, ed. A. Powałowski, Warsaw 2011, p. 297.

of them in the first instance.[84] The price that PSFs pay for having exclusive rights is relatively far-reaching supervision from the administrative authorities over their functioning.

136. Before 2005, the Polish regulations contained a provision which directly specified that only one PSF can operate in a given discipline or area of sports (Article 10 paragraph 2 of the Act on Physical Culture of 1996).[85] The current AoS does not contain such a rule. However, a whole series of provisions of this Act actually introduces such a monopoly. In particular, the introduction of three principles into the AoS – the obligation of the PSF to belong to an international sports federation, the need to obtain a licence from the minister to establish the PSF and the award of exclusive rights to the PSF to handle matches for the title of national champion and the national cup, the selection of a national squad and other exclusive rights referred to in Article 13 AoS – prejudges that PSFs still have a monopolistic position.

137. The existence of a monopoly was also confirmed by the public authorities, both through the statements of the Minister of Sport[86] and in the justification to the bill on sport.[87]

138. Therefore, under the Polish model of organization of sport, PSFs have a monopolistic position on the relevant markets.

139. The above principle that every PSF operates in one sport is correlated with the monopolistic position of PSFs. Only the Minister of Sport has the authority to agree to making an exception to the principle of 'one sport, one PSF' (Article 11, paragraph 4 AoS). It is indicated in the legal doctrine that such consent will be justified not only in all situations where the sport is similar to another sport, but also when the PSF already operates organizationally in another sport where no other PSF is operating, or when the clubs operating in a particular sport (in which no PSF is currently operating) accept the inclusion of this sport into the 'jurisdiction' of the PSF which fundamentally operates in another sport.[88] However, formally, the Minister of Sport is not bound by anything in this respect.

140. The scope of exclusive rights to which PSFs are entitled can be seen at national and international levels.

---

84. Grants are actually awarded – at various amounts – to thirty-five PSFs, which are considered to be so-called Polish Olympic sports associations (of the existing seventy-two PSFs).
85. Likewise, commentaries on the Act on Physical Culture of 1996 acknowledged that 'the Act therefore introduces a monopoly'. *See* Z. Więckowski (in:) W. Sawicki et al., *Ustawa o kulturze fizycznej* … , p. 20.
86. Response from the Minister of Sport and Tourism of 8 Nov. 2012 to interpellation No. 8506 on the clarification of the assumptions to the proposed amendments on the demonopolization of Polish sports federations.
87. *See* justification to the bill on sport, Sejm of the sixth term of office, parliamentary form No. 2313.
88. *See Ustawa o sporcie* … , ed. M. Gniatkowski, p. 70.

141. In practice, the monopoly of the national dimension also means the right of the NFs – which is not directly written into the legislation, but is accepted by the Polish legal doctrine and applied in practice – to transfer the principle of 'one area, one organization' to a lower level of the organizational structure.

142. Of course, there are possible competence conflicts. One of the best-known examples in Polish practice was the dispute between the PZPN and the Polish Federation of Beach Soccer. This latter organization successfully developed beach soccer in Poland in the years 2003–2009. In 2009, during the European Beach Soccer finals tournament, the national team that was selected and entered by the Polish Federation of Beach Soccer was disqualified from the play-offs and the team entered by PZPN played in the tournament. The PZPN referred to the fact that the global beach soccer authorities recognized PZPN's team as the only team representing Poland, as well as the provisions of Article 11, paragraph 1 AoQS, according to which only one PSF can operate in a given discipline. Referring to this provision, PZPN stated that it is the entity representing beach soccer.[89] In practice, PZPN effectively deprived the Polish Federation of Beach Soccer, namely the organization that organized beach soccer matches and intended to represent the beach soccer environment before the relevant international federation, of the ability to operate. The only representative of Polish beach soccer since 2009 has been PZPN.

143. The dispute in this case applied to what the term 'this sport' means when used in Article 13, paragraph 1, item 4 AoS, namely whether beach soccer should be considered as falling within the category of 'football' or whether it is a new sport discipline. If the latter assumption were to be accepted, PZPN's action should be considered unlawful. This was also the direction in which the argumentation of the Polish Federation of Beach Soccer was heading.[90] The arguments of the latter organization finally proved insufficient, while control over beach soccer is exercised in Poland by PZPN. In a certain sense, the Polish discussion was a reflection of the discussion taking place at international level. After initial disputes, FIFA took over the responsibilities for organizing beach soccer matches.

144. There are four types of rights of importance in the national context, which are regulated in two provisions of the AoS. The first is the power to lay down and implement the rules of sports. The second is the right to lay down and implement the organizational rules on competition in sports organized by the association. The next is the right to lay down and implement Disciplinary Rules. The fourth right in the national context is the right to organize and manage sports competitions for the

89. *See* communication of PZPN cited by K. Borawski, *'To skandal', 'PZPN zniszczył wszystko … '*, http://sport.wp.pl/kat,1726,title,To-skandal-PZPN-zniszczyl-wszystko,wid,11152953,wiadomosc.html, accessed on 5 Jun. 2016.

90. The official position of this organization was: 'PZPN cannot put up an official Polish national team in beach soccer because it does not meet the formal requirements, in accordance with the Act on Qualified Sport to which PZPN refers. PZPN never received and therefore does not have the consent of the Minister of Sport to operate in the sports discipline of "Beach Soccer" and it does not satisfy the other formal requirements to call itself the Polish Beach Soccer Association' (quoted from K. Borawski, *'To skandal', 'PZPN zniszczył wszystko … '*).

title of Polish Champion and the Polish Cup in the given sport – with the exclusion of all other entities (Article 13, paragraph 1, item 1 AoS).

145. In practice, the monopoly at national level means the actual right to build a monopolistic structure reaching down to the level of sports associations. The statutory rule of 'one sport, one organization' is therefore supported by the actually applied principle of 'one area, one organization'.

146. The monopoly officially granted to the PSF also encompasses the international aspect. This applies to establishing rights of various natures. These are, in fact, the rights to:

- select the national squad and prepare it for the Olympic Games and Paralympic Games, Deaflympics, World Championships or European championships, namely the selection of the national squad, which will represent Poland abroad; and
- represent the given sport in international sports organizations (Article 13, paragraph 1, items 3 and 4 AoS).

147. In the case of relevant rights at national level, each of them has slightly different characteristics. The scope of this monograph prevents each of them from being discussed in detail. However, let us look at certain issues related to these rights.

148. The right to lay down and implement rules of sports is a natural consequence of awarding the PSF a leading role in Polish sports. The objective of such a shape of the organizational structure is primarily to ensure equal sports rivalry for everyone. This is because it is difficult to imagine, for example, associations organizing volleyball matches competing among themselves as to whether the match is to be held with one ball or two, or whether there are to be six players or seven. Rules of this type must be uniform, observed by all interested parties, for which central administration and management is required which will not allow for full competition. The Polish lawmakers therefore concluded that it would be best to accept that the PSF is responsible for laying down and implementing the sports, organizational and disciplinary rules in sports competitions.[91]

149. But it is clear that despite the provisions of the AoS and the provisions of the statutes, the PSFs do not have the actual powers to lay down the rules of the sports. In practice, the role of the PSF in this respect is negligible, if not to say non-existent. Although the provisions of the statutes of the PSFs contain appropriate clauses duplicating the provisions of the AoS,[92] in fact, the PSFs do not lay down the rules of the sports. This is done by either the international sports organization,

---

91. For more on the nature of the rules of the game, *see* E.J. Krześniak, *Kluby i organizacje sportowe* (…), pp. 414–425.
92. *See* Art. 11, § 1, item 3 of the PZPN's statutes, according to which PZPN's objective is to 'develop rules and regulations on football and secure compliance with them'.

of which the PSF is a member, or – occasionally – another organization or entity designated by the world sports organization (football or golf). The rules are never set by the national association.[93]

150. The German and British legal doctrine consider the rules of the game to be a part of the so-called *lex ludica* and therefore be a part of a set of legal norms that are not legal norms and do not necessarily even need to be consolidated within the framework of international sports federations, but which, nevertheless, are universally applied and respected by the whole of the contemporary world of sport, such as the principle of fair play and the principle of equal opportunities.[94] The Swiss doctrine has taken a similar stance.[95] It is similar to Poland, although the rule determining who has the right to lay down the rules of the game itself is a legal rule.

151. The Polish legal doctrine has also not addressed the issue of the legal nature of the rules of the game in any great detail. Meanwhile, based on the results of foreign authors, the following criteria can be proposed to make a distinction between the sports rules and the organizational and disciplinary rules – sports rules apply to the course of individual sports rivalry, including possible sanctions for non-compliance. Sports rules differ for each sport and, in a sense, determine the specificity of the sport; likewise, they cannot be changed without affecting the given sports discipline. Therefore, rules of this type apply to a limited area, including geographically – on the field of play, wherever sports rivalry is taking place, while their observance is controlled by a referee/umpire or another person appointed for this.[96] The application of these rules does not rule out the possibility of applying other organizational or disciplinary rules, on the basis of the same event. The rules of the game are excluded from any external audit and constitute the exclusive domain of the PSF.

---

93. Attempts to create local rules of the game in recognized sports, where international matches are played, can only be encountered in such exotic countries as North Korea, where basketball matches are held according to modified rules – the team receives eight points for a basket scored in the last three seconds of the match, points are also added for throwing the ball into the basket, while a point is taken away for a missed free throw. *See* P. Wesołowicz, *Rzut za osiem punktów*, Rzeczpospolita of 3 Mar. 2016, p. A16.
94. This subject is discussed more extensively by M.F.P. Borges, *Verbandsgerichtsbarkeit Und Schiedsgerichtsbarkeit Im Internationalen Berufsfussball: Unter Berücksichtigung Der Verbandsinternen FIFA-Rechtsprechung In Bezug Auf Die Lex Sportiva*, Frankfurt am Main 2009, pp. 81–87. *See also* K. Foster, *Lex Sportiva and Lex Ludica: The Court of Arbitration for Sport's Jurisprudence*, 3 Entertainment and Sports Law Journal (2004), http://www.springer.com/cda/content/document/cda_downloaddocument/9789067048286-c2.pdf?SGWID=0-0-45-1293560-p174256763, accessed on 17 Jul. 2016.
95. *See* M. Kummer, *Spielregel und Rechtsregel*, Bern 1973, p. 35. The author specifies the obvious functional difference between the sports rules and the rules of the law – while sports rules determine the method and course of the given sporting event, the rules of law organize our lives (*das Leben ordnen*). *See* M. Kummer, *Spielregel …* , p. 22.
96. S. Jędruch refers to applying 'sports law' directly at the place of the sports event by the arbitrator (S. Jędruch, *Odpowiedzialność za szkody wyrządzone w związku z uprawianiem sportu*, Warszawa 1972, p. 27).

152. The assessment of the same concept of the statutory monopoly is disputed in the Polish legal doctrine. There are numerous critical voices.[97] However, there are many voices that consider the monopolies of PSFs to a specified extent as being a reasonable and correct solution.[98]

153. The principle of 'one sport, one organization' can be seen to work well in practice, whereas the matter of whether this principle is written into the law (as in Poland, Spain and France) or it arises from the rules accepted by the national sports association itself is essentially of secondary importance and does not change the fact that such an organizational model of sport in Europe is applicable.

154. The few exceptions, such as boxing (in many countries),[99] motor racing (in Germany – because of the complex history)[100] or sailing (in Sweden), confirm the rule. They also clearly show that competition between sports associations in the given sports discipline does not lead to either an increase in the popularity of that sport or to an elimination of doping, and does not lead to the disappearance of the suspicion of corruption. Therefore, this is not a legal remedy for all sores in contemporary sport.

III. Sport Outside the Formal Structures of the World and National Federations

155. The fact that almost all contemporary sports in Europe are organized on the basis of the above structure of a pyramid and a monopoly of individual sports associations controlling the given sport, while the IOC and World Anti-Doping Agency (WADA) play an important role, the conclusion should not be drawn that this is the case for all sports activity. The organizational structure may be completely different, especially in the case of sports which are on the borderline between sport and art or sport and broadly understood culture or even religious practices; it may be distributed or may not be present.

156. For example, there is no international yoga federation that would set uniform rules for this activity. All kinds of fitness or pilates classes are also developing on the basis of distributed structures. The same applies to commercial offerings for

97. T.T. Koncewicz, B. Rischka, *Autonomia związków sportowych: europejski ideał, polska karykatura. Rzeczpospolita.*
98. *See* W. Cajsel, *Ustawa o sporcie. Komentarz …* , p. 112.
99. Overall, boxing has fifteen international federations, of which at least four (*World Boxing Association, World Boxing Council, International Boxing Federation* and *World Boxing Organization*) are universally known.
100. Germany has two competing organizations in motor sports. One originating from the former German Democratic Republic and the other from the former Federal Republic of Germany: *Deutsche Motorsport Verband* and *Allgemeine Deutsche Motorsport Verband. See* N. Korff, *Sportrecht …* , p. 12.

spending leisure time, for example, in the gym. Such activities are organized differently to sporting activities and are much more similar to or are even simply business activities. The case will be the same with dance. Dance doubtless satisfies the requirements of the definition of 'sport' under the Polish Act, but, from the organizational point of view, the organization of dance competitions and training is built on a completely different principle than conventional sports.[101] Although there is a Dance Sport Federation Poland, its role is limited. Competitions in different varieties of dances are held by various organizations. The number of competitions of this type is often large and, given the lack of organizations that would be legally or customarily considered to be entities coordinating dance competitions in a given type of dance, it is possible that, at a given moment, there will be several or even many world or national champions in all the varieties of dance. The effect of such diffusion and functioning of this type of organization outside the 'classic' sports structures is that, in the case of this type of physical activity, it is difficult to talk about their legal nature. Such activities may be conducted in any form permitted by law, while any disputes related to such competitions or activity will be considered by the general courts on the appropriate bases for ordinary civil matters.[102]

157. Supplementing these considerations, it should be pointed out that many sporting events organized by private entities outside the formal structures referred to in this monograph refer, as an aid, to the rules and other norms adopted by the international sports federations and PSFs. Therefore, the significance of the NFs extends beyond organized sport in the meaning of the AoS. This is the case, for example, with road running. These events are organized by private entities, which are neither sports clubs nor sports associations which, nevertheless, refer to the rules of both international sports federations and PSFs. For example, the organizer of *Orlen Warsaw Marathon* and the ten-kilometre run[103] specified in the rules of the race (the acceptance of which was a condition for taking part in the race) that all runners are subject to the rules of the International Association of Athletics Federations (IAAF)[104] and the Polish Athletics Association.

101. For more on dance, sports dancing and the point of interconnect of this form of activity with art, *see* the Judgment of the Voivodship Administrative Court of 24 Jan. 2014, VI SA/Wa 1775/13, LEX No. 1577727.
102. Cf. E.J. Krześniak, *Kluby i orgnizacje sportowe* ..., pp. 100–101.
103. A private company, Agencja Live Sp. z o.o., with its registered office in Warsaw.
104. The regulations are available at www.iaaf.org.

Chapter 2. Public Regulation

§1. Fundamental Rights (Freedom of Association, Personality Rights)

158. It is generally accepted in the Polish literature that the regulations laid down by the international federations of sports associations and the national sports associations operating in the form of associations cannot be considered a source of law in the meaning of the Constitution of the Republic of Poland.[105] Views are only occasionally expressed that the internal norms of sports associations, as autonomous, expert regulations of normative subsystems created intentionally and being of a public status, frequently combined with a system of uniform international arbitration, can, perhaps, be compared to common law.[106]

159. Therefore, the rights of the NFs to set the organizational framework for playing sports arise in Poland from both a specific provision of the law and the general principle of the freedom of association of all Polish citizens.

160. However, the question can be asked about where to set the boundary between State regulation imposed by the State on the citizens and associations and self-regulation of sports organizations.

161. The fact is that the people responsible for establishing the applicable norms in the world of sport (both the organizational rules and the rules of the game) are unwilling for the State to interfere at all in any matter for which they are responsible. In practice, the largest world sports federations, such as the FIFA and the Fédération Internationale de Volleyball (International Volleyball Federation) try to operate as quasi-ex-territorial entities. The German researcher, G. Manssen, refers to the 'anationality' (*Anationalität*) of such organizations and claims that such organizations are even trying to gain such anationality.[107] The FIFA has strong instruments for applying pressure and severe sanctions, for the application of which it does not need to benefit from State coercion.

162. Organizations such as FIFA appear to take the stance that the influence of State law on such an area of life as sport means a risk of a loss of the typical features which distinguish sport from other areas. They make the assumption that sport is autonomous of all types of public authority and, as such, should not be subject to its control. An example is even the fundamental principle of the Olympic movement which is written into the Olympic Charter, according to which sports organizations associated in the Olympic movement should have full freedom to decide on

105. *See*, e.g., W. Sanetra, *Zmiana klubu sportowego przez sportowca w świetle polskiego prawa,* p. 81.
106. J. Jabłońska-Bonca, '*Istota spójności regulacji prawnych oraz niesprzeczności regulacji pozaprawnych z regulacjami prawnymi*' (in:) Kompatybilność pozaprawnych regulacji sportowych ..., ed. A.J. Szwarc, pp. 60–61. *See also* E.J. Krześniak, *Kluby i organizacje sportowe* ... .
107. G. Manssen, *Buchbesprechung von: Klaus Vieweg* ..., p. 121.

how they will administer, manage and regulate the Olympic movement and, in this respect, they should have full autonomy (point No. 5 in the chapter named 'Fundamental Principles of Olympism').

163. Concerns of this kind may be more justified in such a legal system as the Polish or the French systems. This is because the lawmakers there make the assumption that there is a need to strictly regulate the world of sport. As the regulation is strict, many of the issues that give rise to the concern of sports organizations are regulated directly in those legal systems. However, in the case of such legal systems as the British or German systems, where there is no act of law regulating sport, this risk appears to be significantly smaller. The State interferes far less in the autonomy of sports associations in these legal systems. State regulations in these latter counties only interfere where the sports associations themselves are unable to appropriately regulate certain issues or wherever an excessive amount of concentration of authority in the hands of such organizations would be unjustified and would be damaging to the interests of the sportspeople.

164. Likewise, the European Commission accepts that there are certain types of rules set by the sports associations as a part of the implementation of the principle of sports autonomy, with respect to which it is difficult to imagine that they could breach the EU's competition law. It is presumed that, in principle, norms of this type are admissible, if only the anti-competitive effect – if it exists – is proportional to the objectives that these rules are to achieve. All the rules of the game fit into this category. Certain organizational rules related to sport also fit into this category, such as, for instance, the rule regarding the selection of players for individual competitions, norms specifying when meetings are played 'at home' and when they are played 'away', as well as norms prohibiting simultaneously holding shares in more than one club (in our legal system, this is actually a provision of the law, Article 10 AoS) and rules on the membership of national teams, anti-doping rules (in Poland also a provision of the law – *see* Chapter 9 of the AoS) and the rules on transfer windows.

165. On the sideline, it should be noted that European law indirectly protects the rights of associations and other legal entities to freely decide on their internal affairs in a certain way. Therefore, for instance, in *Bosman*, the ECJ allowed associations (sports clubs and sports associations) to have the freedom to decide on their own internal affairs and acknowledged that a right of clubs of this type is protected by the fundamental rights secured by European law.

166. However, the autonomy of sport is also the organizational dimension and the need for bodies of public authority to refrain from interfering in the affairs of sports organizations unless social or other justified reasons support otherwise. Although the State has instruments of supervision and control, it frequently does not have the authority to actually take advantage of these instruments. A good example is the right to suspend board members of PSFs from their duties. The public authorities are not concerned about using instruments of this type in the case of small PSFs, which organize competitions in niche sports, such as in the case of the authorities

of the Polish Archery Federation.[108] But in the case of such powerful associations as the PZPN or Polish Volleyball Association (PZPS), the minister is much less inclined to reach out for such sanctions. The threat of exclusion of Polish clubs and the national team from participating in international tournaments and the fear of social anger which would undoubtedly be related to this are the most effective brakes.

§2. Governmental Conditions and Permits (Quotas, Work Restrictions)

167. The establishment of a sports club or a sports association does not require any State permit in Poland.

168. The establishment of a PSF (NF) is only subject to far-reaching regulation. A PSF can only be established by sports associations with the consent of the Minister of Sport. The minister's consent is given or refused by way of an administrative decision. A draft set of statutes of the PSF and a detailed description of the sport in which the PSF intends to organize and hold competitions should be attached to the application for consent, simultaneously giving precise information on the conditions for playing this sport and finally attaching a certificate of membership of an international sports federation operating in an Olympic, Paralympic or other sport recognized by the IOC to the application (Article 11, paragraph 2 AoS).

169. Each of the above-mentioned attachments to the application is related to another issue – the draft statute applies to corporate issues, the detailed description of the sport, with precise information on the conditions of playing that sport, as well as the rules and the system of competing in this sport are related to the matter of the rules of the game and the so-called sports rules, while the certificate of membership of an international sports federation operating in an Olympic, Paralympic or other sports recognized by the IOC or featured in the list published by the Minister of Sport indicates that a given organization functions within international sports structures.

170. Other than this sole exception, sports clubs, sports associations and NGBs are subject to the same requirements as all other legal entities operating in the same legal form (companies or associations).

171. Sports activity in Poland is still, to a certain extent, an administrative law method of regulation. The Minister of Sport has relatively far-reaching rights in this respect.

172. The fact that the Minister of Sport has greater rights in Poland than his counterparts in other countries (as well as the mere fact that we have a Minister of Sport in Poland) is explained in the Polish legal doctrine by the fact that Polish

108. *See* W. Cajsel, *Ustawa o sporcie. Komentarz ...* , p. 51.

NGBs have significant rights awarded directly by the AoS. This makes their actual position comparable, in the area of their competence, with the authoritative position of the administrative authorities. A whole range of powers awarded to the PSFs by the laws actually and legally gives them a monopolistic position in the organization of sports matches in each of the areas of sport. This can cause at least two negative effects.

173. First, giving the PSF exclusive rights can lead to the situation in which these rights are not exercised (for instance, not playing Polish championship matches in some sports discipline).[109] This would obviously have a negative consequence on the sportspeople and all other people involved in the given sport. On the contrary, it is also possible that the monopoly could encourage illegal activities – abuse of the monopolistic position by forcing specific conduct or not allowing for certain conduct (despite the lack of grounds for this). Since this is the case, the Polish lawmakers provided for a system of supervision over the PSFs awarding the appropriate rights and setting the appropriate duties for the respective State authorities.[110] This last argument should also be supplemented by mentioning the historic traditions, as well as the partially interventionist model of sports regulation accepted in Poland, where there is a conviction that strict control of PSFs is necessary due to certain historic 'inertia' – as sport was always under the strict control of the State, it should obviously continue to be subject to it.

174. Under the currently applicable regulations, it is the activities of the PSF authorities and not the authorities of the PSFs themselves or the PSFs which are subject to supervision.[111] Such activities will, obviously, most frequently be taken up by the authorities (governing bodies) of the PSF, so the minister's indirect control over the authorities of the PSFs will be implemented, although monitoring the activities of an entity's authorities (e.g., examining the appropriate qualifications of that entity's authorities) is one thing, while monitoring that entity's activities is another.

175. The criterion of supervision is both compliance with the law and compliance with the provisions of the statutes. This last matter gives rise to some emotion in the Polish legal doctrine. Some authors consider leaving the ability to audit the PSFs for compliance of their activities with their statutes within the responsibilities of the State's supervisory powers to be a doubtful solution.[112] However, it can also be argued that the statutory monopoly that has been awarded requires balancing through audit instruments. Likewise, it cannot be forgotten that only the members of the PSFs, namely the sports associations and sports clubs, have the legal instruments for monitoring the decisions made by the authorities of those PSFs. It is those

109. Cf. M. Bidziński, *Kontrola i nadzór nad polskimi związkami sportowymi* (in:) Problemy prawne na styku sportu i medycyny ed. T. Gardocka, D. Jagiełło, Warsaw 2015, pp. 178–179.
110. M. Bidziński, *Kontrola i nadzór* ... , p. 179.
111. Cf. R. Hauser, *Aspekty administracyjnoprawne w ustawie o sporcie*, (in:) A.J. Szwarc (ed.), *Ustawa o sporcie*, p. 34.
112. *See* P. Łebek, *Autonomia organizacji sportowych. Problemy Współczesnego Prawa Mi ędzynarodowego Europejskiego i Porównawczego 2011*, p. 170.

entities that can contest resolutions of the PSF or take other legal steps with respect to the PSF's authorities, exercising the rights possessed by all members of the associations and entities with respect to which the provisions of the Law on Associations applies by analogy. Natural persons on whom sport is based, namely the sportspeople, trainers and referees/umpires, are not members of the PSF, so they do not have such rights. Simultaneously, they are subject to the actual 'jurisdiction' of the PSF and, furthermore, the internal deeds of the PSF sometimes refer to the sanction of exclusion from the PSF. Therefore, it is reasonable for the supervisory authority to be able to audit the activities of the PSF from the point of view of compliance of its activity with the provisions of the statutes.

176. Disciplinary and rules-related decisions of the authorities of PSFs related to the organization and handling of sports competitions have been excluded from the supervisory rights of the Minister of Sport. It has been acknowledged by the Polish legal doctrine that this exclusion arises from the monopoly and the autonomy of the PSF encompassing the organization and handling of competitions in the given sport.[113] This regulation is generally considered appropriate, assuming that the exclusivity of the right to organize and manage competitions in a given sport must go hand in hand with the inability of the supervisory authority to interfere with the disciplinary and rules-related settlements. It is only the combination of these two elements that gives a guarantee that the PSF will maintain its autonomy.[114]

177. However, there is no agreement in the legal doctrine as to how far this exclusion reaches. Some authors accept that this should be interpreted strictly, which means that the two types of rules-related and disciplinary decisions of the PSF authorities would need to be distinguished – those which are related to the organization and course of sports competitions and those which are not related to this. Decisions on imposing a fine on a club, sportsperson, coach, instructor, referee/umpire and activists for failing to perform legally binding judgments of the PZPN jurisdictional and disciplinary authorities can be mentioned as an example of the latter.[115] Other authors believe that, since the lawmakers excluded rules-related and disciplinary decisions on organizing and handling sports competitions from the supervision of the respective authorities, it should be accepted that this principle should not have any restrictions on the enforcement of their implementation. According to these authors, proceedings initiated by the relevant authorities of the PSF in order to enforce previously issued decisions and decisions which are issued during the proceedings are of the nature of disciplinary decisions related to the organization and handling of sports competitions because they exert a direct influence

113. *See* D. Bidziński, *Kontrola i nadzór* ..., p. 183.

114. *See* D. Bidziński, *Kontrola i nadzór* ..., pp. 183–184; W. Cajsel, *Ustawa o sporcie. Komentarz* ..., p. 143; M. Badura, H. Basiński, G. Kałużny, M. Wojcieszak, *Ustawa o sporcie* ..., p. 281; *Ustawa o sporcie* ..., ed. M. Gniatkowski, pp. 99–100 oraz P. Łebek, *Autonomia organizacji* ..., pp. 169–170. Similarly, justification to the bill on sport (Sejm of the sixth term of office, parliamentary form No. 2313, p. 7).

115. Example from W. Cajsel, *Ustawa o sporcie. Komentarz* ..., p. 144.

on the legal situation of their participant or another person to whom they apply with regard to participation in sports competitions.[116]

178. The authors who are proponents of the strict interpretation are more convincing and therefore appear to be correct. They distinguish two types of rules-related and disciplinary decisions of the PSF authorities – namely those related to the organization and handling of sports competitions (not subject to audits) and those who are not related to this (who are subject to such audits).

179. The next right of the Minister of Sport with regard to the supervision of the NGBs is the right to approve the statutes of the given NGB and giving consent to the conclusion of an agreement between the PSF and the company managing the professional league specifying the principles of functioning of this league (Article 15, paragraph 5 AoS).

180. The minister responsible for physical culture shall refuse to agree to the conclusion of this agreement only if its provisions are inconsistent with the law, but he does not have the right to do so if the provisions of the agreement are consistent with it. This rule has little point, because the provisions of an agreement which are in conflict with the law would be invalid *ex lege*. An additional examination by the minister in this respect is therefore unnecessary. For this reason, the author of this monograph has been postulating the complete elimination of the regulation of Article 15, paragraph 5 AoS from Polish law.[117]

181. The Minister of Sport is also entitled to stricto penalizing rights. In the first instance, this will be the right to give the authorities of the given NGB a warning (Article 22, paragraph 1, item 1 AoS). By imposing a sanction in the form of a warning, the minister should simultaneously specify the deadline by which action should be taken to ensure that a condition which is consistent with the law is restored. Although Article 22, paragraph 1, item 1 AoS does not specify that such actions should be taken up within a specified time, according to the Voivodship Administrative Court in Warsaw, a different (strictly literal) interpretation of this provision would prevent the performance of the obligation by the association; the lack of specification of the time frames would lead to a situation which prevents further steps being taken by the supervisory authority.[118] At the same time, this deadline cannot be discretionary; it should be based on the actual time that is needed to resolve the matter.[119] In issuing the decision, the minister is also required to explain why he accepted that the specified deadline is reasonable – the inclusion of this

116. M. Badura, H. Basiński, G. Kałużny, M. Wojcieszak, *Ustawa o sporcie* … , p. 282.
117. E.J. Krześniak, *Kluby i organizacje sportowe* … , pp. 482–483.
118. *See* Judgment of the Voivodship Administrative Court in Warsaw of 7 Jan. 2014 VI SA/Wa 2072/13, LEX No. 1577785.
119. *See* Judgment of the Voivodship Administrative Court in Warsaw of 7 Jan. 2014 VI SA/Wa 2072/13, LEX No. 1577785.

explanation as late as in the response to the party's complaint is too late, as the response to the complaint cannot constitute a supplement to the contested decision.[120]

182. However, the judicature is not consistent on whether the enforceability of a decision regarding a warning and ordering the authorities of the PSF to take steps to ensure the restoration of a condition which is consistent with the law can be withheld. Two different adjudicating panels of voivodship administrative courts issued two different decisions in factual situations which were essentially identical.[121] The argument that is admissible to withhold the enforceability of a decision regarding a warning appears to be more convincing.

183. However, the administrative courts exercise control over the activities of public administration and therefore also over the activities of the minister. This control is exercised in terms of compliance with the law, unless acts of law provide otherwise. Therefore, this is about examining acts and activities of public administration in terms of their compliance with substantive law and the procedural regulations and not according to criteria of justness.[122] In the first instance, cases within the jurisdiction of the administrative courts are examined by the voivodship administrative courts. An appeal may be filed with the Voivodship Administrative Court with jurisdiction against the decisions issued by the minister in the supervisory procedure. A relatively large number of judgments was passed in the first instance on matters related to the issue of establishing a PSF (requirement of consent from the minister for establishing a PSF) and the approval of amendments to the PSF's statutes.

184. The furthest-reaching sanction that can be applied to a PSF is the suspension of the authorities of the PSF and the dissolution of the PSF. Both these sanctions may only be applied by the court.

185. Before the lawmakers decided to award the right to the court to suspend the authorities of a PSF, the voivods and (in the case of national associations) the President of the Office of Physical Culture and Tourism had such a right (Article 16, item 3 in connection with Article 15, paragraphs 1 and 2 of the Act on Physical Culture of 1996), followed by the POC CAS (Article 23a AoQS).

186. Today, the actual applicant in the case of both these sanctions is the Minister of Sport. The Minister of Sport may apply for the application of the sanction of suspending the authorities of the PSF if the activities of the PSF are in breach of the law or a provision of the statutes, whereas the minister may apply for the court

---

120. *See* Judgment of the Voivodship Administrative Court in Warsaw of 7 Jan. 2014 VI SA/Wa 2072/13, LEX No. 1577785.

121. *See* decision of the Voivodship Administrative Court in Warsaw of 27 Nov. 2013, VI SA/Wa 2373/13, LEX No. 1585607 and decision of the Voivodship Administrative Court in Warsaw of 12 Feb. 2014, VI SA/Wa 2338/13, LEX No. 1577840.

122. *See* decision of the Voivodship Administrative Court in Warsaw of 7 Jan. 2014, VI SA/Wa 2072/13, LEX No. 1577785 of 20 Nov. 2013, VI SA/Wa 1944/13, LEX No. 1729618.

to apply the most serious measure, namely the actual 'death penalty' for the PSF, which will effectively mean the dissolution of the PSF by the court if the activities of that PSF demonstrate gross or persistent breaches of the law or the provisions of the statutes and there are no conditions for recovering a situation which is compliant with the law or the statutes (Article 22, paragraph 1, item 4 AoS in connection with Article 23, paragraph 2 AoS).

187. When suspending the authorities of the PSF, the court simultaneously appoints a trustee, who is required to hold elections for new authorities of the PSF. However, during the time that passes from the appointment of the trustee to the moment that new authorities are elected, the trustee exercises actual authority at the federation – he is entitled to the rights of the authority of the PSF (Article 23, paragraph 3 AoS). And this is where we encounter a problem. This is because world sports federations defend their independence. Attempts of the public authorities to interfere directly in the federation's matters are treated as an attack on the neutrality of these organizations. The provisions of the statutes of international sports federations provide directly that the decisions of any authorities that are not appointed completely independently and freely by the national organization (namely also in a manner which is free of any pressure from the public authorities) will not be acknowledged by the international federations. PSFs should be considered the national organizations in this context and this principle applies to them. The respective provisions of the statutes of these organizations emphasize that this also applies to authorities and persons appointed temporarily, as if they wanted to clearly emphasize that they will not recognize the provisions of national legal orders providing for the appointment of trustees.

188. In practice, this means that any attempts to appoint a trustee for PZPN (admissible under Polish law) will quickly end in the failure of the applicants and the executors of this step – the public authority. The best-known case is the suspension of PZPN's authorities in 2007 by the Minister of Sport of that time. The matter started in September 2006 with the initiation of administrative proceedings with respect to PZPN. In the media, the Minister of Sport explained this by the desire to clarify 'whether the law was being breached at PZPN and why this association is doing nothing about the corruption scandal in Polish football', and demanded the election of new authorities for the association.[123] On 18 January 2007, after arresting and pressing corruption charges on one of the members of PZPN's Management Board, the Minister of Sport demanded that the management board is to step down; on the next day, the management board set a date for Congress on 31 January 2007, simultaneously rejecting the minister's demands. The minister suspended the Management Board of PZPN with immediate effect and appointed a trustee. After several weeks, the Minister of Sport withdrew the suspension of PZPN's Management Board and recalled the trustee. From the formal point of view, he cancelled his own decision of 19 January 2007 awarding the decision to appoint a trustee for the sanction of immediate enforceability. The matter was subject to mediation at the highest

123. *See Minister sportu Tomasz Lipiec odwiesił zarząd PZPN (opis)*, 5 Mar. 2007, http://www.slask.sport.pl/sport-slask/1,121857,3964927.html, accessed on 7 Jun. 2016.

level – the Polish President of the time, Lech Kaczyński, and the head of FIFA of that time, Sepp Blatter, mediated. As the attempt in 2007 and the later events showed, the threat of the expulsion of Polish clubs and the national team from matches organized by Union of European Football Associations (UEFA) and FIFA is a sufficiently effective threat that it actually deprives the public authorities of the ability to take advantage of the instruments to which they are entitled to discipline PSFs, or at least some of them.

189. A historic analysis of the laws on the supervision of (Polish) sports federations shows that Poland is missing a certain amount of continuity and consistent leading thoughts. It is sufficient to look at the supervisory measure in the form of the ability to suspend the Polish authorities of a sports association. The voivod and (in the case of national associations) the President of the Office of Physical Culture and Tourism were initially entitled to this right (Article 16, item 3 in connection with Article 15, paragraphs 1 and 2 of the Act on Physical Culture of 1996). Next, the minister responsible for physical culture was equipped with this power (Article 23 in connection with Article 18 of the Act on Physical Culture of 1996). This right was taken away from the minister and awarded to the POC CAS (Article 23a of the Act on Physical Culture of 1996).[124] After several years, the whole of the regulation on the arbitration court was deleted from the AoS, as a result of which the court was awarded the right to suspend the authorities of PSFs (at the request of the minister) (Article 23, paragraph 1, item 1 of the AoS).

§3. Tort Law (Civil and Criminal Liability, Gambling, Public Safety)

190. This part of the monograph will discuss very different issues. Therefore, in order to enable the arguments to be followed, I have divided this section into subsections.

I. Safety of Mass Events

191. Playing sports is related to safety of mass events, which is a part of the issue of the principles of organizing sports events. The matter of the responsibility of the organizer of a sports event to its participants, spectators and third parties, as well as the matter of insurance related to playing sports constitute topics of interest to both legal theoreticians and lawyers advising sports clubs, sportspeople and people who have suffered injury or damage to property in connection with watching sports events.

192. Of practical importance is the matter of liability of sports clubs for damage caused by people who are contractually related to the club (players, trainers, activists) as well as people who are not in such a relationship but are related directly to

124. The court's decision was made at the minister's request.

the sport (referees/umpires) or people who do not have such a relationship (so-called pseudo-fans demolishing shops at the time of a sports event for which they do not have tickets). This subject is well written in foreign literature,[125] somewhat less in Poland.

193. The rules on safety and security of mass events have been separated into a separate legal act – the Act on Safety and Security of Mass Events of 2009 (Journal of Laws of 2015, item 2139). Not only does this regulation apply to sports events but also, for instance, to musical concerts. In the first instance, the provisions of this Act implement the principles arising from the European Convention on Spectator Violence and Misbehaviour at Sports Events and in particular at Football Matches (Journal of Laws of 1995, No. 129, item 625) and incorporate them into Polish law.

194. In handling matters of safety at mass events, the Polish Supreme Court held in one of its judgments that the civil liability of the organizer of a mass event is of a practically absolute nature; in other words, the organizer is responsible for almost everything that takes place during the mass event.[126] The judgment was criticized in the doctrine,[127] although it demonstrates the tendency to assign responsibility to an almost unlimited extent to sports clubs and other entities, such as the organizers of sports events. Therefore, the Polish regulations can be summed up as follows – if anything bad happens at the stadium, the organizer is responsible.

II. Overstepping the Rules of the Game as a Criterion of Liability

195. The boundary between causing injury as a result of the normal, but unintentional result of sports rivalry and such injury that could result in criminal liability of the perpetrator is not unambiguous. However, it is obvious that this boundary lies in a slightly different place to that of so-called normal life. This does not change the fact that sport is not an area in which the legal norms, including the norms of criminal law, do not apply. They are fully applicable, although it can be argued from the same provisions of criminal law that they will not apply in specific sporting situations. This subject was well written in the Polish literature – as early as in 1971,

125. Cf. based on German law: U. Haas, D.-R. Martens, *Sportrecht – ...* , Zürich 2011, pp. 178–209; based on Russian law: O. Rymkevich, *International Encyclopaedia of Law. Sports Law. Russia* (Kluwer Law International, 2021); based on Slovak law: T. Gábriš, *International Encyclopaedia of Law. Sports Law. Slovakia* 74–84 (Kluwer Law International, 2015).

126. Judgment of the Supreme Court of 26 Sep. 2003, IV CK 8/02, LEX No. 84305.

127. *See*, among others, M. Dróżdż, *Potrzeba zmian ustawy o bezpieczeństwie imprez masowych. Praktyczne problemy z jej zastosowaniem – wybrane zagadnienia*, pp. 76–77; M. Dróżdż, *Glosa do wyroku Sądu Najwyższego z dnia 19 października 2012 r., IV CSK 439/11*, Ius Novum 2013, No. 2; M. Dróżdż, *Odpowiedzialność deliktowa oraz kontraktowa organizatora imprezy masowej*, PS 2002, No. 10, p. 41.

A.J. Szwarc mentioned the key theories in this respect.[128] In the German legal system, the matter of overstepping the sports rules (or not) is treated as a key circumstance in the assessment of whether there can be talk of criminal liability. In the event that the sports rules are not overstepped, the person who, despite not overstepping the rules, causes injury to another person who was also competing in the same event (and in the extreme case, causes that person's death), is not liable under criminal law. If these norms are slightly overstepped (which is typical of normally playing the given sport – e.g., the collision of two basketball players), there will also not be such liability. Only in the case of seriously overstepping the norms, or even wilful misconduct, with the intention of causing injury to the other person, can there be talk under German criminal law of potential criminal liability.[129] The German arguments can also be applied, in principle, to the Polish regulations.

196. The rules of the game can also be significant in specifying possible civil law liability of participants of sports events. There can be no doubt that the participants of a sports event (players) are not in any contractual relationship with each other.[130] Therefore, if one player causes injury to another, only the rules on delict (tort), as specified in the Polish Civil Code (Articles 415 et seq. PCC), can be applicable. It also appears that it should be accepted that all players taking part in a sports event (and this term should also be understood to mean training) are obliged to apply due diligence with respect to each other.

197. In this context, advantage can be taken of the rules of the game, treating them as a measure of this diligence. The general requirement to apply due diligence should be additionally specified in the case of individual sports. Therefore, it should be possible to apply the sports rules which are typical of a given sport. For example, the rules of football prohibit so-called sliding tackles to an opponent's legs. The breach of these rules can result in the infringer's civil law liability. There is no available data on the approach of the Polish courts to these issues, although I believe that, when assessing the justification for awarding compensation, the court should also assess whether the sports rules of the game were breached. In this sense, the rules of the game can be an additional criterion for assessing a player's negligence.

198. Furthermore, if there is a list of norms and rules of the game in a given sport, which should be observed if the sport is to be played safely, everyone who plays this sport, including as a hobby, should be required to comply with these

---

128. In other words, the exclusion of the so-called objective essence of the deed, the lack of guilt, normal practice, the theory of the so-called professional law, the theory of the objective, the concept of the State permit, the theory of the so-called admissible sports risk, the consent of the victim, acting within the limits of the law or the legal obligation, playing sports on order (e.g., in the army), the permission of the authorities for organizing a sports event, the theory of the so-called dominating public interest, cultural norms and theories based on sports regulations. *See* A.J. Szwarc, *Sport a prawo karne. Wprowadzenie do problematyki karnoprawnej oceny tzw. naruszeń sportowych*, pp. 99–121.

129. *See* Haas, Martens, *Sportrecht*, pp. 207–208. *See also* A.J. Szwarc, *Sport a prawo karne* ... , p. 118.

130. As a rule, such a legal relationship arises between the player and the sports club and not between players.

norms, while it should be possible to apply the 'test of the rules of the game' as a measure of due diligence, even in the case of amateurs and people who are not members or players of sports clubs. An attempt could be made to highlight the rules of the game that contain provisions intended to minimize injury that could be sustained during sports and therefore rules containing the principles of safety (this will be the situation in the case of contact sports, such as boxing), as well as those not containing such rules (most frequently individual sports, where there is no contact between players, such as in the case of tennis). It is also possible to analyse the issue of seriously overstepping the rules and a minor breach of the rules, which is essentially the norm in every sport and can justify the acceptance of the argument of the lack of liability for injury caused by slightly breaching the rules (but only if such a breach is committed by a player and not, for instance, a coach, who is rather appointed to ensure the observance of the rules). Consideration can also be given to the assessment of the situation in which the breach of the norms arises from the player's fatigue.[131]

III. Structure of the Club's Fault and Civil Law Liability

199. The matter of the fault of the sports club is disputed in the Polish legal doctrine. Although it is universally accepted in the doctrine that an act resulting in disciplinary liability can be committed by both a natural person (sportsperson or coach) and a legal person (sports club), this still does not dispel all the doubts.

200. The study of criminal law presents two possible concepts of guilt, described as the so-called psychological theory and normative theory.[132] The psychological theory emphasizes the perpetrator's internal mental experience which, for obvious reasons, would make it difficult to assign or even prevent the assignment of guilt understood in this way to a sports club or sports association. The normative theory gives slightly greater opportunities because it refers to the external guilt of given conduct.[133] According to one Polish author, it is possible to imagine the formulation of an allegation on the basis of an external assessment (which is typical of this concept) of an internal decision of the collective will created by a sports club or sports association that the club wanted something that it should not have wanted because, if the club had acted in accordance with the principles of fair play, it would not have performed this deed.[134] However, the author clearly points out that the acceptance of such a structure would require further research work.

201. An alternative structure would be reference not so much to criminal concepts of guilt, as to civil law concepts, which do not directly refer to and are not

131. Cf. E.J. Krześniak, *Kluby i organizacje sportowe* (...), pp. 422–424.
132. Interesting arguments on 'criminal law' elements in sports disciplinary liability can be found in the study by A.J. Szwarc, *Karny charakter odpowiedzialności dyscyplinarnej w sporcie* (in:) Rozważania o prawie karnym. Księga pamiątkowa z okazji siedemdziesięciolecia urodzin Profesora Aleksandra Ratajczaka, ed. A.J. Szwarc, Poznań 1999, pp. 279–292.
133. *See* P. Jóźwiak, *Odpowiedzialność dyscyplinarna w sporcie, Poznań 2001*, p. 326.
134. P. Jóźwiak, *Odpowiedzialność dyscyplinarna* ... , p. 326.

based on the principles of guilt in its dogmatic approach, but rather a quasi-guilt concept in which the classic forms of guilt (such as *culpa in eligendo,*[135] *culpa in custodiendo*[136] or organizational guilt)[137] are, in a way, transposed into criminal type guilt.[138] Looking at the direction in which practice has gone, it would be necessary to agree with such a view.

202. There is a tendency to attribute responsibility to sports clubs regardless of whether or not any fault can be attributed to the club. It is a common practice in PSFs to introduce the principle of joint and several liability of the clubs for anyone related to that club in any way.[139] Therefore, the reality of sport is that disciplinary liability of collective entities, in the first instance, sports clubs, is actually based on the principle of risk. The illegality of a given act, understood as non-compliance of an act or omission with the disciplinary regulations is sufficient to accept the existence of this liability.

203. Liability of this type is attributed regardless of the existence of any written rule on this, even in the internal regulations of PSFs (associations or federations). Only a very small proportion of disciplinary regulations directly state that disciplinary liability is based on the principle of risk. However, the decided majority of disciplinary regulations do not have such provisions, which is correct, because this liability arises from the law itself.

204. After all, the search for legal possibilities of increasing the grounds for liability of legal persons (in the first instance, sports clubs) involved in sport as much as possible is not unique to Poland. The battle against stadium hooliganism, especially in football, requires far-reaching steps.[140] The legal literature contains an extensive description of the imposition of a disciplinary penalty of exclusion from the UEFA play-offs and the imposition of a penalty of CHF 100,000 on Feyenord Rotterdam in 2006 after Feyenord Rotterdam's match with AS Nancy, even though Feyenord Rotterdam took far-reaching steps to prevent the riots involving its own fans. The compliance with Swiss law of the UEFA rules specifying that football clubs are liable for the damage caused by fans and pseudo-fans identifying themselves with the club was confirmed by the Lausanne CAS in the award issued in

135. Guilt in choice; in the context of disciplinary liability in sport, this would apply, for example, to the allegation of a lack of choice of appropriate person to make decisions on behalf of the club.
136. Guilt in supervision; in the context of disciplinary liability in sport, this would apply, for example to the allegation of a lack of supervision by the club over the people who, through their conduct, performed an act which, in accordance with the disciplinary regulations, is treated as the disciplinary guilt of the club itself.
137. The structure is similar to the institution of liability for fiscal infringements, involving the inadvertent performance of a prohibited act.
138. *See* P. Jóźwiak, *Odpowiedzialność dyscyplinarna* ... , pp. 328–330.
139. *See*, e.g., PZPN's disciplinary regulations, https://www.pzpn.pl/public/system/files/site_content/635/562-PDF%20REGULAMIN%20DYSCYPLINARNY%20UCHWALONY%20NA%20WALNYM%20ZGROMADZENIU%20DELEGAT%C3%93W%20W%20DNIU%2027%20MAJA%202014.pdf, accessed on 6 Jun. 2016.
140. Cf. on this, among others, J. Räker, '*Odpowiedzialność cywilnoprawna klubów piłkarskich za wykroczenia kibiców*' (in:) *Prawne problemy sportu piłkarskiego* ... , ed. A.J. Szwarc, pp. 130–162.

this case.[141] The award simultaneously confirmed the earlier, similar decision of the CAS issued in *PSV Eindhoven v. UEFA*.[142]

205. Likewise, in Poland, such a situation as described above could end with the imposition of a disciplinary penalty on the club, all the more so that PZPN's disciplinary regulations provide directly for liability on the principle of risk.

IV. Disciplinary Liability and Civil Law Liability

206. The clear assignment of liability to clubs or players with respect to fans and other spectators of a sports event will not always be straightforward. Whether sportspeople (and indirectly also the clubs, as the entities responsible for those sportspeople) incur civil law liability as an actual consequence of a disciplinary delict (tort) will depend on the specific circumstances of the given case. For example, there could be situations in which the damage arises from the sportsperson's lack of appropriate skills or other errors he commits during the sports event. Can there be talk, in such a situation, of the fact that the spectators accept a potential risk to some extent (e.g., while watching motor racing)? Does the spectator at a football match have the right to sue two players and the club for a fist fight that spread to the stands? Similarly, if a spectator at a golf tournament suffers injury because of a defective demonstration of a golf swing by a player away from the place where the ball is struck, can it be considered whether this type of unsporting conduct on the part of the player resulting in the emergence of injury should automatically result in his liability.

207. Without a more detailed analysis, it could be argued that perhaps no injuries of this type which are suffered by the spectators and third parties, which arise directly from the sports rivalry itself, should result in the liability of the sportspeople and the clubs with respect to these people, whereas all injuries arising from events that are indirectly related to the sports event (such as the few examples presented above) should result in such liability.

208. Likewise, the assessment of who the liability should be attributed to in the case of injury caused to people who are not formally spectators of the sports event but found themselves in the place where the sport is played by chance can give rise to doubt.[143]

---

141. Award of the CAS of 9 Feb. 2007, Az.: 2007/A/1217. This judgment is extensively discussed by B. Haslinger, *Die Rechtsprechung der CAS zur Haftung bei Zuschauerausschreitungen vir dem Hintergrund statuarischer Regelungen internationaler Verbände* (in:) Verantwortlichkeiten und Haftung im Sport, Baden-Baden 2012, pp. 34–36. A critical assessment of this award of the CAS is presented by J. Räker, *Odpowiedzialność cywilnoprawna* ... , pp. 137–162.
142. Award of the CAS of 3 Jun. 2003, Az.: 2002/A/423. The award is extensively discussed by B. Haslinger, *Die Rechtsprechung* ... , pp. 30–34.
143. Cf. more on this topic, E.J. Krześniak, *Kluby i organizacje sportowe* (...), pp. 544–545.

V. Gambling

209. Gambling in Poland is still associated more with scenes from F.F. Coppola's 'New York Stories' than the elegant casinos in Las Vegas or the Ascot races. This translates directly into the legal regulations on gambling which are more restrictive in Poland than almost anywhere else in the world. The political anti-gambling campaign that was taken up several years ago by the authorities of that time in response to the scandal uncovered by the authorities in which the main roles were played by a politician from the governing party and one of the businessmen from the gambling sector, which resulted in the introduction of far-reaching restrictions on the ability to conduct business in this area. A large proportion of the market, including that, which applied to betting on the results of sports events, is therefore actually controlled by entities operating abroad, which also try to offer their products to Polish consumers openly to a greater or lesser extent (they cannot do this directly because of statutory restrictions).

210. In the area of sports, the criminal regulations introducing sanctions for 'fixing' the results of sports events are also particularly important. The mere acceptance of financial or personal benefits or the offer of this in exchange for dishonest conduct, which can affect the result of sports competitions organized by a PSF or an entity acting on contract to it, is punishable with imprisonment for up to eight years (ten if the benefit is of substantial value) (Article 46 AoS). Intermediation in fixing a specific result of sports competitions in exchange for financial or personal benefit is also punishable (Article 48 AoS). The conduct described above is punishable regardless of whether or not anyone bet on the result of the sports competition in which the result of the match was fixed or such an attempt was made. Taking advantage of knowledge of fixing the result of a match or another sports event in order to bet on the result of the match in bets, which, one way or another are legal, or even informing someone, who wants to place a bet, about the fixing of the result of the match is punishable separately and independently with a penalty imprisonment of up to five years (Article 47 AoS).

211. Conviction for the offences specified in Article 46, paragraphs 1, 2 and 4, Article 47 and Article 48, paragraphs 1 and 2 may result in the deprivation of public rights, as well as the prohibition of holding a position or occupation or working in state and local government bodies and institutions (Article 49a AoS).

§4. Tax

I. General Principles of Taxation in Poland

212. The main taxes which taxpayers are required to settle in Poland are:

– personal income tax (PIT – discussed in Sport and Employment);
– corporate income tax (CIT); and
– value added tax (VAT).

A. CIT

213. Taxation with CIT is governed by the provisions of the Act on Corporate Income Tax of 15 February 1992 (Act on CIT).

214. According to the general principles, the CIT tax base is income regardless of the type of sources of income from which the income is earned. Income is the surplus of the sum of revenues over the costs of generating that income, which is generated in the tax year, whereby deductible expenses are the costs incurred on generating revenue or preserving or securing sources of revenue.

215. CIT amounts to:

- 19% of the tax base;
- 9% of the taxable base on revenue (income) other than from capital gains – in the case of taxable persons whose revenue earned in a fiscal year did not exceed the PLN equivalent of EUR 2,000,000, converted according to the average EUR exchange rate announced by the National Bank of Poland as at the first working day of the fiscal year, rounded to PLN 1,000.15% of the tax base – for small taxpayers and taxpayers starting business – in the tax year in which they start their business, provided that they satisfy the conditions laid down in the Act on CIT.

B. VAT

216. Taxation with VAT is governed by the provisions of the Act on VAT of 11 April 2002 (Act on VAT).

217. Taxpayers are legal persons, unincorporated organizational units and self-employed people, regardless of the objective or result of such activity, whereby sales made by taxpayers whose total net sales value did not exceed PLN 200,000 in the previous year are exempt from this taxation.

II. Special Regulations on Sports Clubs and Sports Associations

A. CIT

218. In principle, sports clubs and sports associations are CIT taxpayers.

219. The part of the income of taxpayers, whose statutory objectives are activities of physical culture and sport, which arises from these objectives is exempt from CIT, whereby this exemption applies, among others to entities managed in the form of a company and therefore the exemption primarily applies to sports clubs or sports associations operating in the form of associations.

220. In addition, the income of the sports clubs referred to in the AoS, which is assigned to or disbursed on sports training and competitions of children and adolescents in the age categories of children, younger juniors, juniors and youths aged up to 23 years during the tax year or the following year is also exempt from CIT.

B. VAT

221. Services strictly related to sports or physical education provided by sports clubs, sports associations and federations, as well as other legal entities, the statutory objective of which is to develop and promote sports, are exempt from VAT, provided that:

(1) they are necessary for organizing and playing sport or organizing and participating in physical education;
(2) the service providers are not profit-oriented; and
(3) they are provided to people who play sports or participate in physical education.

222. These exclude services related to marketing, as well as advertising and promotional activities, admission to sports events, paid services of managing sport and recreational facilities, paid services of accommodation related to sports and physical education, as well as rental of sports equipment and sports facilities services for a fee.

223. However, the exemption described above is applicable on condition that the entities performing the activities referred to above do not systematically generate profits from such activities, and in the event that they are generated, they are assigned in whole for continuing or improving the services provided.

224. Even so, the VAT exemptions cannot be applied to the provision of services that are strictly related to the basic services if they are not necessary for the performance of the basic service, which is exempt from tax, or their main objective is for the taxpayer to obtain additional income from the competitive performance of these activities for taxpayers not benefiting from such an exemption.

C. Transfer of Tax to the Club

225. Sports clubs that are not profit-oriented companies may also be considered to be public benefit organizations. Clubs with such a status may ask their supporters to transfer 1.5% of the tax that these people pay each year to them. The introduction of the ability to transfer 1.5% of the tax that is payable to a public benefit organization of the taxpayer's choice was a result of the efforts of the non-governmental organization sector to strengthen the role of the civic society.

§5. Sports Justice

I. Disciplinary Liability

226. Disciplinary liability is not something that is unique to sport. However, in sport, it has a special function. It has top priority.[144] Even so, it can be speculated that the analysis of numerous Disciplinary Rules in PSFs suggests that one of the fundamental objectives, if not the basis of all of these rules, is the desire to leave all 'intra-association' or 'intra-federation' issues within the sports organizations on their own without the involvement in (although perhaps it may be more appropriate to say – without admission to) these matters of the administrative authorities and the general courts.

227. The principles of disciplinary liability in sport are not based on the concept of arbitration. Penalization of activities under the rules on disciplinary liability should not be treated as arbitration in the formal sense. Significant consequences arise from this fact alone, for instance, those which, in the context of disciplinary proceedings, the arbitration rules on admissibility or the taking of evidence, most frequently modelled on the principles of Civil Procedures Code (CPC), do not apply classically. In this respect, the respective NGBs have far greater freedom than any arbitration court.

228. However, this does not mean that the system of disciplinary liability can be entirely arbitrary. It should satisfy at least some of the basic standards of the principles of social coexistence and may be assessed according to them and, in the case of conflicts, priority should be given to the norms of social coexistence. Disciplinary proceedings themselves should be transparent and conducted comprehensibly for those who participate in them. As far as possible – simultaneously fast, as required by the nature of modern sport, and inexpensive.

229. It may be difficult to reconcile all of these objectives. For example, a process that is fast and inexpensive, most frequently takes place without legal counsels; the inclusion of lawyers in this procedure means that the proceedings will be more expensive, while the time that passes from the start of the case to the moment when the decision is issued will certainly be longer. Therefore, all these issues need to be addressed and a system needs to be built that will implement them as fully as possible.

230. Disciplinary liability should also not be equated to statutory rules-related liability, although the boundary between the two types of proceedings is vague and can, in itself, lead to disputes.

---

144. With regard to disciplinary liability in sport, *see*, among others A.J. Szwarc, *Znaczenie i problemy odpowiedzialności dyscyplinarnej w sporcie* (in:) Odpowiedzialność dyscyplinarna w sporcie, ed. A.J. Szwarc Poznań 2001, pp. 21–48. *See also* J. Giezek, *Sportowe sankcje dyscyplinarne* (in:) Odpowiedzialność dyscyplinarna w sporcie, ed. A.J. Szwarc, Poznań 2001, pp. 93–118.

231. Disciplinary liability may either be based on a specific statutory provision or it may arise from the provisions of the statutes of associations or federations. The Polish legal regulations do not contain rules on disciplinary liability, but do not rule out the possibility of establishing specific standards within associations or federations and imposing sanctions for non-compliance, which is a typical feature of any disciplinary liability.[145] It does not even need to be called disciplinary liability – the terms 'rules-related liability', 'statutory liability' or 'organizational liability' are frequently used, but the difference is mainly semantic and, in most cases, we will be dealing with disciplinary liability.

232. There can be talk of disciplinary liability in the Polish legal system not only with respect to natural persons – sportspeople, activists or referees/umpires – but also with respect to sports clubs and other legal entities operating in sport.[146] This is in conflict with the traditional legal understanding of the term 'disciplinary liability', which is understood as the rules that specify who is liable for what, whereby 'who' in this case (in other areas of life) always means a natural person.[147] When regulating disciplinary liability in other areas of life outside sport, the lawmakers almost always refer to specific groups of people. They will be, for instance, central or local government administration employees, people practising professions related to the administration of the law, including attorneys-at-law, legal counsels, notaries public, prosecutors, court bailiffs, tax advisers and patent attorneys, as well as judges of both general courts and administrative courts, the Supreme Court and the Constitutional Tribunal. Likewise, people working in the so-called uniform services – officers of the Police, the State Fire Brigade, the Border Guards or the Customs Service – are subject to disciplinary liability, as are employees of the Internal Security Agency and the Intelligence Agency, the State Protection Service and the Prison Service. In all these cases, we are dealing with the liability of specific individuals for specific breaches. It is different in sport.

233. The AoS governs disciplinary liability to a limited extent. Article 13, paragraph 1 item 2 AoS specifies that the PSF has the exclusive right to establish and enforce both sports and organizational, as well as Disciplinary Rules in competitions organized by the association, excluding the anti-doping rules. Disciplinary liability in sport is therefore a liability of PSFs to the extent defined in the Disciplinary Rules adopted by the meeting of members or delegates of that association.[148]

234. In turn, Article 45b AoS contains rules on the basis of disciplinary liability and a list of penalties (not exclusive – the rules may provide for penalties other than

145. *See* P. Suski, *Stowarzyszenia i fundacje, Warszawa 2008*, p. 245.
146. More on this in P. Jóźwiak, *Odpowiedzialność dyscyplinarna ...*, Poznań 2014, pp. 32–33, 317–333. *See also* P. Sławicki, *Odpowiedzialność dyscyplinarna w sporcie w świetle nowej ustawy*, PiP 2012, book 4, pp. 67–77.
147. Cf. Z. Leoński, *Odpowiedzialność dyscyplinarna słuchaczy państwowych szkół wyższych w prawie polskim*, Zeszyty Naukowe Uniwersytetu im. A. Mickiewicza, 1955, book 1, pp. 131–133.
148. *See also* P. Jóźwiak, *Odpowiedzialność dyscyplinarna ...*, p. 32.

those specified in the provisions of the law). The law also defines two main principles of disciplinary liability – the right to a defence and two instances of proceedings.

235. Handling civil, criminal or administrative proceedings against an accused does not rule out the possibility of taking disciplinary action for the same offence. The principle of independence of disciplinary liability from other types of liability is one of the key features of disciplinary liability in general.[149] In the case of a disciplinary offence, the defendant is subject to disciplinary liability regardless of whether or not he can also be liable, for example, for a crime, if his offence bears the signs of a crime. In practice, it is obviously possible to suspend disciplinary proceedings until the end of the criminal or administrative proceedings, but this is not obligatory.

236. In the case of sport, disciplinary liability is not limited to just natural persons but also legal entities and potentially other entities.

237. The rules regarding disciplinary liability in sport are supplemented to a great extent by the statutes of the Polish NFs and the relevant rules. The analysis of these statutes and rules gives an understanding of how individual NFs deal with this problem. Tables 1 and 2 summarize the solutions implemented in PSFs regarding disciplinary liability.

149. Z. Leoński, *Odpowiedzialność dyscyplinarna* ... , book 1 p. 133, quotation from P. Jóźwiak, *Odpowiedzialność dyscyplinarna* ... , p. 25.

Table 1 Disciplinary Liability in Individual Sports (PSFs)

Name of the Association	*Regulation on Disciplinary Liability in the Association's Statutes (Yes/No Specifying the Provisions of the Statutes)*	*Existence of Separate Rules on Discipli nary Liability (Yes/No)*	*Which Authorities Are Entitled to Impose Disciplinary Penalties (Indicating Where They Have Been Regulated)*	*How Many Instances in Disciplinary Proceedings (Indicating Where This Has Been Regulated)*	*Is It Possible to Appeal Against the Disciplinary Penalties to the POC Court of Arbitration for Sport (Yes/No Indicating Where This Has Been Regulated)*	*Is It Possible to Appeal Against the Disciplinary Penalties to CAS in Lausanne (Yes/No Indicating Where This Has Been Regulated)*	*Is It Possible to Appeal Against the Disciplinary Penalties to Another Arbitration Court (Yes/ No Indicating Where This Has Been Regulated)*	*Is It Possible to Appeal Against the Disciplinary Penalties to a General Court (Yes/No Indicating Where This Has Been Regulated)*
1	2	3	4	5	6	7	8	9
Polish Mountai neering Association	No – Article 25, clause 5 of the Statutes specifies that: 'Penalties and sanctions at the disposal of the	Yes	Pursuant to Article 6 of the Disciplinary Rules: 'The authorities responsible for disciplinary hearings (disciplinary bodies of the Polish Mountaineering Association) are:	Two instances (Pursuant to Articles 12, 13, 14 and 15 of the Disciplinary Rules.)	Yes – In 'cassation' proceedings, an appeal to the Tribunal is possible under Article 87 of the Disciplinary Rules:	No	No	No

Name of the Association	*Regulation on Disciplinary Liability in the Association's Statutes (Yes/No Specifying the Provisions of the Statutes)*	*Existence of Separate Rules on Discipli nary Liability (Yes/No)*	*Which Authorities Are Entitled to Impose Disciplinary Penalties (Indicating Where They Have Been Regulated)*	*How Many Instances in Disciplinary Proceedings (Indicating Where This Has Been Regulated)*	*Is It Possible to Appeal Against the Disciplinary Penalties to the POC Court of Arbitration for Sport (Yes/No Indicating Where This Has Been Regulated)*	*Is It Possible to Appeal Against the Disciplinary Penalties to CAS in Lausanne (Yes/No Indicating Where This Has Been Regulated)*	*Is It Possible to Appeal Against the Disciplinary Penalties to Another Arbitration Court (Yes/ No Indicating Where This Has Been Regulated)*	*Is It Possible to Appeal Against the Disciplinary Penalties to a General Court (Yes/No Indicating Where This Has Been Regulated)*
	Association's Judicial Panel are included in the Rules on Disciplinary Proceedings of the Polish Mountaineering Association.'		(1) the disciplinary authorities of the full members of the Polish Mountaineering Association; (2) leaders of expeditions, groups and ex-Tatra courses; (3) managers of national and Tatra groups and courses; (4) the Polish Mountaineering Association's Judicial Panel;		'After exhausting the association's internal disciplinary procedure, disciplinary decisions issued in disciplinary proceedings related to a breach of the anti-doping rules			

Name of the Association	*Regulation on Disciplinary Liability in the Association's Statutes (Yes/No Specifying the Provisions of the Statutes)*	*Existence of Separate Rules on Discipli nary Liability (Yes/No)*	*Which Authorities Are Entitled to Impose Disciplinary Penalties (Indicating Where They Have Been Regulated)*	*How Many Instances in Disciplinary Proceedings (Indicating Where This Has Been Regulated)*	*Is It Possible to Appeal Against the Disciplinary Penalties to the POC Court of Arbitration for Sport (Yes/No Indicating Where This Has Been Regulated)*	*Is It Possible to Appeal Against the Disciplinary Penalties to CAS in Lausanne (Yes/No Indicating Where This Has Been Regulated)*	*Is It Possible to Appeal Against the Disciplinary Penalties to Another Arbitration Court (Yes/ No Indicating Where This Has Been Regulated)*	*Is It Possible to Appeal Against the Disciplinary Penalties to a General Court (Yes/No Indicating Where This Has Been Regulated)*
			(5) Management Board of the Polish Mountaineering Association; (6) The General Meeting of Delegates.'		may be contested before the POC Court of Arbitration for Sport in accordance with the provisions referred to in § 3, clause 1, item 2 of the Rules' (which provides that 'The provisions of the Disciplinary Rules shall be applied accordingly to disciplinary proceedings related to the use of doping in sport').			

Name of the Association	*Regulation on Disciplinary Liability in the Association's Statutes (Yes/No Specifying the Provisions of the Statutes)*	*Existence of Separate Rules on Discipli nary Liability (Yes/No)*	*Which Authorities Are Entitled to Impose Disciplinary Penalties (Indicating Where They Have Been Regulated)*	*How Many Instances in Disciplinary Proceedings (Indicating Where This Has Been Regulated)*	*Is It Possible to Appeal Against the Disciplinary Penalties to the POC Court of Arbitration for Sport (Yes/No Indicating Where This Has Been Regulated)*	*Is It Possible to Appeal Against the Disciplinary Penalties to CAS in Lausanne (Yes/No Indicating Where This Has Been Regulated)*	*Is It Possible to Appeal Against the Disciplinary Penalties to Another Arbitration Court (Yes/ No Indicating Where This Has Been Regulated)*	*Is It Possible to Appeal Against the Disciplinary Penalties to a General Court (Yes/No Indicating Where This Has Been Regulated)*
Polish Badminton Association	Yes (§§ 51–52 of the Statutes)	Yes – PZBad Referee Rules and Sports Rules.	Disciplinary and Arbitration Committee (§ 52 of the Statutes), National Delegates Convention (§ 32 of the Statutes)	One instance (a principle that is not directly expressed, possibly Sports Tribunal at the POC)	Implicit rule	No	No	No
Polish Biathlon Association	Yes – Article 30 of the Statutes describes disciplinary liability; the	Yes	Pursuant to Article 5 of the Disciplinary Rules: The Disciplinary Authorities are: the Disciplinary Ombudsman, the Disciplinary Commission, as the first instance ruling authority, and	Two instances (Pursuant to Article 6 of the rules: 'Disciplinary proceedings are	§ 7 item 5: Final decision issued the disciplinary proceedings is appealable to the Arbitration Tribunal for Sport with the POC.	No	No	No

Name of the Association	*Regulation on Disciplinary Liability in the Association's Statutes (Yes/No Specifying the Provisions of the Statutes)*	*Existence of Separate Rules on Discipli nary Liability (Yes/No)*	*Which Authorities Are Entitled to Impose Disciplinary Penalties (Indicating Where They Have Been Regulated)*	*How Many Instances in Disciplinary Proceedings (Indicating Where This Has Been Regulated)*	*Is It Possible to Appeal Against the Disciplinary Penalties to the POC Court of Arbitration for Sport (Yes/No Indicating Where This Has Been Regulated)*	*Is It Possible to Appeal Against the Disciplinary Penalties to CAS in Lausanne (Yes/No Indicating Where This Has Been Regulated)*	*Is It Possible to Appeal Against the Disciplinary Penalties to Another Arbitration Court (Yes/ No Indicating Where This Has Been Regulated)*	*Is It Possible to Appeal Against the Disciplinary Penalties to a General Court (Yes/No Indicating Where This Has Been Regulated)*
	elaboration on this is contained in the Disciplinary Rules.		the Appeals Commission, as the second instance ruling authority. It is possible to appoint more disciplinary ombudsmen, it being understood that they act individually. The Disciplinary Authorities and their particular members are appointed by the PZBiath Review Commission.	governed by the dual instance principle.')				
Polish Bobsleigh and Skeleton Federation	Yes – § 34 of the Statute sets forth the general rules of disciplinary liability; this issue has been	Yes	Pursuant to § 5, 6, 10 and 11 of the Disciplinary Rules, the disciplinary authorities are: PZBiS Disciplinary Commission (main disciplinary authority), PZBiS Management Board, General Delegates	Two instances (§ 33 of the Rules)	Yes – § 53 of the Disciplinary Rules and § 34 of the Statutes.	No	No	No

Name of the Association	Regulation on Disciplinary Liability in the Association's Statutes (Yes/No Specifying the Provisions of the Statutes)	Existence of Separate Rules on Discipli nary Liability (Yes/No)	Which Authorities Are Entitled to Impose Disciplinary Penalties (Indicating Where They Have Been Regulated)	How Many Instances in Disciplinary Proceedings (Indicating Where This Has Been Regulated)	Is It Possible to Appeal Against the Disciplinary Penalties to the POC Court of Arbitration for Sport (Yes/No Indicating Where This Has Been Regulated)	Is It Possible to Appeal Against the Disciplinary Penalties to CAS in Lausanne (Yes/No Indicating Where This Has Been Regulated)	Is It Possible to Appeal Against the Disciplinary Penalties to Another Arbitration Court (Yes/ No Indicating Where This Has Been Regulated)	Is It Possible to Appeal Against the Disciplinary Penalties to a General Court (Yes/No Indicating Where This Has Been Regulated)
	addressed in greater detail in the Disciplinary Rules.		Meeting. The Disciplinary Commission rules as the first instance authority, except in matters of excluding or suspending a Management Board member; the Management Board rules as the first instance authority in matters of excluding or suspending a Management Board member and as the second instance authority for the Disciplinary Commission rulings. The General Delegates Meeting considers the appeal measures for the Management Board's first instance rulings.					

Name of the Association	*Regulation on Disciplinary Liability in the Association's Statutes (Yes/No Specifying the Provisions of the Statutes)*	*Existence of Separate Rules on Discipli nary Liability (Yes/No)*	*Which Authorities Are Entitled to Impose Disciplinary Penalties (Indicating Where They Have Been Regulated)*	*How Many Instances in Disciplinary Proceedings (Indicating Where This Has Been Regulated)*	*Is It Possible to Appeal Against the Disciplinary Penalties to the POC Court of Arbitration for Sport (Yes/No Indicating Where This Has Been Regulated)*	*Is It Possible to Appeal Against the Disciplinary Penalties to CAS in Lausanne (Yes/No Indicating Where This Has Been Regulated)*	*Is It Possible to Appeal Against the Disciplinary Penalties to Another Arbitration Court (Yes/ No Indicating Where This Has Been Regulated)*	*Is It Possible to Appeal Against the Disciplinary Penalties to a General Court (Yes/No Indicating Where This Has Been Regulated)*
Polish Gymnastics Association	Yes – Disciplinary liability is regulated in § 37 of the statutes and addressed in greater detail in the Disciplinary Rules.	Yes	Pursuant to Article 5 of the Disciplinary Rules: 'The authorities responsible for disciplinary hearings (disciplinary bodies of the Polish Gymnastics Association) are: (1) the Disciplinary Committee of the Polish Gymnastics Association; (2) Management Board of the Polish Gymnastics Association; (3) The General Meeting of Delegates.'	Two instances (Pursuant to Article 36, clause 1 of the Disciplinary Rules; 'Disciplinary proceedings shall take place in at least two instances'.)	Yes – Pursuant to Article 56 of the Disciplinary Rules: 'After exhausting the internal disciplinary process, disciplinary decisions issued in disciplinary proceedings related to a breach of the anti-doping rules may be contested before the POC Court of Arbitration for Sport.'	No	No	No

Name of the Association	*Regulation on Disciplinary Liability in the Association's Statutes (Yes/No Specifying the Provisions of the Statutes)*	*Existence of Separate Rules on Discipli nary Liability (Yes/No)*	*Which Authorities Are Entitled to Impose Disciplinary Penalties (Indicating Where They Have Been Regulated)*	*How Many Instances in Disciplinary Proceedings (Indicating Where This Has Been Regulated)*	*Is It Possible to Appeal Against the Disciplinary Penalties to the POC Court of Arbitration for Sport (Yes/No Indicating Where This Has Been Regulated)*	*Is It Possible to Appeal Against the Disciplinary Penalties to CAS in Lausanne (Yes/No Indicating Where This Has Been Regulated)*	*Is It Possible to Appeal Against the Disciplinary Penalties to Another Arbitration Court (Yes/ No Indicating Where This Has Been Regulated)*	*Is It Possible to Appeal Against the Disciplinary Penalties to a General Court (Yes/No Indicating Where This Has Been Regulated)*
Polish Golf Union	Yes (§§ 24–25 of the Statutes)	Yes	First instance – Disciplinary and Rules-related Committee. Second instance – the Union's Management Board. (§ 27 of the statutes)	Two instances (§ 25 item 5 of the statutes and § 15 item 1 of the Disciplinary Rules)	Yes (§ 4 item 6 and § 15 item 2 of the Disciplinary Rules)	No	No	No

Name of the Association	*Regulation on Disciplinary Liability in the Association's Statutes (Yes/No Specifying the Provisions of the Statutes)*	*Existence of Separate Rules on Disciplinary Liability (Yes/No)*	*Which Authorities Are Entitled to Impose Disciplinary Penalties (Indicating Where They Have Been Regulated)*	*How Many Instances in Disciplinary Proceedings (Indicating Where This Has Been Regulated)*	*Is It Possible to Appeal Against the Disciplinary Penalties to the POC Court of Arbitration for Sport (Yes/No Indicating Where This Has Been Regulated)*	*Is It Possible to Appeal Against the Disciplinary Penalties to CAS in Lausanne (Yes/No Indicating Where This Has Been Regulated)*	*Is It Possible to Appeal Against the Disciplinary Penalties to Another Arbitration Court (Yes/No Indicating Where This Has Been Regulated)*	*Is It Possible to Appeal Against the Disciplinary Penalties to a General Court (Yes/No Indicating Where This Has Been Regulated)*
Polish Kickboxing Association	No – Pursuant to Article 39 of the Statutes: 'The disciplinary procedure and types of penalties are specified in detail in the Association's Disciplinary Rules adopted by the General Congress of Delegates.'	Yes	Pursuant to Article 4, item 2 of the Disciplinary Rules: 'The bodies authorized to exercise disciplinary authority at the Polish Kickboxing Association, hereinafter referred to as the disciplinary bodies, are: – the Management Board of the Polish Kickboxing Association; – the Disciplinary Committee of the Polish Kickboxing Association; – the Judicial Committee of the Polish Kickboxing Association; – the Club's Management Board or its Disciplinary Committee.'	Two instances (Pursuant to § 5 of the Disciplinary Rules: 'The principle of two instances applies in disciplinary proceedings.')	No	No	Yes – Pursuant to § 41 of the Statutes, disciplinary rulings may be protested to the Association's Management Board or using legal measures available under applicable laws.	Yes – Pursuant to § 41 of the statutes, disciplinary rulings may be protested to the Association's Management Board or using legal measures available under applicable laws.

Name of the Association	*Regulation on Disciplinary Liability in the Association's Statutes (Yes/No Specifying the Provisions of the Statutes)*	*Existence of Separate Rules on Discipli nary Liability (Yes/No)*	*Which Authorities Are Entitled to Impose Disciplinary Penalties (Indicating Where They Have Been Regulated)*	*How Many Instances in Disciplinary Proceedings (Indicating Where This Has Been Regulated)*	*Is It Possible to Appeal Against the Disciplinary Penalties to the POC Court of Arbitration for Sport (Yes/No Indicating Where This Has Been Regulated)*	*Is It Possible to Appeal Against the Disciplinary Penalties to CAS in Lausanne (Yes/No Indicating Where This Has Been Regulated)*	*Is It Possible to Appeal Against the Disciplinary Penalties to Another Arbitration Court (Yes/ No Indicating Where This Has Been Regulated)*	*Is It Possible to Appeal Against the Disciplinary Penalties to a General Court (Yes/No Indicating Where This Has Been Regulated)*
Polish Athletic Association	Yes – The general principles of disciplinary liability are specified on the basis of Article 34 of the Statutes, whereas the extension of this issue is contained in the Disciplinary Rules.	Yes	Pursuant to Article 58 of the Disciplinary Rules: the following bodies are authorized to adjudicate in cases of disciplinary offences ('Disciplinary bodies'): (1) the National Congress of Delegates of the Polish Athletic Association; (2) the Management Board of the Polish Athletic Association; (3) the Committee on Awards, Discipline and Combating Doping of the Polish Athletic Association; (4) the Disciplinary Committee of the Voivodship Athletic Association;	Two instances (Pursuant to Article 62, clause 1 of the Disciplinary Rules; 'The principle of two instances applies in disciplinary proceedings.')	Yes – § 34 item 6 of the Statutes.	Yes – § 63 of the Disciplinary Liability Rules: 'The second instance authorities competent to rule in disciplinary matters are: (4) the Court of Arbitration for Sport (CAS) – for	Yes – Article 88 of the Disciplinary Rules states that 'In matters specified in the IAAF Statutes, a competitor may appeal against decisions of the Disciplinary Bodies to the IAAF.'	No

Name of the Association	*Regulation on Disciplinary Liability in the Association's Statutes (Yes/No Specifying the Provisions of the Statutes)*	*Existence of Separate Rules on Discipli nary Liability (Yes/No)*	*Which Authorities Are Entitled to Impose Disciplinary Penalties (Indicating Where They Have Been Regulated)*	*How Many Instances in Disciplinary Proceedings (Indicating Where This Has Been Regulated)*	*Is It Possible to Appeal Against the Disciplinary Penalties to the POC Court of Arbitration for Sport (Yes/No Indicating Where This Has Been Regulated)*	*Is It Possible to Appeal Against the Disciplinary Penalties to CAS in Lausanne (Yes/No Indicating Where This Has Been Regulated)*	*Is It Possible to Appeal Against the Disciplinary Penalties to Another Arbitration Court (Yes/ No Indicating Where This Has Been Regulated)*	*Is It Possible to Appeal Against the Disciplinary Penalties to a General Court (Yes/No Indicating Where This Has Been Regulated)*
			(5) the disciplinary committees or management boards of the clubs.			second instance rulings of the Disciplinary Panel with the Committee on Combating Doping in Sport, referred to in item 8.1.1 of the Polish Anti-Doping Rules to the		

Name of the Association	*Regulation on Disciplinary Liability in the Association's Statutes (Yes/No Specifying the Provisions of the Statutes)*	*Existence of Separate Rules on Discipli nary Liability (Yes/No)*	*Which Authorities Are Entitled to Impose Disciplinary Penalties (Indicating Where They Have Been Regulated)*	*How Many Instances in Disciplinary Proceedings (Indicating Where This Has Been Regulated)*	*Is It Possible to Appeal Against the Disciplinary Penalties to the POC Court of Arbitration for Sport (Yes/No Indicating Where This Has Been Regulated)*	*Is It Possible to Appeal Against the Disciplinary Penalties to CAS in Lausanne (Yes/No Indicating Where This Has Been Regulated)*	*Is It Possible to Appeal Against the Disciplinary Penalties to Another Arbitration Court (Yes/ No Indicating Where This Has Been Regulated)*	*Is It Possible to Appeal Against the Disciplinary Penalties to a General Court (Yes/No Indicating Where This Has Been Regulated)*
						extent arising from item 13.2.1 of the Polish Anti-Doping Rules.'		

Name of the Association	*Regulation on Disciplinary Liability in the Association's Statutes (Yes/No Specifying the Provisions of the Statutes)*	*Existence of Separate Rules on Discipli nary Liability (Yes/No)*	*Which Authorities Are Entitled to Impose Disciplinary Penalties (Indicating Where They Have Been Regulated)*	*How Many Instances in Disciplinary Proceedings (Indicating Where This Has Been Regulated)*	*Is It Possible to Appeal Against the Disciplinary Penalties to the POC Court of Arbitration for Sport (Yes/No Indicating Where This Has Been Regulated)*	*Is It Possible to Appeal Against the Disciplinary Penalties to CAS in Lausanne (Yes/No Indicating Where This Has Been Regulated)*	*Is It Possible to Appeal Against the Disciplinary Penalties to Another Arbitration Court (Yes/ No Indicating Where This Has Been Regulated)*	*Is It Possible to Appeal Against the Disciplinary Penalties to a General Court (Yes/No Indicating Where This Has Been Regulated)*
Polish Ski Federation	No – Article 33 of the Statutes provides that disciplinary liability issues are addressed in the manner and under the principles laid down in the Disciplinary Rules.	Yes	'Pursuant to Article 5 of the disciplinary rules, the body that is authorized to adjudicate in the 1st instance is the Disciplinary Committee, while, pursuant to Article 6 of the rules, the body is the Management Board in the 2nd instance.'	Two instances (Pursuant to Article 6 of the Rules: 'The principle of two instances applies in disciplinary proceedings.')	Yes – Pursuant to Article 13, clause 6b, an appeal may be filed with the POC Court of Arbitration for Sport on matters related to doping tests: 'in cases involving national sports people who are subject to the Anti-Doping Agency, who are not entitled to appeal under clause 6, item a) above, these people are entitled to appeal	Yes – Pursuant to Article 13, clause 6a, an appeal may be filed with the CAS on matters related to doping tests: 'in cases related to participation in international sporting	No	No

Name of the Association	*Regulation on Disciplinary Liability in the Association's Statutes (Yes/No Specifying the Provisions of the Statutes)*	*Existence of Separate Rules on Discipli nary Liability (Yes/No)*	*Which Authorities Are Entitled to Impose Disciplinary Penalties (Indicating Where They Have Been Regulated)*	*How Many Instances in Disciplinary Proceedings (Indicating Where This Has Been Regulated)*	*Is It Possible to Appeal Against the Disciplinary Penalties to the POC Court of Arbitration for Sport (Yes/No Indicating Where This Has Been Regulated)*	*Is It Possible to Appeal Against the Disciplinary Penalties to CAS in Lausanne (Yes/No Indicating Where This Has Been Regulated)*	*Is It Possible to Appeal Against the Disciplinary Penalties to Another Arbitration Court (Yes/ No Indicating Where This Has Been Regulated)*	*Is It Possible to Appeal Against the Disciplinary Penalties to a General Court (Yes/No Indicating Where This Has Been Regulated)*
					against the decision to the independent and impartial appeal body at national level, which is the POC Court of Arbitration for Sport'.	events or in cases involving international class sports people, an appeal may only be filed against the decision with the Court of Arbitration in Sport (CAS) in accordance with the rules in force in		

Name of the Association	*Regulation on Disciplinary Liability in the Association's Statutes (Yes/No Specifying the Provisions of the Statutes)*	*Existence of Separate Rules on Discipli nary Liability (Yes/No)*	*Which Authorities Are Entitled to Impose Disciplinary Penalties (Indicating Where They Have Been Regulated)*	*How Many Instances in Disciplinary Proceedings (Indicating Where This Has Been Regulated)*	*Is It Possible to Appeal Against the Disciplinary Penalties to the POC Court of Arbitration for Sport (Yes/No Indicating Where This Has Been Regulated)*	*Is It Possible to Appeal Against the Disciplinary Penalties to CAS in Lausanne (Yes/No Indicating Where This Has Been Regulated)*	*Is It Possible to Appeal Against the Disciplinary Penalties to Another Arbitration Court (Yes/ No Indicating Where This Has Been Regulated)*	*Is It Possible to Appeal Against the Disciplinary Penalties to a General Court (Yes/No Indicating Where This Has Been Regulated)*
						proceedings before that court'.		
Polish Modern Pentathlon Association	Yes (§§ 33–35 of the Statutes)	No	First instance – Disciplinary Committee; second instance – the Association's Management Board (§§ 34–35 of the Statutes)	Two instances (§§ 34–35 of the Statutes)	Yes (§ 35 of the Statutes)	No	No	No
Polish Swimming Federation	Yes (§§ 58–61 of the Statutes)	Yes	First instance – Disciplinary Committee; second instance – the Association's Management Board (or the National Congress in matters of expulsion of a member by the Management Board) pursuant to § 60 of the statutes and § 5 of the Disciplinary Rules	Two instances (§ 61 item 1 of the Statutes)	Yes (§ 61 item 2 of the Statutes)	No	No	No

Name of the Association	*Regulation on Disciplinary Liability in the Association's Statutes (Yes/No Specifying the Provisions of the Statutes)*	*Existence of Separate Rules on Discipli nary Liability (Yes/No)*	*Which Authorities Are Entitled to Impose Disciplinary Penalties (Indicating Where They Have Been Regulated)*	*How Many Instances in Disciplinary Proceedings (Indicating Where This Has Been Regulated)*	*Is It Possible to Appeal Against the Disciplinary Penalties to the POC Court of Arbitration for Sport (Yes/No Indicating Where This Has Been Regulated)*	*Is It Possible to Appeal Against the Disciplinary Penalties to CAS in Lausanne (Yes/No Indicating Where This Has Been Regulated)*	*Is It Possible to Appeal Against the Disciplinary Penalties to Another Arbitration Court (Yes/ No Indicating Where This Has Been Regulated)*	*Is It Possible to Appeal Against the Disciplinary Penalties to a General Court (Yes/No Indicating Where This Has Been Regulated)*
Polish Weightlifting Federation	Yes – The general principles of disciplinary liability are specified on the basis of Articles 43–44 of the Statutes, whereas the extension of this issue is contained in the Disciplinary Rules.	Yes	All first instance disciplinary matters fall within the jurisdiction of the Disciplinary and Club Change Commission of PZPC in the panel of three arbiters. The second instance disciplinary authority is the Disciplinary Commission, ruling in the panel of three arbiters who have not participated in issuing the protested ruling (§§ 5–6 of the Rules).	Two instances (§ 44 item 4 point 2 of the Statutes and § 30 of the Disciplinary Rules)	Yes – § 44 of the Statutes and § 35 item 2 of the Disciplinary Rules.	No	No	No

Name of the Association	*Regulation on Disciplinary Liability in the Association's Statutes (Yes/No Specifying the Provisions of the Statutes)*	*Existence of Separate Rules on Discipli nary Liability (Yes/No)*	*Which Authorities Are Entitled to Impose Disciplinary Penalties (Indicating Where They Have Been Regulated)*	*How Many Instances in Disciplinary Proceedings (Indicating Where This Has Been Regulated)*	*Is It Possible to Appeal Against the Disciplinary Penalties to the POC Court of Arbitration for Sport (Yes/No Indicating Where This Has Been Regulated)*	*Is It Possible to Appeal Against the Disciplinary Penalties to CAS in Lausanne (Yes/No Indicating Where This Has Been Regulated)*	*Is It Possible to Appeal Against the Disciplinary Penalties to Another Arbitration Court (Yes/No Indicating Where This Has Been Regulated)*	*Is It Possible to Appeal Against the Disciplinary Penalties to a General Court (Yes/No Indicating Where This Has Been Regulated)*
Polish Luge Federation	Yes – blanket regulation (§§ 32–33 of the Statutes)	Yes	First instance – the management boards of the clubs, the management boards of the regional associations; second instance – the regional management boards of the associations, the Management Board of the Federation, the General Meeting of Delegates (§§ 18–19 of the Rules).	Two instances (§ 5 of the Rules)	Yes (§ 11 item 4 of the Rules)	No	No	No
Polish Sport Shooting Federation	Yes (§§ 34–39 of the Statutes)	Yes	First instance – Disciplinary Committee, the Federation's Management Board; second instance – the Association's Management Board, the General Meeting (§§ 10–12 of the Rules)	2 (§ 37 item 1 of the Statutes)	Yes (§ 37 item 3 of the Statutes)	No	No	No

Name of the Association	*Regulation on Disciplinary Liability in the Association's Statutes (Yes/No Specifying the Provisions of the Statutes)*	*Existence of Separate Rules on Discipli nary Liability (Yes/No)*	*Which Authorities Are Entitled to Impose Disciplinary Penalties (Indicating Where They Have Been Regulated)*	*How Many Instances in Disciplinary Proceedings (Indicating Where This Has Been Regulated)*	*Is It Possible to Appeal Against the Disciplinary Penalties to the POC Court of Arbitration for Sport (Yes/No Indicating Where This Has Been Regulated)*	*Is It Possible to Appeal Against the Disciplinary Penalties to CAS in Lausanne (Yes/No Indicating Where This Has Been Regulated)*	*Is It Possible to Appeal Against the Disciplinary Penalties to Another Arbitration Court (Yes/ No Indicating Where This Has Been Regulated)*	*Is It Possible to Appeal Against the Disciplinary Penalties to a General Court (Yes/No Indicating Where This Has Been Regulated)*
Polish Chess Federation	Yes – General principles of disciplinary liability are specified on the basis of Article 31 of the Statutes, whereas the extension of this issue is contained in the Disciplinary Rules.	Yes	Pursuant to Article 5 of the Disciplinary Rules: 'The following are authorized to adjudicate on disciplinary matters in the 1st instance: (a) the club and section management board; (b) the voivodship chess associations; (c) the Board of Judges of the Polish Chess Federation; (d) the Electronic Doping Committee; (e) the Awards and Discipline Committee of the Polish Chess Federation.	Two instances (Pursuant to § 13 the Disciplinary Rules: 'The principle of two instances applies in disciplinary proceedings.')	Yes (§ 31 item 4 of the Statutes and § 5 item 4 of the Disciplinary Rules)	No	No	No

Name of the Association	*Regulation on Disciplinary Liability in the Association's Statutes (Yes/No Specifying the Provisions of the Statutes)*	*Existence of Separate Rules on Discipli nary Liability (Yes/No)*	*Which Authorities Are Entitled to Impose Disciplinary Penalties (Indicating Where They Have Been Regulated)*	*How Many Instances in Disciplinary Proceedings (Indicating Where This Has Been Regulated)*	*Is It Possible to Appeal Against the Disciplinary Penalties to the POC Court of Arbitration for Sport (Yes/No Indicating Where This Has Been Regulated)*	*Is It Possible to Appeal Against the Disciplinary Penalties to CAS in Lausanne (Yes/No Indicating Where This Has Been Regulated)*	*Is It Possible to Appeal Against the Disciplinary Penalties to Another Arbitration Court (Yes/ No Indicating Where This Has Been Regulated)*	*Is It Possible to Appeal Against the Disciplinary Penalties to a General Court (Yes/No Indicating Where This Has Been Regulated)*
			(Furthermore) The authorities responsible for adjudicating in disciplinary cases in the 2nd instance are: (a) the voivodship chess associations; (b) the Awards and Discipline Committee of the Polish Chess Federation; (c) the Management Board of the Polish Chess Federation;’					

Name of the Association	*Regulation on Disciplinary Liability in the Association's Statutes (Yes/No Specifying the Provisions of the Statutes)*	*Existence of Separate Rules on Discipli nary Liability (Yes/No)*	*Which Authorities Are Entitled to Impose Disciplinary Penalties (Indicating Where They Have Been Regulated)*	*How Many Instances in Disciplinary Proceedings (Indicating Where This Has Been Regulated)*	*Is It Possible to Appeal Against the Disciplinary Penalties to the POC Court of Arbitration for Sport (Yes/No Indicating Where This Has Been Regulated)*	*Is It Possible to Appeal Against the Disciplinary Penalties to CAS in Lausanne (Yes/No Indicating Where This Has Been Regulated)*	*Is It Possible to Appeal Against the Disciplinary Penalties to Another Arbitration Court (Yes/ No Indicating Where This Has Been Regulated)*	*Is It Possible to Appeal Against the Disciplinary Penalties to a General Court (Yes/No Indicating Where This Has Been Regulated)*
Polish Table Tennis Association	Yes – General principles of disciplinary liability are specified on the basis of Article 37 of the Statutes, whereas the extension of this issue is contained in the Disciplinary Rules.	Yes	Pursuant to Article 58 of the Disciplinary Rules: 'The following bodies are authorized to adjudicate in cases of disciplinary offences ('Disciplinary bodies'): (1) the General Meeting of Delegates of the Polish Table Tennis Association; (2) the Management Board of the Polish Table Tennis Association; (3) the Disciplinary Committee of the Polish Table Tennis Association; (4) the Disciplinary Committee of the Voivodship Table Tennis Associations;	Two instances (Pursuant to Article 62, clause 1 of the Disciplinary Rules: 'The principle of two instances applies in disciplinary proceedings.')	No	No	Yes – Article 88 of the Disciplinary Rules states that 'In matters specified in the ITTF Statutes, a competitor may appeal to the ITTF against decisions of the Disciplinary Bodies.'	No

Name of the Association	*Regulation on Disciplinary Liability in the Association's Statutes (Yes/No Specifying the Provisions of the Statutes)*	*Existence of Separate Rules on Discipli nary Liability (Yes/No)*	*Which Authorities Are Entitled to Impose Disciplinary Penalties (Indicating Where They Have Been Regulated)*	*How Many Instances in Disciplinary Proceedings (Indicating Where This Has Been Regulated)*	*Is It Possible to Appeal Against the Disciplinary Penalties to the POC Court of Arbitration for Sport (Yes/No Indicating Where This Has Been Regulated)*	*Is It Possible to Appeal Against the Disciplinary Penalties to CAS in Lausanne (Yes/No Indicating Where This Has Been Regulated)*	*Is It Possible to Appeal Against the Disciplinary Penalties to Another Arbitration Court (Yes/ No Indicating Where This Has Been Regulated)*	*Is It Possible to Appeal Against the Disciplinary Penalties to a General Court (Yes/No Indicating Where This Has Been Regulated)*
			(5) the disciplinary committees or management boards of the clubs.'					
Polish Tennis Association	Yes – blanket regulation (§ 36 of the Statutes)	Yes	Pursuant to Article 5 item 1 of the Disciplinary Rules: 'first instance disciplinary penalties are inflicted collectively by the Disciplinary Commission in the panel of at least 3, while in the second instance – by the PZT Management Board in the panel of at least 5'.	Two instances (Article 18 of the Disciplinary Rules)	Yes (Pursuant to § 20 of the Disciplinary Rules, the disciplinary rulings of the PZT Management Board may be appealed to the Court of Arbitration for Sport with the POC.)	No	No	No

Name of the Association	*Regulation on Disciplinary Liability in the Association's Statutes (Yes/No Specifying the Provisions of the Statutes)*	*Existence of Separate Rules on Discipli nary Liability (Yes/No)*	*Which Authorities Are Entitled to Impose Disciplinary Penalties (Indicating Where They Have Been Regulated)*	*How Many Instances in Disciplinary Proceedings (Indicating Where This Has Been Regulated)*	*Is It Possible to Appeal Against the Disciplinary Penalties to the POC Court of Arbitration for Sport (Yes/No Indicating Where This Has Been Regulated)*	*Is It Possible to Appeal Against the Disciplinary Penalties to CAS in Lausanne (Yes/No Indicating Where This Has Been Regulated)*	*Is It Possible to Appeal Against the Disciplinary Penalties to Another Arbitration Court (Yes/ No Indicating Where This Has Been Regulated)*	*Is It Possible to Appeal Against the Disciplinary Penalties to a General Court (Yes/No Indicating Where This Has Been Regulated)*
Polish Wrestling Federation	Yes (§§ 48–51 of the Statutes)	Yes	The first instance disciplinary authorities competent to rule on disciplinary matters are: the Disciplinary and Arbitration Commission – in all matters related to disciplinary transgressions during or in connection with participating in wrestling competitions; the Association's Management Board – in matters of excluding a member from the Association. The second instance authorities are: the Association's Management Board – as the appeal authority for first instance and	Two instances (§ 49 ust. 3 of the Statutes)	Yes (§ 51 of the Statutes and § 98 of the Disciplinary Rules)	No	No	No

Name of the Association	*Regulation on Disciplinary Liability in the Association's Statutes (Yes/No Specifying the Provisions of the Statutes)*	*Existence of Separate Rules on Disciplinary Liability (Yes/No)*	*Which Authorities Are Entitled to Impose Disciplinary Penalties (Indicating Where They Have Been Regulated)*	*How Many Instances in Disciplinary Proceedings (Indicating Where This Has Been Regulated)*	*Is It Possible to Appeal Against the Disciplinary Penalties to the POC Court of Arbitration for Sport (Yes/No Indicating Where This Has Been Regulated)*	*Is It Possible to Appeal Against the Disciplinary Penalties to CAS in Lausanne (Yes/No Indicating Where This Has Been Regulated)*	*Is It Possible to Appeal Against the Disciplinary Penalties to Another Arbitration Court (Yes/No Indicating Where This Has Been Regulated)*	*Is It Possible to Appeal Against the Disciplinary Penalties to a General Court (Yes/No Indicating Where This Has Been Regulated)*
			Disciplinary and Arbitration Commission rulings; the General Delegates Meeting – as the appeal authority for Management Board rulings in matters of excluding a member from the Association (§ 80 of the Disciplinary Rules).					

Source: Own study. The table in the Polish language version was included for the first time in the book E.J. Krześniak, *Kluby i organizacje sportowe* (…), pp. 520–527, updated as of March 2021.

Table 2 Disciplinary Liability in Team Sports (PSFs)

Name of the Association	*Regulation on Disciplinary Liability in the Association's Statutes (Yes/No Specifying the Provisions of the Statutes)*	*Existence of Separate Rules on Disciplinary Liability (Yes/No)*	*Which Authorities Are Entitled to Impose Disciplinary Penalties (Indicating Where They Have Been Regulated)*	*How Many Instances in Disciplinary Proceedings (Indicating Where This Has Been Regulated)*	*Is It Possible to Appeal Against the Disciplinary Penalties to the POC Court of Arbitration for Sport (Yes/No Indicating Where This Has Been Regulated)*	*Is It Possible to Appeal Against the Disciplinary Penalties to CAS in Lausanne (Yes/No Indicating Where This Has Been Regulated)*	*Is It Possible to Appeal Against the Disciplinary Penalties to Another Arbitration Court (Yes/No Indicating Where This Has Been Regulated)*	*Is It Possible to Appeal Against the Disciplinary Penalties to a General Court (Yes/No Indicating Where This Has Been Regulated)*
1	2	3	4	5	6	7	8	9
Polish Ice Hockey Federation (PZHL)	No – Article 33 of the Statutes specifies that: 'The types of disciplinary penalties and the procedure and principles of their adjudication, as well as the structure of the bodies adjudicating	Yes	Pursuant to § 9 of the Disciplinary Rules, the first instance ruling authority is the Disciplinary Arbiter, ruling individually in disciplinary matters. The Arbiter is appointed by the PZHL Management Board. In particularly complex matters, as well as at the behest of the Disciplinary Arbiter, a disciplinary ruling is issued by the Arbitration Panel comprising the Disciplinary	Two instances of implicit rule	No	No	No	No

Name of the Association	*Regulation on Disciplinary Liability in the Association's Statutes (Yes/No Specifying the Provisions of the Statutes)*	*Existence of Separate Rules on Disciplinary Liability (Yes/No)*	*Which Authorities Are Entitled to Impose Disciplinary Penalties (Indicating Where They Have Been Regulated)*	*How Many Instances in Disciplinary Proceedings (Indicating Where This Has Been Regulated)*	*Is It Possible to Appeal Against the Disciplinary Penalties to the POC Court of Arbitration for Sport (Yes/No Indicating Where This Has Been Regulated)*	*Is It Possible to Appeal Against the Disciplinary Penalties to CAS in Lausanne (Yes/No Indicating Where This Has Been Regulated)*	*Is It Possible to Appeal Against the Disciplinary Penalties to Another Arbitration Court (Yes/No Indicating Where This Has Been Regulated)*	*Is It Possible to Appeal Against the Disciplinary Penalties to a General Court (Yes/No Indicating Where This Has Been Regulated)*
	in disciplinary cases, are specified by the Federation's Disciplinary Rules, which are adopted by the General Assembly of the Federation.'		Arbiter and two of its deputies. Pursuant to § 13, however, the parties may appeal such rulings to the PZHL Appeals Commission.					

Name of the Association	*Regulation on Disciplinary Liability in the Association's Statutes (Yes/No Specifying the Provisions of the Statutes)*	*Existence of Separate Rules on Disciplinary Liability (Yes/No)*	*Which Authorities Are Entitled to Impose Disciplinary Penalties (Indicating Where They Have Been Regulated)*	*How Many Instances in Disciplinary Proceedings (Indicating Where This Has Been Regulated)*	*Is It Possible to Appeal Against the Disciplinary Penalties to the POC Court of Arbitration for Sport (Yes/No Indicating Where This Has Been Regulated)*	*Is It Possible to Appeal Against the Disciplinary Penalties to CAS in Lausanne (Yes/No Indicating Where This Has Been Regulated)*	*Is It Possible to Appeal Against the Disciplinary Penalties to Another Arbitration Court (Yes/ No Indicating Where This Has Been Regulated)*	*Is It Possible to Appeal Against the Disciplinary Penalties to a General Court (Yes/ No Indicating Where This Has Been Regulated)*
Polish Hockey Association	Yes (§ 38 of the statutes)	Yes	Pursuant to § 4 of the Disciplinary Rules, the PZHT authorities with disciplinary powers are: PZHT Management Board, PZHT Disciplinary Commission, PZHT Games and Discipline Department, technical delegate, PZHT Referees College, voivodeship Field Hockey Federation's management board and its executive authorities, as well as camp management (with regard to orderly penalties). Sections 31 and 32 set forth in detail the competences, which authorities rule in the first and sccond instances.	2 (§ 31 of the statutes)	Yes – § 37 item 2 of the Disciplinary Rules	No	No	No

Name of the Association	*Regulation on Disciplinary Liability in the Association's Statutes (Yes/No Specifying the Provisions of the Statutes)*	*Existence of Separate Rules on Disciplinary Liability (Yes/No)*	*Which Authorities Are Entitled to Impose Disciplinary Penalties (Indicating Where They Have Been Regulated)*	*How Many Instances in Disciplinary Proceedings (Indicating Where This Has Been Regulated)*	*Is It Possible to Appeal Against the Disciplinary Penalties to the POC Court of Arbitration for Sport (Yes/No Indicating Where This Has Been Regulated)*	*Is It Possible to Appeal Against the Disciplinary Penalties to CAS in Lausanne (Yes/No Indicating Where This Has Been Regulated)*	*Is It Possible to Appeal Against the Disciplinary Penalties to Another Arbitration Court (Yes/No Indicating Where This Has Been Regulated)*	*Is It Possible to Appeal Against the Disciplinary Penalties to a General Court (Yes/No Indicating Where This Has Been Regulated)*
Polish Basketball Association (PZKosz)	No – Article 48 of the Statutes specifies that: 'The types of penalties and the conditions and rules for inflicting them are set forth in the Disciplinary Rules featured in the applicable bylaws developed and approved by the Association's Management Board.'	Yes	Pursuant to Article 13 of the Disciplinary Rules: 'The disciplinary body of the 1st instance is the Disciplinary Judge who makes a decision individually on disciplinary matters. In particularly complicated matters, by a decision of the Disciplinary Judge, the disciplinary decision is issued by an Arbitral Panel, which consists of a Disciplinary Judge and a maximum of his five substitutes' and, pursuant to Article 16 of the Disciplinary Rules: 'Disciplinary decisions issued by the adjudicating body in the 1st instance may be contested by the parties before the appeal	Two instances (Pursuant to the provisions of the Disciplinary Rules)	Tak – § 49 of the Statutes	No	Pursuant to Article 16, clause 2 of the Disciplinary Rules: 'In tournaments, in matters involving disqualification pursuant to § 13 item 7, the appeal body is the Jury d'Appel consisting of representatives of the teams participating in the	No

Name of the Association	*Regulation on Disciplinary Liability in the Association's Statutes (Yes/No Specifying the Provisions of the Statutes)*	*Existence of Separate Rules on Disciplinary Liability (Yes/No)*	*Which Authorities Are Entitled to Impose Disciplinary Penalties (Indicating Where They Have Been Regulated)*	*How Many Instances in Disciplinary Proceedings (Indicating Where This Has Been Regulated)*	*Is It Possible to Appeal Against the Disciplinary Penalties to the POC Court of Arbitration for Sport (Yes/No Indicating Where This Has Been Regulated)*	*Is It Possible to Appeal Against the Disciplinary Penalties to CAS in Lausanne (Yes/No Indicating Where This Has Been Regulated)*	*Is It Possible to Appeal Against the Disciplinary Penalties to Another Arbitration Court (Yes/No Indicating Where This Has Been Regulated)*	*Is It Possible to Appeal Against the Disciplinary Penalties to a General Court (Yes/No Indicating Where This Has Been Regulated)*
			body, which is the Appeals Board of the Polish Basketball Association.'				tournament, the referees and a representative of the Training Department of the Sports Department.' Further, pursuant to § 47 of the Statutes, the Association's Management Board may appoint a Court of Arbitration to resolve	

Name of the Association	*Regulation on Disciplinary Liability in the Association's Statutes (Yes/No Specifying the Provisions of the Statutes)*	*Existence of Separate Rules on Disciplinary Liability (Yes/No)*	*Which Authorities Are Entitled to Impose Disciplinary Penalties (Indicating Where They Have Been Regulated)*	*How Many Instances in Disciplinary Proceedings (Indicating Where This Has Been Regulated)*	*Is It Possible to Appeal Against the Disciplinary Penalties to the POC Court of Arbitration for Sport (Yes/No Indicating Where This Has Been Regulated)*	*Is It Possible to Appeal Against the Disciplinary Penalties to CAS in Lausanne (Yes/No Indicating Where This Has Been Regulated)*	*Is It Possible to Appeal Against the Disciplinary Penalties to Another Arbitration Court (Yes/No Indicating Where This Has Been Regulated)*	*Is It Possible to Appeal Against the Disciplinary Penalties to a General Court (Yes/No Indicating Where This Has Been Regulated)*
							disputes, including property disputes, as well as to decide on matters of disciplinary liability. The Court of Arbitration with the Polish Basketball Association, referred to as the 'Court Arbitration for Sport', is a separate,	

Name of the Association	*Regulation on Disciplinary Liability in the Association's Statutes (Yes/No Specifying the Provisions of the Statutes)*	*Existence of Separate Rules on Disciplinary Liability (Yes/No)*	*Which Authorities Are Entitled to Impose Disciplinary Penalties (Indicating Where They Have Been Regulated)*	*How Many Instances in Disciplinary Proceedings (Indicating Where This Has Been Regulated)*	*Is It Possible to Appeal Against the Disciplinary Penalties to the POC Court of Arbitration for Sport (Yes/No Indicating Where This Has Been Regulated)*	*Is It Possible to Appeal Against the Disciplinary Penalties to CAS in Lausanne (Yes/No Indicating Where This Has Been Regulated)*	*Is It Possible to Appeal Against the Disciplinary Penalties to Another Arbitration Court (Yes/ No Indicating Where This Has Been Regulated)*	*Is It Possible to Appeal Against the Disciplinary Penalties to a General Court (Yes/ No Indicating Where This Has Been Regulated)*
							stand-alone unit appointed to resolve disputes which have arisen in connection with particular property and non-property disputes, which may be subject to a court settlement. The proceedings	

Name of the Association	*Regulation on Disciplinary Liability in the Association's Statutes (Yes/No Specifying the Provisions of the Statutes)*	*Existence of Separate Rules on Disciplinary Liability (Yes/No)*	*Which Authorities Are Entitled to Impose Disciplinary Penalties (Indicating Where They Have Been Regulated)*	*How Many Instances in Disciplinary Proceedings (Indicating Where This Has Been Regulated)*	*Is It Possible to Appeal Against the Disciplinary Penalties to the POC Court of Arbitration for Sport (Yes/No Indicating Where This Has Been Regulated)*	*Is It Possible to Appeal Against the Disciplinary Penalties to CAS in Lausanne (Yes/No Indicating Where This Has Been Regulated)*	*Is It Possible to Appeal Against the Disciplinary Penalties to Another Arbitration Court (Yes/No Indicating Where This Has Been Regulated)*	*Is It Possible to Appeal Against the Disciplinary Penalties to a General Court (Yes/No Indicating Where This Has Been Regulated)*
							before the Court are conducted pursuant to the Court Rules adopted by the PZKosz Management Board.	

Name of the Association	*Regulation on Disciplinary Liability in the Association's Statutes (Yes/No Specifying the Provisions of the Statutes)*	*Existence of Separate Rules on Disciplinary Liability (Yes/No)*	*Which Authorities Are Entitled to Impose Disciplinary Penalties (Indicating Where They Have Been Regulated)*	*How Many Instances in Disciplinary Proceedings (Indicating Where This Has Been Regulated)*	*Is It Possible to Appeal Against the Disciplinary Penalties to the POC Court of Arbitration for Sport (Yes/No Indicating Where This Has Been Regulated)*	*Is It Possible to Appeal Against the Disciplinary Penalties to CAS in Lausanne (Yes/No Indicating Where This Has Been Regulated)*	*Is It Possible to Appeal Against the Disciplinary Penalties to Another Arbitration Court (Yes/ No Indicating Where This Has Been Regulated)*	*Is It Possible to Appeal Against the Disciplinary Penalties to a General Court (Yes/ No Indicating Where This Has Been Regulated)*
Polish Football Association	Yes – Chapter 38 of the Statutes describes disciplinary liability, while the elaboration on this contained is in the Disciplinary Rules.	Yes	Pursuant to Article 121 of the Disciplinary Rules: 'The authorities responsible for adjudicating in disciplinary cases in the 1st instance are: 1) the club's management board or another disciplinary body of the club; 2) the disciplinary committee of the voivodship football association with territorial jurisdiction; 3) the disciplinary committee of the voivodship football association, managing 3rd division matches on behalf of the Polish Football Association; 4) the appropriate disciplinary authority of Ekstraklasa S.A.;	Two instances (Pursuant to Article 120 of the Disciplinary Rules: 'The two-instance rule applies to proceedings before the disciplinary authorities, unless otherwise provided in specific regulations.')	Yes – Pursuant to Article 54 of the Statutes: 'The Court of Arbitration with the Polish Olympic Committee is competent, by operation of the law, to consider disputes arising from protesting final rulings of PZPN's	Yes – Article 56 of the Statutes: 'According to the respective articles of the FIFA and / or UEFA Statutes, any appeal against a final and binding decision of FIFA or UEFA shall be settled by the Court of Arbitration	Yes – The Football Court of Arbitration is appointed to consider any property and non-property disputes which may be subject to a settlement, including those regarding players' contractual stability and club licence issues arisen	No

Name of the Association	*Regulation on Disciplinary Liability in the Association's Statutes (Yes/No Specifying the Provisions of the Statutes)*	*Existence of Separate Rules on Disciplinary Liability (Yes/No)*	*Which Authorities Are Entitled to Impose Disciplinary Penalties (Indicating Where They Have Been Regulated)*	*How Many Instances in Disciplinary Proceedings (Indicating Where This Has Been Regulated)*	*Is It Possible to Appeal Against the Disciplinary Penalties to the POC Court of Arbitration for Sport (Yes/No Indicating Where This Has Been Regulated)*	*Is It Possible to Appeal Against the Disciplinary Penalties to CAS in Lausanne (Yes/No Indicating Where This Has Been Regulated)*	*Is It Possible to Appeal Against the Disciplinary Penalties to Another Arbitration Court (Yes/ No Indicating Where This Has Been Regulated)*	*Is It Possible to Appeal Against the Disciplinary Penalties to a General Court (Yes/ No Indicating Where This Has Been Regulated)*
			5) the Disciplinary Committee on behalf of the Polish Football Association.' However, pursuant to Article 122 of the Disciplinary Rules: 'the disciplinary bodies with the jurisdiction to adjudicate in the 2nd instance in appeals against judgements of bodies of the 1st instance are: 1) the disciplinary committee of the voivodship football association; 2) the Disciplinary Committee of the Polish Football Association; 3) the disciplinary authority of Ekstraklasa S.A.; 4) the appeal committee of the voivodship football association; 5) the Supreme Board of Appeal'.		disciplinary authorities, as well as other domestic football disputes to which PZPN is a party, submitted to the Court's jurisdiction pursuant to a separate arbitration agreement.'	for Sport (CAS) in Lausanne, Switzerland. PZPN shall ensure full compliance with every final decision issued by FIFA and / or UEFA or CAS, by its governing bodies and its members, and the individuals subject to PZPN rules.'	with regard to entitlement, popularization and development of football, to be settled by arbitration as provided for in the statutes and bylaws of FIFA, UEFA and PZPN. More on that in Articles 50–53 of the statutes and in the Football Court of Arbitration Bylaws.	

Name of the Association	*Regulation on Disciplinary Liability in the Association's Statutes (Yes/No Specifying the Provisions of the Statutes)*	*Existence of Separate Rules on Disciplinary Liability (Yes/No)*	*Which Authorities Are Entitled to Impose Disciplinary Penalties (Indicating Where They Have Been Regulated)*	*How Many Instances in Disciplinary Proceedings (Indicating Where This Has Been Regulated)*	*Is It Possible to Appeal Against the Disciplinary Penalties to the POC Court of Arbitration for Sport (Yes/No Indicating Where This Has Been Regulated)*	*Is It Possible to Appeal Against the Disciplinary Penalties to CAS in Lausanne (Yes/No Indicating Where This Has Been Regulated)*	*Is It Possible to Appeal Against the Disciplinary Penalties to Another Arbitration Court (Yes/ No Indicating Where This Has Been Regulated)*	*Is It Possible to Appeal Against the Disciplinary Penalties to a General Court (Yes/ No Indicating Where This Has Been Regulated)*
Polish Volleyball Federation	Yes – Articles 39–40 of the Statutes describes disciplinary liability, although an elaboration on this is contained in separate Disciplinary Rules.	Yes	Pursuant to Article 106 of the Disciplinary Rules, the first instance authorities ruling on disciplinary matters are: the Disciplinary Commission with the Professional League Management and the PZPS Disciplinary Division. The second instance authority competent to rule on appealed first instance disciplinary rulings is the Court of Appeals with PZPS (Article 107).	Two instances (Pursuant to Article 48 of the Disciplinary Rules: 'The disciplinary proceedings are in two instances.')	Yes – Pursuant to Article 41 of the Statutes, an appeal may be filed with the Tribunal at the POC.	No	No	No

Name of the Association	*Regulation on Disciplinary Liability in the Association's Statutes (Yes/No Specifying the Provisions of the Statutes)*	*Existence of Separate Rules on Disciplinary Liability (Yes/No)*	*Which Authorities Are Entitled to Impose Disciplinary Penalties (Indicating Where They Have Been Regulated)*	*How Many Instances in Disciplinary Proceedings (Indicating Where This Has Been Regulated)*	*Is It Possible to Appeal Against the Disciplinary Penalties to the POC Court of Arbitration for Sport (Yes/No Indicating Where This Has Been Regulated)*	*Is It Possible to Appeal Against the Disciplinary Penalties to CAS in Lausanne (Yes/No Indicating Where This Has Been Regulated)*	*Is It Possible to Appeal Against the Disciplinary Penalties to Another Arbitration Court (Yes/ No Indicating Where This Has Been Regulated)*	*Is It Possible to Appeal Against the Disciplinary Penalties to a General Court (Yes/ No Indicating Where This Has Been Regulated)*
Polish Floorball Association	No – Article 34 of the Statutes provide that disciplinary liability is included in the Disciplinary Rules.	Yes	Article 3 of the Disciplinary Rules provides that: 'The following bodies are authorized to adjudicate on disciplinary matters: a) the Management Board of the Polish Floorball Association; b) the Games and Disciplinary Department of the Polish Floorball Association; c) the Judicial Department of the Polish Floorball Association on matters regarding referees; d) the Management Boards of the clubs.'	Two instances (Pursuant to Article 10 of the Disciplinary Rules: 'The principle of two instances applies in disciplinary proceedings.')	Yes – Pursuant to § 22: 'The final rulings of the Polish Floorball Association are appealable to the Court of Arbitration for Sport with the Polish Olympic Committee as provided for in the generally applicable laws.'	No	Yes – Pursuant to Article 19 of the Disciplinary Rules: 'A complaint may be filed with the Management Board of the Polish Floorball Association with respect to legally binding disciplinary judgements passed by	No

Name of the Association	*Regulation on Disciplinary Liability in the Association's Statutes (Yes/No Specifying the Provisions of the Statutes)*	*Existence of Separate Rules on Disciplinary Liability (Yes/No)*	*Which Authorities Are Entitled to Impose Disciplinary Penalties (Indicating Where They Have Been Regulated)*	*How Many Instances in Disciplinary Proceedings (Indicating Where This Has Been Regulated)*	*Is It Possible to Appeal Against the Disciplinary Penalties to the POC Court of Arbitration for Sport (Yes/No Indicating Where This Has Been Regulated)*	*Is It Possible to Appeal Against the Disciplinary Penalties to CAS in Lausanne (Yes/No Indicating Where This Has Been Regulated)*	*Is It Possible to Appeal Against the Disciplinary Penalties to Another Arbitration Court (Yes/ No Indicating Where This Has Been Regulated)*	*Is It Possible to Appeal Against the Disciplinary Penalties to a General Court (Yes/ No Indicating Where This Has Been Regulated)*
							the bodies of the Polish Floorball Association within 7 days of the date on which the judgement becomes final. The decision of the Management Board of the Polish Floorball Association is final.'	

Name of the Association	*Regulation on Disciplinary Liability in the Association's Statutes (Yes/No Specifying the Provisions of the Statutes)*	*Existence of Separate Rules on Disciplinary Liability (Yes/No)*	*Which Authorities Are Entitled to Impose Disciplinary Penalties (Indicating Where They Have Been Regulated)*	*How Many Instances in Disciplinary Proceedings (Indicating Where This Has Been Regulated)*	*Is It Possible to Appeal Against the Disciplinary Penalties to the POC Court of Arbitration for Sport (Yes/No Indicating Where This Has Been Regulated)*	*Is It Possible to Appeal Against the Disciplinary Penalties to CAS in Lausanne (Yes/No Indicating Where This Has Been Regulated)*	*Is It Possible to Appeal Against the Disciplinary Penalties to Another Arbitration Court (Yes/No Indicating Where This Has Been Regulated)*	*Is It Possible to Appeal Against the Disciplinary Penalties to a General Court (Yes/No Indicating Where This Has Been Regulated)*
Polish Handball Federation	Yes – blanket regulation (§§ 51–53 of the Rules)	Yes	The association's disciplinary authorities are: 1) ZPRP Disciplinary Commission; 2) ZPRP Appeals Commission; 3) ZPRP Management Board; 4) ZPRP General Delegates Meeting. 3. In matters referred to in Chapter 11a (Arbitration Proceedings at ZPRP), arbitration is also permissible. (§ 50 of the rules) – casuistic instances.	Two instances (§ 50 of the rules)	Yes – The penalized and injured parties to the disciplinary or membership proceedings before ZPRP authorities have the right to appeal to the CAS, hereinafter referred to as the Court (§ 78 item 1 of the Disciplinary Rules).	No	Yes – Pursuant to the ZPRP Court of Arbitration Rules, the Court is competent to resolve property disputes related to handball sports activities, as well as disputes subject to its jurisdiction by the	No

Name of the Association	*Regulation on Disciplinary Liability in the Association's Statutes (Yes/No Specifying the Provisions of the Statutes)*	*Existence of Separate Rules on Disciplinary Liability (Yes/No)*	*Which Authorities Are Entitled to Impose Disciplinary Penalties (Indicating Where They Have Been Regulated)*	*How Many Instances in Disciplinary Proceedings (Indicating Where This Has Been Regulated)*	*Is It Possible to Appeal Against the Disciplinary Penalties to the POC Court of Arbitration for Sport (Yes/No Indicating Where This Has Been Regulated)*	*Is It Possible to Appeal Against the Disciplinary Penalties to CAS in Lausanne (Yes/No Indicating Where This Has Been Regulated)*	*Is It Possible to Appeal Against the Disciplinary Penalties to Another Arbitration Court (Yes/No Indicating Where This Has Been Regulated)*	*Is It Possible to Appeal Against the Disciplinary Penalties to a General Court (Yes/No Indicating Where This Has Been Regulated)*
							parties pursuant to an arbitration clause (Article 3 of the Court of Arbitration Rules).	

Source: Own study. The table in the Polish language version has been included in the book, E.J. Krześniak, *Kluby i organizacje sportowe* (…), pp. 528–533, updated as of March 2021.

238. An analysis of the statutes and Disciplinary Rules of the PSFs, the results of which have been presented above, suggest that the issue of disciplinary liability and the desire to 'maintain' disputes within the organization itself is important to a large proportion of sports associations. The reference to the association's internal dispute resolution procedure is most frequently found in the association's statutes themselves. The detailed procedure is, however, regulated in a separate document – the rules or the statutes of the arbitration court, if such rules or statutes have been established within a given association.

239. With few exceptions,[150] the PSFs analysed have adopted disciplinary regulations.[151] The part of the statutes that applies to disciplinary liability and disputes is not developed uniformly in every case. In several cases (e.g., the Polish Luge Federation, the Polish Badminton Association, the Polish Handball Federation, the Polish Bobsleigh and Skeleton Federation and the Polish Weightlifting Federation), the statutes can be defined as essentially blanket regulations, referring only to separate rules.

240. Many of the Disciplinary Rules do not describe procedures for settling disputes through arbitration, but purely focus on penalties.

241. The Disciplinary Rules applied by the Polish NGBs are similar to each other. The differences arise from the characteristics that are unique to the given sport – the descriptions of scoring, the duties of the referees/umpires or activists and other similar issues. The differences between disciplines also arise in the list of penalties and offences, the direct effect of which is the degree of expansion of the given documents. Team sports – handball, football and hockey – clearly stand out against the rest, while the Disciplinary Rules of the respective associations are the most extensive. At the other extreme is the modern pentathlon, the rules on penalties and disputes of which are contained in the three provisions of the statutes.

242. When defining the penalties, the Disciplinary Rules simultaneously define prohibited acts that are punishable with a disciplinary penalty. The analysis of the rules suggests a substantial difference between the norms of criminal law and the disciplinary norms in this respect. This is because, in the case of disciplinary liability, a prohibited act is usually so-called unsportsmanlike behaviour,[152] namely behaviour which cannot be unequivocally defined. Disciplinary rules frequently introduce an additional gradation, referring to 'highly unsportsmanlike behaviour'[153] or 'grossly unsportsmanlike behaviour'.[154] Grading of breaches of this type

150. The Statutes of the Polish Modern Pentathlon Association contain a wide range of norms of litigation and do not refer to any separate rules.
151. The nomenclature can vary, sometimes referred to as 'disciplinary board rules' or 'disciplinary rules'.
152. English language rules use such notions as a '*breach of good sportsmanship*'.
153. *See* § 22, clause 1, item 7 of the Disciplinary Rules of the Polish Basketball Association.
154. *See*, for instance, § 22, clause 1, items 1, 2, 3 and 4 of the Disciplinary Rules of the Polish Basketball Association.

in the Disciplinary Rules should be considered acceptable. The rules that are applicable under criminal law, which require the strict and unambiguous specification of the prohibited conduct, do not apply to disciplinary liability in sport.

243. Additionally, the sanctioning of conduct defined as 'unsportsmanlike behaviour', 'a breach of the principles of sports ethics' or other similar activities is necessary from the point of view of the essence of sport and the need for fair sports rivalry. This is similar to the German doctrine.[155]

244. It is also worth adding that none of the NGBs operating in Poland transfers disciplinary matters to the jurisdiction of general courts or 'non-sports' arbitration courts.

245. References to disciplinary decisions of sports associations are discussed by the POC CAS, as will be discussed further below.

II. Alternative Dispute Resolution in Polish Sport

246. Virtually the entire world of sport is of the opinion that the less frequently disputes go to the courts, the better.[156] The German doctrine refers to the fact that it is often not only not in the interests of the clubs or sports associations but also the sportspeople themselves to entrust the verification of the decisions of the federal authorities to the State courts. This is primarily due to the fact that the career of leading sportspeople is short – it lasts a few or a maximum a dozen or so years and, in such a case, going through all the instances of the courts, which usually takes years, can effectively ruin a sportsperson's career.[157] It is also believed in the British doctrine that the principle that sports federations and their decisions may only be contested before the internal quasi-judicial bodies of these organizations, with a possible appeal to independent arbitration, is the basis of sports autonomy, while the British courts strongly defend the rights of sports associations to subject sports disputes to arbitration in special arbitration courts handling sports matters.[158]

247. In practice, almost all people and entities involved in a given sport (clubs, sportspeople, sports associations, PSFs and other entities) accept the 'dominance' of the arbitration court over the general court in the area of sport. Many international sports federations introduce a rule that obligates the national sports associations not only to entrust cases to which they are parties themselves but also for this type of requirement to apply to the counterparties to these disputes, namely the

155. Haas, Martens, *Sportrecht*, pp. 98–99.
156. *See*, among others, the positions of German doctrine and German sports activists in Haas, Martens, *Sportrecht*, pp. 89–91.
157. The German literature refers to the example of Katrin Krabbe, who filed a complaint against the disciplinary penalty imposed on her (Haas, Martens, *Sportrecht*, p. 22).
158. J. Taylor & J. Herbert, *Sports Governance*, in *Sport: Law and Practice* Ch. A2, 87 (Bloomsbury Professional, 2014).

sports clubs and the sportspeople themselves.[159] The way in which this is to be achieved is most frequently left to national sports associations.

248. The Polish Government, as well as both houses of the Polish Parliament (the Sejm and the Senate), has acknowledged, as indicated in the justification of the draft of the Polish AoS, that 'the statutes of international sports federations exclude the possibility of referring the cases in question [namely matters related to the settlement of court disputes – added by E.J.K.] to the state judiciary'.[160] Since this is the case, a whole range of instruments have been developed to make disputes related to playing and organizing sport appear before the general courts very rarely. The fundamental instrument is the actual compulsion for interested parties to use arbitration dedicated to sport.

249. In this respect, the Polish solutions should be considered innovative on a global scale.

250. This is because the Polish Parliament adopted a regulation ordering people and entities involved in sport to refer disputes to arbitration courts, avoiding the courts. In the vast majority of sports-related cases in Poland, the interested parties are directed to the arbitration by law.

251. The Polish lawmakers therefore gave priority to the requirements of practice (disputes in sport are still dealt with by the arbitration courts) over the theory of the law (the right to a court hearing, as under constitutional law). At this point, it would be appropriate to mention that in 2012 the European Parliament passed a resolution in which it recognized the legitimacy of 'sports courts' for settling sports disputes, as long as they respected the fundamental rights of everyone to a fair hearing.

252. It would be necessary to agree with this last position of the European Parliament. The advantages of arbitration in sport override any possible disadvantages. The nature of today's sport approximates it to international trade. Just as in international trade, the speed of the decision and the international aspect and long-term legal relations are important. In addition, in the case of sport, we are dealing with far-reaching commercialization. In international trade, arbitration is a widely used instrument for settling disputes.[161] Therefore, it should come as no surprise that arbitration is often used in the case of sports disputes.

253. It is also obvious that, in many respects, the arbitration court offers an advantage over the State judiciary. The key advantages of arbitration, with a particular focus on organized sport, are the speed of the proceedings, the ability to

159. An example is Art. 68.1 of the FIFA statutes.
160. Justification to the bill on sport, Sejm of the seventh term of office, parliamentary form No. 3161.
161. For more on this subject, *see* E.J. Krześniak, *Wybrane elementy z problematyki rozstrzygania sporów w obszarze sportu na drodze arbitrażu* (in:) B. Jelonek-Jarco, R. Kos, J. Zawadzka (ed.) *Usus magister est Optimus. Rozprawy prawnicze ofiarowane profesorowi Andrzejowi Kubasowi, Warsaw 2016*, p. 704.

select experts and competent people for settling disputes, lower costs, a greater sense of connection between the parties and the people who decide and issue the award, as well as confidentiality of the proceedings. Obviously, of these advantages, the most important is speed of the proceedings. This issue is absolutely fundamental in the case of sport. In practice, a sportsperson's career is short, while the exclusion of a sportsperson from competitions for a specified period or the penalty of disqualification, if not confirmed or overruled quickly, can ruin a sportsperson's career. At the same time, the speed of arbitration in sports is so spectacular[162] that it gives rise to the highest respect. The British doctrine uses a good expression for this – 'justice delayed is justice denied'. This last sentence is especially true in the case of sport.[163]

III. POC Court of Arbitration for Sport

A. Introduction

254. The most important Court of Arbitration in Polish sport is the POC CAS.

255. The CAS was established on 17 November 1994.[164] It received statutory grounds for its functioning in 1996, under the Act on Physical Culture which was adopted at that time, several provisions of which (Articles 40 and 41) were devoted to this institution. The statutory regulation regarding the court did not present any specific difference from other arbitration courts, other than the clear indication that appeals may be filed with the court against disciplinary and rules-related decisions of the competent authorities of PSFs, imposing the most severe disciplinary sanctions, such as the lifetime disqualification of sportspeople, referees/umpires or sports activists, the deprivation of a player or team of the title of national champion or winner of the Polish Cup, the relegation of the team to a lower division or the prohibition to represent Polish sport in international competitions or international sports tournaments (Article 41, paragraph 1 Act on Physical Culture of 1996).

256. In its initial years, the Court focused on issuing of individual consultative opinions and considering a few appeals against decisions of the authorities of PSFs, the statutes of which provided that this Court of Arbitration has the jurisdiction to consider such appeals.[165]

162. For example, matters considered by the so-called ad hoc divisions within the CAS are dealt with on the same day that the complaint is lodged.
163. *See* A. Lewis & J. Taylor, *Remedies and Procedure in the Courts on a Challenge to the Actions of a Sports Governing Body*, in *Sport: Law and Practice* Ch. E1, 966 (Bloomsbury Professional, 2014). More is discussed there about the importance of time in dealing with sports-related disputes.
164. The court acted on the basis of a resolution of the Management Board of the POC.
165. A. Wach (in:) System prawa handlowego, t. 8, Arbitraż handlowy. ed. A. Szumański, Warszawa 2015, p. 962.

257. The Polish Constitutional Tribunal and the Supreme Court have also addressed the role of the Court of Arbitration. Both of these Supreme Courts in Poland have confirmed that the Court of Arbitration does not belong to any of the segments of authority in the meaning of Article 10 of the Polish Constitution and, in particular, it cannot be included among the judiciary. It is a standing arbitration court, of the nature of an internal court of sports associations, operating exclusively in cases which are subject to its jurisdiction on the basis of an arbitration clause and those specified in the relevant provisions of the AoS.[166]

258. A dozen or so years after its establishment, the Court was treated as being among the top five best organized arbitration courts considering sports matters in the world.[167] In terms of the number of cases, it was just behind the Lausanne CAS. After all, some of the solutions accepted with respect to the POC CAS are modelled on the solutions adopted with respect to the said CAS, which is the key arbitral tribunal in the world of sport.

B. The Court's Powers and Membership

259. Starting from 2004 (with a break in 2010–2015), the POC Court of Arbitration necessarily considered – by virtue of a specific provision of Polish law – appeals against disciplinary and rules-related decisions of PSFs. In other words, unlike in the case of classic arbitration, a particular provision of the Act specifies the Court of Arbitration as the body considering certain categories of cases. Therefore, appeals against the most severe disciplinary sanctions are referred to the court not as a result of an agreement between the parties, but on the basis of the applicable provisions of the law. Therefore, we are dealing here not so much with compulsory arbitration imposed by statutes and other rules of world sports federations, but 'normative compulsory arbitration', directly imposed by the lawmakers.

260. As can easily be imagined, such a non-standard solution resulted in intensive discussion in the Polish legal doctrine. For some of its representatives, this solution is almost sacrilegious. One of the most prominent representatives of the Polish legal doctrine, F. Zedler, repeatedly emphasized that if something is compulsory it is certainly not arbitration – as this always requires the voluntary consent of the parties.[168] Those authors also argue that matters which, according to Polish law cannot be subject to arbitration at all (disciplinary matters which are not of the

166. Judgment of the Constitutional Tribunal of 19 Oct. 2010, P 10/10, LEX, No. 607436 and decision of the Supreme Court of 13 Dec. 2012, III PO 15/12, LEX No. 1667677.

167. *See* A. Wach, M. Wach, *Spór o spory sądowe*, Rzeczpospolita of 9 Jun. 2010, http://www.rp.pl/artykul/491340-Spor-o-spory-sportowe.html, accessed on 24 Jul. 2016.

168. F. Zedler, *Postępowanie polubowne* ..., pp. 47–61. A similar position is taken by A. Szumański, who positively assessed the fact that the AoS – in contrast with the AoQS – does not regulate sports through arbitration (A. Szumański, *Prawne instrumenty reagowania na niedopuszczalną niekompatybilność pozaprawnych regulacji sportowych z regulacjami prawnymi w systemie rozstrzygania sporów sportowych na drodze arbitrażu* (in:) Kompatybilność pozaprawnych regulacji sportowych z regulacjami prawnymi (ed. *A.J. Szwarc), Poznań 2014*, pp. 206–207).

nature of arbitration matters) have been transferred to the jurisdiction of the Court of Arbitration. In their opinion, the Polish regulations are in conflict with the applicable legal regulations on arbitration and give rise to serious doubts about compliance with the constitutional principle of the right to a court hearing.[169] According to F. Zedler, the very concept of 'forced arbitration' is grossly in conflict with the essence of arbitration, based on the agreement of the parties, which, like every agreement, must be voluntary.[170] F. Zedler also draws attention to the fact that compulsory arbitration originated in two legal institutions in the disgraceful times of the pre-1989 era – the State Economic Arbitration and the arbitration of civil law disputes arising from economic and scientific/technical cooperation based on the convention signed in Moscow on 26 May 1972.[171]

261. Other authors are appreciative of the rules that oblige interested parties to use – under duress – the arbitration court, while they consider the grounds for introducing such atypical solutions to be the fact that it best suits the needs of practice.[172] General courts were and are tardy in Poland, while arbitration courts operate much faster. Time is of the essence in sport. A sports career is short; sportspeople sometimes only have the opportunity to take part in major competitions such as the Olympic Games or the World Championships once in their lives. In team sports, league matches start every year on the same date and a player not included in the team before the respective date loses the whole season.[173] Disputes between sportspeople and clubs, clubs and sports federations and between sportspeople and both national and international sports federations have to end quickly. This does not mean that arbitration in sports has no disadvantages. It is pointed out, however, that the speed of proceedings is so important that it is sometimes necessary to simply ignore the limitations of arbitration and continue as normal. Sometimes defects in sports realities, especially professional sport, can prove to be an advantage (primarily holding sessions behind closed doors[174] and the single instance nature). The Polish model of settling sports disputes seems to be well appreciated by many sports environments abroad.[175]

262. The dispute in the doctrine between proponents and opponents of introducing provisions on sports arbitration into Polish law, or, in other words, the dispute about de facto and *de iure* forced arbitration, has resulted in a great deal of volatility in the Polish regulations on this. Initially, the supporters of the practical approach had the advantage – provisions introducing compulsory arbitration at the

169. F. Zedler, *Postępowanie polubowne* ..., pp. 52–53.
170. F. Zedler, *Postępowanie polubowne* ..., p. 49.
171. Journal of Laws of 1974, No. 7, item 37.
172. A. Wach, *Jaki arbitraż w sporcie*, Rzeczpospolita of 1 Oct. 2013.
173. This rule is widely applied throughout the world, including in Poland – the aim is not to interrupt sports rivalry during the season, e.g., shortly before the key championship meetings and player transfers.
174. For example, A. Wach considers this to be as an advantage of sports arbitration. *See* A. Wach (in:) System ..., p. 966.
175. This is mentioned by A. Wach, M. Wach, *Spór o spory sądowe*, Rzeczpospolita z dnia 9 czerwca 2010 r.

CAS and regulating organizational matters related to this arbitration court, such as the method of appointing arbitrators and their number, were introduced into Polish law and were applicable for almost ten years. Next, the advocates of the 'purist' approach, according to whom 'compulsory' arbitration' is an oxymoron – either something is arbitration or it is compulsory – gained the advantage in 2010. As a result, all the rules on both the said court and other arbitration courts were removed from the current AoS. But it was only for five years. Despite opposition from a part of the environment, the provisions on the CAS were introduced into the AoS in 2015. They largely duplicate the solutions in force until 2010.

263. It was pointed out, in both the justification to the amendment in 2015 and the justification to the bill on sport that the decisions of the lawmakers on the normative regulation regarding the functioning and powers of the Court of Arbitration were based on foreign experience. In the justification to the amendment of 2015, it was stated, *inter alia*, that 'international sports federations rule out the possibility of referring the cases in question [i.e., matters regarding the settlement of court disputes – added by E.J.K.] to the state courts in their statutes. This is because, in this way, they want to avoid the inconsistent national decisions of courts made on the basis of the same federal rules, all the more so that this takes place after conducting the two-instance proceedings of the association in similar disciplinary or rules-related proceedings'.[176] It is stated in the justification that the jurisdiction of the CAS for resolving international disciplinary or rules-related disputes is accepted in connection with such an approach of international sports federations. It was also pointed out that the bill on sport eliminates the possibility of appealing against awards issued by the CAS, because that is how it is done around the world. It was written directly into the justification that 'the exclusion of judgments of this kind from the jurisdiction of the general court is applied in practice in all sports organizations and arises from the specifics of sports disciplinary case law, which is essentially neither administrative proceedings nor, all the more so, the settlement of disputes of a civil law nature'.[177]

264. It is true to say that CAS' function is more akin to that of a court of law and less to commercial arbitration. Disputes between players and clubs or between clubs and sports associations and world sports federations almost never end up in the general courts.

265. Nevertheless, the Polish solutions regarding the provision of access to specialized arbitration go further than the solutions encountered in most other legal systems, while the structure itself (imposed by law) of compulsory arbitration is an innovative idea of the Polish doctrine. It is difficult to find a similar solution in other countries. Some authors refer to the Spanish regulation, but this does not appear to

176. Justification to the Act on the Amendment of the Act on Sport and the Act on Personal Income Tax, Sejm of the seventh term of office, parliamentary form No. 3161.
177. Justification to the bill on sport, Sejm of the sixth term of office, parliamentary form No. 2313.

be an appropriate comparison. Although the jurisdiction of the Spanish Sports Disciplinary Committee is set out in detail in the Spanish AoS, the Spanish laws regulate the matter of disciplinary liability in sport differently (primarily because Spanish law, in contrast to Polish law, is based on the concept of the comprehensive regulation of disciplinary liability in the Act).

266. The court consists of twenty-four arbitrators appointed by the Management Board of the POC for a term of office of four years (Article 45a, paragraph 4 AoS)[178] from among the people who satisfy the formal criteria.

C. *Types of Proceedings Before the POC Court and Appeals Against Awards of the Court*

267. The POC CAS considers cases in three types of proceedings: (1) classical arbitration proceedings (e.g., financial disputes between owners of sports clubs), (2) disciplinary disputes, and (3) rules-related issues. There are significant differences between the disciplinary category and the rules-related category. First of all, the provisions of the Criminal Procedures Code of 6 June 1997[179] (Article 17, clause 2 of the Statutes of the Court and § 82 of the Rules) are applied accordingly in disciplinary cases, whereas the provisions of the CPC (Article 17, paragraph 1 of the Statutes of the Court) are applied in rules-related matters.

268. As a result, we are therefore dealing with three types of court judgments.

269. First, they are classic arbitral awards with respect to which an appeal may be filed for the annulment of the arbitral award.

270. Second, they are rulings on disciplinary matters with respect to which a cassation complaint may be filed (according to different conditions, in a different procedure and, obviously, to a different court) with the Supreme Court.

271. Third, they are judgments in rules-related issues in the case of which no appeal is available.

272. The Polish regulations differ from many other legal systems in this respect. For example, in Germany, an appeal may be filed with respect to rules-related decisions, including those regarding licences issued by sports associations. The same is true of the British doctrine. M. Beloff, T. Kerr, M. Demetriou and R. Beloff explicitly state that any attempt to rule out the jurisdiction of the common courts of England and Wales is doomed to fail because everyone's constitutional right to the

178. Previously, half of the members of the court were appointed by the POC Management Board and half by the minister responsible for physical culture.
179. Consolidated text: Journal of Laws of 20221, item 5341375, as amended.

hearing of his case by an independent court may only be limited or ruled out by a parliamentary decision.[180] Such an exclusion was introduced by law in Poland.

273. The Polish Supreme Court also plays an important role in the Polish system of dealing with disputes in sport. In the event of a gross breach of the law or an obvious inadmissibility of a decision of the POC CAS, a cassation complaint may be filed with the Supreme Court. The grounds for appeal have been narrowly specified in the amended AoS – only a gross breach of the law or the obvious lack of justness of the award give hope of effectiveness of the complaint.

D. POC Court of Arbitration and CAS

274. The key differences between the CAS and the POC Court of Arbitration have been presented below for those readers who regularly handle cases before the CAS or adjudicate at the CAS, or who know how this arbitration court operates from other sources.

275. The POC CAS has been modelled on CAS, yet there are significant differences. In particular, proceedings held before the POC CAS regarding appeals against rules-related and disciplinary decisions are neither arbitration procedures nor procedures conducted within the structure of general courts. Decisions of this Court of these types are subject to verification by the common courts only to a limited extent, that is, only in the event of a gross breach of the regulations or an obviously unjust judgment.[181] In comparison, CAS judgments cannot be challenged before a Swiss court only if neither party has its registered office or domicile and does not conduct business in Switzerland, while, simultaneously, the parties have expressly ruled out the possibility of challenging a CAS judgment before the State courts in an arbitration agreement (or an agreement with similar content entered into after the emergence of a dispute). In most cases it is possible to take a verdict to the Swiss Federal Tribunal, although the actual recourse to the Tribunal is allowed on a very limited number of grounds, such as lack of jurisdiction.[182]

276. The background of both courts was somewhat similar. Both were set up on the initiative of key personalities of the Olympic world – the head of the IOC in the case of CAS and the head of the POC in the case of the Polish Court. Also, only the

180. 'Any attempt in the courts of England and Wales to oust jurisdiction of the courts is necessarily doomed to fail, for the constitutional right of access to the courts cannot be removed or bargained away except by Parliament. Sports administrators therefore have to lower their sight and concentrate not on immunizing their governing bodies from legal attack, but fortifying them against challenges, recognizing that such challenges cannot be stopped but seeking to ensure that, if made, they will not succeed' (M. Beloff, T. Kerr, M. Demetriou, R. Beloff, *Sports Law* ... , p. 198).

181. E.J. Krześniak, *The Court of Arbitration for Sport at the Polish Olympic Committee v The Court of Arbitration* for Sport (CAS) – *Background, Powers and Authority* 199–209 (Young Arbitration No. 24, Apr. 2016).

182. Compare, for example, judgment of the Swiss Supreme Court (Swiss Federal Tribunal) of 22 Mar. 2007, ATF 133 III 235. p. 1082.

intervention of the lawmakers (in the case of the POC CAS) and international sports federations (in the case of the CAS) ordering these institutions to hear certain categories of cases has led to a substantial increase in the number of cases considered and a related increase in the importance of both institutions in the worlds of sports and law.[183]

277. The number of judges in the CAS is substantially higher, as is the number of cases handled each year.

IV. Other Arbitration Courts and 'Bodies with Jurisdiction' in Polish Sport

278. The POC CAS is not the only Polish arbitration court. Arbitrary courts have also been established under some NFs, but it should be noted that the establishment of arbitration courts by the NFs is not a common phenomenon in Polish sport. Only some PSFs have established their own arbitration courts. In addition, even if the statutes of a given PSF mention the possibility of establishing an arbitration court, an arbitration court is not often established, and there is no information in the public domain on their operation, which could suggest that they have not been established at all, or that they are completely inactive. Therefore, although arbitration courts were established and operate, for example, within the PZPN, the Polish Basketball Association (PZKosz) and the Polish Volleyball Federation, they have not been established – despite the fact that the statutes of the PSF provide for their establishment – at the Polish Chess Federation, the Polish Sport Shooting Association, the Polish Swimming Federation, the Polish Handball Association and the Polish Hockey Association.

279. The key factors for the existence of developed dispute settlement procedures in the statutes and internal acts of PSFs and the appointment of autonomous arbitration are the existence of a strong professional league and extensive club structures, popularity and media coverage, as well as profitability of the sport (the more profitable and the greater the media coverage of the sport, the more developed the dispute resolution system and the more probable it is that the sport will have its own arbitration court) and whether or not this is a team sport. Factors such as whether the sport is an Olympic sport or not do not affect the method of regulating the dispute resolution procedure and the possibility of establishing an arbitration court.

280. One of the most important and most active arbitration courts is certainly the Football Court of Arbitration, the actual founder of which, Prof. Andrzej Wach, is also one of the most prominent representatives of the doctrine of Polish sports law ever. The large number of cases handled in this arbitration court arises from the fact that football generates a great deal of interest, transfers of players are frequent and

183. E.J. Krześniak, *The Court of Arbitration for Sport at the Polish Olympic Committee v The Court of Arbitration for Sport (CAS) – Background, Powers and Authority*, 24 Young Arbitration 199–209 (April 2016).

big money, which encourages the assertion of rights if they are breached. In accordance with the respective FIFA, UEFA and PZPN regulations, disputed matters are necessarily settled by the arbitration courts. The establishment of the PZPN Football Arbitration Court should therefore be closely related to the adoption of FIFA's transfer regulations in 1990 and the related resolutions of the PZPN Management Board of 29 June 1992 on the status of Polish players and changes in club membership.

281. The membership of the Football Arbitration Court consists of twenty-one to twenty-three arbitrators appointed by the Management Board of PZPN for a four-year term of office. Panels consist of three people, each party selects one arbitrator and these arbitrators choose the chairperson. An arbitrator cannot assume a function in a given case if there is any suspicion about his impartiality or independence. Formally, a condition for the Football Court of Arbitration to consider a case is the existence of a valid provision for this court and hence the consent of both parties to the dispute. In fact, neither players nor coaches, instructors nor managers have any choice in this. Let us look at PZPN's statutes. Article 47, § 3 (in connection with Article 47, § 1 of PZPN's statutes) explicitly provides for the obligation of these people to agree to all disputes arising from playing, organizing, promoting and developing the sport of football being settled by the Football Court of Arbitration if the FIFA, UEFA and PZPN statutes and rules provide for their settlement through arbitration.[184]

282. The documents of the PZKosz also contain unique regulations compared to the other PSFs. This association established its own arbitration court, the work of which is organized by separate statutes and rules, while the principles of its operation differ from those of similar arbitration courts. Therefore, just as in the case of the Football Court of Arbitration, the PZKosz Management Board appoints the Chairperson and Deputy Chairperson of the Court of Arbitration for a four-year term of office, although they must have legal qualifications. The procedure for appointing people to the list of arbitrators and appointing an arbitrator who hears the given case is atypical – the Chairperson of the court is entitled to individually make the decision in both cases, while awards are made through a sole arbitrator based on general principles of justice (*ex aequo et bono*).[185] Just as the authorities of the PZPN, the authorities of the PZKosz have also assured themselves of a steady stream of cases to the court by actually enforcing a provision regarding this court. A provision regarding this Court or the international Basketball Arbitral Tribunal is required in order for a player to obtain a periodic player's licence in the Polish Basketball League and for matches organized by the PZKosz. The same requirement applies to contracts with players and coaches in the men's and women's Ekstraklasa leagues.[186]

184. Cf. E.J. Krześniak, *Kluby i organizacje sportowe* (…), pp. 628–629.
185. Clause 1.2b of the Rules of the Polish Basketball Association's Basketball Court of Arbitration.
186. Cf. E.J. Krześniak, *Kluby i organizacje sportowe* (…), pp. 629–630.

283. However, a difference appears in the case of the Professional Volleyball League Arbitration Court compared with the institutions previously discussed – this Court of Arbitration does not operate under the Polish Volleyball Federation but under the company named Profesjonalna Liga Piłki Siatkowej S.A. Ten people nominated by this company and five people nominated by the Polish Volleyball Federation are entered into the list of arbitrators; the group of arbitrators selects a chairperson from among themselves. Panels consist of three people, each party selects one arbitrator and these arbitrators choose the chairperson, who must be a qualified lawyer. Arbitrators adjudicate on the basis of 'the applicable provisions of the law, the content of the contracts binding the parties and established customs' and, with the consent of the parties given in writing, they may adjudicate on the basis of equity, although 'decisions may not breach the principles of the rule of law of the Republic of Poland'.[187]

V. Mediation in Sport

284. It is worth devoting a few words to mediation, which has been popular recently in the daily media and the legal doctrine. Mediation should not be considered to be very useful in sport.[188] Primarily because it is based on trying to find a compromise that will satisfy both sides to the dispute. Its objective is not to quickly resolve the dispute, which, in itself, disqualifies this form of seeking solutions to contentious issues. However, it should also be added that PSFs do not have the capacity to mediate in most of the cases in dispute at all because the disputes that are settled within PSFs and then by the arbitration courts are not normal disputes between two or more entities. These are rather disputes based on events that have breached the interests of many other people and entities (third parties), even those participating in matches, which also involved, for instance a player committing a disciplinary infringement. As such, they are unsuitable for mediation, because it is difficult to imagine all other sportspeople participating in them. Besides, what would such mediation involve? – the establishment that the guilty competitor will lose his first place and be shifted, for example, to fifth? This is unthinkable for obvious reasons. In principle, mediation is only suitable for trade disputes.

285. The Sports Dispute Resolution Chamber at the PZPN can be considered an example of a quasi-mediating body. This body has been appointed to adjudicate on the existence, validity or termination of football contracts, make other decisions 'on the assurance of the contractual stability of players who are parties to such a contract' and on matters related to the so-called solidarity mechanism (Article 46, § 2 of the PZPN statutes). Therefore, this chamber is also appointed to adjudicate on the existence, validity or termination of employment contracts with football players (Article 7, § 2 of the PZPN statutes).[189]

187. E.J. Krześniak, *Kluby i organizacje sportowe* (…), p. 630.
188. In contrast T. Cyrol, *Mediacja sportowa w Polsce*, ADR Arbitraż i Mediacja 2012, No. 4, p. 32.
189. As well as civil law contracts.

286. According to Article 1164 CPC, an arbitration clause contained in an employment contract will be invalid (more on this below). Therefore, in the case of employment contracts, the only role that this body can play is a mediation role – seeking solutions, but not authoritatively ruling on the rights and duties arising from employment contracts. The case is different with civil law contracts, in which the chamber may have jurisdiction.

287. Other than this sole exception, mediation in sport in Poland is not used at all, while mediation in proceedings before the POC Court of Arbitration is a purely theoretical solution, which is not applicable in practice.[190]

190. *See* T. Cyrol, *Mediacja sportowa* ..., p. 31.

Part II. Sport and Employment

Chapter 1. Sources of Employment Law (Ordinary Law and CBA)

§1. Legal Status of Players

288. The status of Polish players depends on the type of relationships that connect them with the club. In the event of concluding an employment contract, they will have the status of a regular employee (rarity). In the event of concluding a civil law contract (a personal service contract or service-provision contract, to which the provisions on contracting are applied accordingly), their legal situation will be a derivative of the contract that is concluded and will be specified in the first instance on the basis of the content of that contract.

289. In addition, Polish NFs generally apply different types of licensing systems. Only people with an appropriate licence can take part in competitions organized or supervised by the given NGB. Systems used by the individual NGBs differ from each other. For example, no licensing system has been introduced in the PZPN for players,[191] whereas the association has introduced and applies a procedure for obtaining the right to play. In the case of a player obtaining the right to play, the applicant is the club that employs him. The club files an application for this to the authority responsible for handling the given competition. The procedure itself is formalized – the application is filed on the appropriate form and the authority managing the matches is required to 'authorize' the player in the shortest possible time, but no later than within ten days of receipt of the application. The refusal of the permission to play must be justified in writing. A player, who has not received a licence to play, cannot represent the club in championships and cup competitions, under the pain of losing the matches by a walkover and the application of the sanctions provided for by PZPN's Disciplinary Rules.

290. These issues have been resolved differently at the Polish Volleyball Federation. A player's licence is not issued by the PSF or entity managing the matches, but by the sports club employing the player. The club has the right to register a player throughout the whole of the match season if he is a member of that club for at least one match season or when a professional licence is issued to the player for the first time. However, a player is entitled to file protests and appeals to the Polish

191. *See* S. Fundowicz, *Prawo sportowe* ..., p. 54.

Volleyball Federation with respect to actions or decisions of the club which are in conflict with the regulations of the Polish Volleyball Federation.

291. At this point, it would be appropriate to point out that the regulations of some NGBs regarding club licences are directly in conflict with the applicable law in Poland. For example, the Polish Automobile and Motorcycle Association has a licence system for clubs and contestants, as described in the relevant rules. The rules on granting and withdrawing the contestant's licence in motorsports (appendix to the resolution of the Management Board of the Polish Automobile and Motorcycle Association No. 1/2006 of 8 April 2006)[192] contains a provision that a complaint about a decision of the Court of the Polish Automobile and Motorcycle Association may be filed with the Voivodship Administrative Court. Such a regulation is obviously in conflict with the law – it tries to introduce a procedure for appealing against the court's decision to the administrative court, which is not provided for or is inadmissible by law. All competition, coaching and club licences – are currently of a civil law nature and any interference from the voivodship administrative courts in the procedure for granting or withdrawing them is inadmissible in the current legal situation.

292. On the sideline, it can be added that coaching licences are also commonly used. Remaining with the example of football, it can be stated that one of the requirements for obtaining a coaching licence is to have an appropriate coaching level in the UEFA system. The coaching licence is granted or renewed for a period of one to three years. The decision to award, refuse to award or extend or suspend the coaching licence is made by the appropriate authority within the PZPN – PZPN Coach Training and Licensing Team, acting within the PZPN Technical Commission, on the basis of its rules. An appeal may be filed with the PZPN Supreme Appeal Commission against the decision of the PZPN Coach Training and Licensing Team refusing to award or extend a licence, or suspending the coaching licence, within fourteen days of the date of receipt of the decision.

§2. The Employment Relationship

293. The main legal act governing work in the Polish labour system is the LC. Labour law is considered to be a separate branch of law, which is isolated from civil law, having its own, exhaustive regulation in its Code. Article 22, § 1 LC defines the fundamental features of the employment relationship. According to this article, when initiating an employment relationship, the employee undertakes to perform a specific type of work for the employer and under his management, as well as in the time and place specified by the employer, while the employer undertakes to employ the employee for a salary. The doctrine of labour law defines the employment relationship as being voluntary, paid, characterized by employment subordination (also referred to as the employer's management) and personal (the employee's work is of

192. *See,* https://www.pzm.pl/pliki/zg/prezydialny/2012/regulaminy_wew/licencje_zawod_28_01_2012.doc, accessed on 6 Jun. 2016.

a personal nature). If the relationship binding two entities demonstrates the above features, the parties are bound by the employment relationship regardless of the name that the parties give to the contract (Article 22, § 11 LC) with all the consequences. The employment relationship carries numerous obligations, primarily for the employer. The employer is required, among others, to keep records of working time, pay the remuneration for the overtime worked, grant leave, hold training on occupational safety and health and pay the social security contributions at the amount provided for by law.

294. The employment of sportspeople on employment contracts was the rule in Poland until 1989. Together with the development and commercialization of sport, there was a move away from employment contracts in favour of civil law contracts. The main agreement on the basis of which sportspeople are employed by sports clubs is the contract on the provision of services to which the provisions on contracting apply accordingly (Article 750 PCC). An agreement binding a player with a club can have multiple names, e.g., contract on playing professional sports, contract on the representation of the club, competition contract, etc. The term 'professional sports contract' is frequently used in the case law. This is a best-efforts contract, in which the competitor/sportsperson undertakes to work to achieve the best sports results. A contract on playing professional sports is not an obligation to achieve a specific result because the result in sport depends on many factors. Moreover, it is specified in the case law that, in addition to the sportsperson's commitment to train and to participate in sports events, in the professional sports contract, he also assumes other commitments, such as living a hygienic lifestyle (which is necessary to remain in top physical form) and fulfilling the coach's instructions. In the case law, doctrine and contractual practice of sports clubs, it is indisputable that such a professional sports contract is not an employment contract and is not regulated by labour law. The doctrine emphasizes that the need for the sportsperson to fulfil the instructions of the coach or the sports club's authorities is not evidence of employee subordination and does not prejudge the employment nature of the relationship binding the sportsperson with the sports club. For this reason, civil law contracts should not be considered to be seeming. It is mentioned in the doctrine of labour law and sports law that the freedom to establish the legal relationship between the professional sportsperson and the sports club is a derivative of the autonomy of sport and the general directive of the lack of State interference in sport, which is considered an area which remains within the domain of the broadly understood civic society and self-regulation.

295. Sports associations frequently prejudge the form of employment by sportspeople, introducing internal rules providing for the conclusion of contracts with sportspeople on professionally playing sports. An example here may be the PZPN resolution of 27 March specifying the minimum requirements for standard contracts of players in the football sector. According to this resolution, all provisions of the contracts with players which are in conflict with the resolution or with the objectives and principles of playing football are invalid. The resolution contains detailed guidelines on the regulation of the rights and duties of the parties to the professional contract (e.g., the obligation to participate in training, the content of the obligation to respect the principles of fair play, the obligation to undergo medical examinations etc.). Such multilevel regulation is a typical feature of contracts in professional sports. These contracts refer to the rules and resolutions of sports associations, as well as the resolutions and internal legal acts of international sports associations. The question arises about the legal nature of these provisions. In practice, contracts concluded with the players contain a reference to the resolutions of sports associations or internal acts of international organizations. In such a case, the regulations contained in these resolutions should be treated as elements determining the contractual obligations of the parties which the parties to the contract considered as shaping their obligations. It is stated in the doctrine that the regulations of resolutions and the rules of sports associations cannot provide for penalties of warnings or reprimands to professional sportspeople if the sportsperson is bound to the club with a civil law contract on professionally playing sports and not a civil law contract. The award to the sports club of the right to reprimand a sportsperson is inconsistent with the nature of the relationship binding the player with the club; this is a punishment for the sportsperson and, as such, cannot be provided for in a contractual relationship. It happens that the rules and resolutions of the sports associations contain provisions that are difficult to recognize as being binding on the parties to the civil law relationship.

296. There is no obstacle to sportspeople professionally playing sport as sole proprietors. In such a case, the contract binding the player with the club will be a contract between two entrepreneurs. From the point of view of civil law, such a contract will not differ significantly from a normal contract on professionally playing sports. Significant differences occur in tax law and in the social security of the sportsperson/entrepreneur.

297. The bond connecting the player with the club is only one of the material legal ties that specifies the sportsperson's/professional's rights under Polish law. The so-called licence granted by the Polish NFs giving the player the right to participate in competitions organized by the NGB (e.g., league matches, Polish Championships) is equally important. For clubs and players, having such a licence is crucial – without it, even the best player will not be able to participate in competitions and will be of no value to the club.

§3. Fundamental Rights and Obligations of Clubs and Players

298. As described in the preceding paragraph, the contract between the player and the club is a so-called best-efforts contract. In this contract, the player undertakes to make every effort to achieve the best possible sports results. These efforts include the player's obligation to train and to take part in sports events. The player's basic duties will also frequently include living a healthy lifestyle, the obligation to observe the rules of fair play, the obligation to undergo medical examinations and to follow the coach's instructions. The club's main duties include paying the salary and providing the conditions for safely playing sport and training.

§4. AGENTS' REGULATIONS

299. A sports agent in Poland is considered to be a person (although there are also opinions that a legal entity, such as a company, may also be an agent) representing a player or a sports club. Unlike in France, for example, Polish law does not contain separate regulations regarding this professional group. Therefore, the Polish literature uses the terms 'sports agent', 'sports manager', 'player's representative' and 'transfer agent' interchangeably. All these people mean the person who professionally handles the intermediation between the player and the sports club in order to bring about the conclusion of an employment contract or a similar agreement between them. Therefore, a sports agent helps the player find a club for a fee. The reverse situation is also possible – the agent helps the club find a player for a fee. The agent also participates, sometimes actively, in negotiating the contract between a club and the player. In Polish practice, he also frequently assumes the role of a lawyer, even if he does not have legal qualifications, and advises on the content of the individual provisions of the contract.[193] More in-depth studies additionally distinguish the sports agent in the sense described above from the sports manager, namely the person associated with the sports club, whose duties, apart from finding players for the club (or, in other words, acting as a sports agent), also include other activities related to managing the sports club.[194]

300. In addition to intermediating in the conclusion of employment contracts or similar agreements, a sports agent usually provides a number of other services to a player – he looks for sponsors and negotiates advertising contracts, he publicly promotes the player and handles the media relations, as well as organizing promotional events.

301. Sports agents conduct their activities on their own or within sports agencies.

302. As mentioned, in some countries, the activities of sports agents are governed by law. The United States is a leader here, as the regulations governing sports agents and numerous court judgments devoted to them in the USA constitute a major part of sports law. American regulations are very detailed and apply both to the agent-player relationship and to the agent-sports club relationship.

---

193. *See* M. Leciak, *Agent sportowy* (in:) Leksykon prawa sportowego. 100 podstawowych pojęć, M. Leciak (ed.), C.H. Beck, Warsaw 2017, pp. 1–3.

194. P. Gulak-Lipka writes extensively about the role of a sports manager, *Rola menadżera sportowego w dwutorowej karierze sportowca*, Quality in Sport 2, 2016 and M. Wasylkowska, *Rola menadżera sportowego w zarządzaniu klubami sportowymi*, Zeszyty Naukowe Uniwersytetu Szczecińskiego, 2011, No. 685, 2011 and – unpublished – paper by U. Gulan, *Uwarunkowania tworzenia profesji menadżerów sportowych w Polsce*, doctoral thesis, University of Warsaw, Management Department, June 2012.

303. The generally applicable provisions of the law in these countries are supplemented by the internal regulations of sports associations. The right of sports organizations to regulate the profession of sports agents has been confirmed at the EU level in the *Piau* case (ECJ T-193/02), in which it was acknowledged that the regulation of access to the profession is justified in terms of qualitative (rather than quantitative) restrictions.

304. In Polish law, the role of an agent is assessed from the point of view of the generally applicable regulations regarding persons other than a sports agency, albeit providing similar services – in other words, persons intermediating professionally, for a fee, in concluding contracts of a particular type. Therefore, these will be legal regulations governing, *inter alia*, the conclusion of contracts (Articles 66–72 of the PCC); representation, including powers of attorney (Articles 98–109 of the PCC); general regulations on liabilities (Articles 353–3651 of the PCC); provisions on the agency contracts (Articles 758–7649 of the PCC), although this group applies to the situation where the agent and the player are entrepreneurs, as well as the provisions of the Act on the Promotion of Employment and Labour Market Institutions of 20 April 2004 (Consolidated Text, Journal of Laws of 2016, item 645, as amended), with regard to an employment agency and the Business Activity Freedom Act of 2 July 2004 (Journal of Laws of 2016, item 1829, as amended).[195]

305. However, the internal norms imposed by both international sports federations and those applied by the Polish sports associations are of key significance. The latter sometimes apply extended licensing systems. The regulations of Polish sports associations most frequently transpose the regulations of international sports federations. However, although such sports as football or basketball most frequently apply extensive rules governing the activities of sports agents, such regulations are not applied in other popular sports. Examples of the latter disciplines can be volleyball or handball.[196]

306. The scope of these regulations varies in different sports. The regulations of sports organizations are targeted at the licensing of the activities of sports agents, the specification of the conditions of access and the rules for performing the functions of the agent. They may also deal with such issues as the minimum level of qualifications that the agent should have, the obligation to hold insurance, the principle of transparency (disclosure of earnings by the agent), the prohibition to incite players to breach the terms of the contracts concluded, or the rules governing the required content of the contract between the agent and the player. As a rule, the principles of representing underage players and the requirement to avoid conflicts of interest are specifically regulated.

195. List of regulations by M. Leciak, *Agent sportowy*, p. 2.

196. However, the Polish Handball Federation adopted the Rules of a Handball Agent in 2017, while the first agency licences are planned to be issued by December 2017. Cf. *Agenci w piłce ręcznej musz ąprzyzwyczaić się do zmian,* available at, http://sponsoringsport.pl/aktualnosci/agencji-pilce-recznej-musza-przyzwyczaic-sie-zmian/.

307. The scale of activity of sports agents in Poland is incomparable with the scale of their activity, for instance, in the UK, while the amount of GBP 130 million that English football clubs were supposed to have paid in commission to agents in the 2014–2015 season is considered astronomical in Poland.[197] Even so, some of the most famous football agents are almost as well known as the footballers themselves.[198] This does not change the fact that they often have to explain what representatives of sports clubs and Polish sports associations consider to be their excessive earnings and non-transparent principles of operation.[199]

§5. Settlement of Employment and Economic Disputes

308. Polish law does not allow for the introduction of arbitration clauses into employment contracts. In accordance with Article 1164 CPC, an arbitration clause contained in an employment contract will be invalid – an arbitration clause regarding labour law disputes can only be prepared after the emergence of a dispute and must be made in writing, whereby, in this case, provisions mitigating the requirement of the written form are not applicable. It has been clearly accepted in the legal doctrine that an employee cannot be forced to enter into a contract containing an arbitration clause; it is inadmissible to include arbitration clauses in employment contracts.[200] Briefly speaking, it clearly arises from the wording of the provision that it is inadmissible to include a clause providing for the jurisdiction of an arbitration court in an employment contract or another contract between an employee and an employer for disputes which can only arise between the parties in the future.[201] This applies to the protection of the employee's rights and the avoidance of the situation in which the employee would have to accept an arbitration clause when entering into the employment contract (as one of its integral provisions) for fear of otherwise not entering into that contract.[202] It arises from the justification of the Codification Commission's draft that the above restrictions on the arbitration clause in labour law cases were introduced in order to 'protect the employee's rights'.[203] This also applies to sportspeople.

---

197. This is also presented in a number of statistical listings. For example, in 2011, Jarosław Kołkowski, having contracts with seventy-nine players, was in the thirty-first place in the world in terms of the number of players managed, whereas, in terms of the market value of the players, he was outside the top 100 agents. Cf. Z. Pawlak, A. Smoleń, *Etyczne aspekty agentów w piłce nożnej* [in:] *Annales. Etyka w życiu gospodarczym*, 2012, vol. 15, p. 134.
198. An example may be Cezary Kucharski, former deputy of the Polish Sejm and sports agent of the best-known Polish sportsperson, Robert Lewandowski.
199. Cf. J. Węglarski, Ł. Klenczon, *Agent piłkarski, czyli zło futbolu. Jaki nie powinien być 'opiekun' piłkarza*, available at, http://juniorfutbol.pl/agent-pilkarski-czyli-zlo-futbolu-jaki-nie-powinien-byc-opiekun-pilkarza,artykul.html?material_id=55155ef6e1e17ddb7f9e9459.
200. *See* A. Zieliński (in:) Kodeks postępowania cywilnego. Komentarz, ed. A. Zieliński, K. Flaga-Gieruszyńska, Legalis/el. *Komentarz do art. 1164.*
201. *See* R. Golat, *Specyfika polubownego rozstrzygania sporów w stosunkach pracowniczych*, Służba Pracownicza 2006, No. 9, LEX No. 53982, p. 9.
202. R. Flejszar, *Ugodowe rozwiązywanie sporów z zakresu prawa pracy*, Studia z zakresu prawa pracy i polityki społecznej 2010, No. 1, pp. 315–328.
203. *See* R. Morek (in:) Kodeks postępowania cywilnego. Komentarz, ed. E. Marszałkowska-Krześ, Legalis/el., *Komentarz do art. 1164.*

309. The basis of the Court of Arbitration possibly examining labour law cases is the contract between the parties. In procedural terms, one of the elements determining the specificity of the arbitration clause in labour law cases is the moment in which the conclusion of the arbitration clause becomes admissible. The lawmakers relate this moment exclusively to the existence of a dispute. The contract should contain the subject matter of the dispute or the legal relationship from which the dispute arose, while the parties may only decide to subject the dispute to arbitration after the emergence of the specific event. Since the necessary condition for making the decision on the clause is the existence of a dispute, this provision is essentially an independent arbitration agreement. The existence of a dispute arising from the obligating bond binding the parties (employment relationship) is therefore a necessary condition of arbitration.[204]

310. In practice, however, authorities operate within PSFs, which, de facto, take over the review of disputes between sportspeople and sports clubs in an effort to remain in compliance with the law in force in Poland.

311. The so-called form of self-employment is used for this purpose (as well as to obtain tax savings), which means the acceptance that the sportsperson is not an employee, but a sole proprietor or a person collaborating with the club on the basis of a service-provision contract. Labour law protection does not encompass the rights of these people.

312. Additionally, the appropriate authorities in the NGBs settle disputes between sports clubs and sportspeople on the principle of consent to a kind of mediation, to which the employee is also entitled.

313. For example, the Sports Dispute Resolution Chamber at the PZPN can be mentioned, which examines disputes between footballers and football clubs. The Chamber is appointed for adjudicating on the existence, validity or termination of football contracts, making other decisions 'on the assurance of contractual stability of players who are parties to the contract', as well as on matters regarding the so-called solidarity mechanism (Article 46, § 2 of the PZPN statutes). In accordance with a literal wording of the PZPN statutes, the chamber is appointed to adjudicate on the existence, validity or resolution of both civil law contracts[205] and employment contracts with footballers (Article 7, § 2 of the PZPN statutes).[206]

314. As noted in the literature, certain shortcomings of this body (the Chamber can be considered to be an arbitration court) mean that the conclusion of a contract

204. M. Bąba, *Zapis na sąd polubowny w sporach z zakresu prawa pracy*, ADR. Arbitration and Mediation 2009, No. 4, p. 5.

205. In practice, these contracts are of key importance and are concluded most frequently. If an employment contract is concluded at all, it most frequently does not cover the whole spectrum of legal relationships which bind the player with the football club. They also do not include the whole of the remuneration that the player receives.

206. E.J. Krześniak, *Kluby i organizacje sportowe* (…), pp. 626–628.

by and between a player and a football club, in accordance with the relevant resolutions of the PZPN Management Board, followed by the confirmation of this fact by the Chamber does not guarantee the clubs a favourable result in a dispute of an international dimension (i.e., with a foreign player or coach).[207]

§6. Social Security

315. Polish law provides for four main types of social security: pension, disability, sickness (in the case of sickness and maternity) and accident insurance (for accidents at work and occupational diseases). People who have the appropriate title have the above social security. The insurance itself and the legal titles to it are governed by the provisions of the Act on the Social Security System (AoSSS).

316. In accordance with the provisions of the AoSSS, sportspeople employed by the clubs under an employment contract are subject to all four types of insurance: pension, disability, sickness and accident insurance. The club/employer is obliged to pay the contributions for the above insurance. The contributions to the pension and disability insurance are covered equally by the player and club/employer. The part of the contribution due from the sportsperson is deducted by the club from his due remuneration for his work. Accident and sickness insurance contributions are borne by the sportsperson/employee (they are deducted from the remuneration due to him).

317. As mentioned above, employment contracts are becoming less frequently encountered. The question therefore arises from the legal title to the social insurance of sportspeople who have concluded civil law contracts with the club for professionally playing sports. As indicated above, according to the Polish law, such a contract is a contract on the provision of services, to which the provisions on contracting apply accordingly. In such a case, the sportspeople are covered by the disability, pension and accident insurance under Article 6, paragraph 1, item 4 AoSSS.[208] The only difference in comparison with sportspeople/employees is being subject to sickness insurance. The sportsperson/employee is covered by sickness insurance by law, while the sportsperson/contractor is covered by this insurance on request. The principles of payment of social insurance contributions (and therefore also their split between the club and the player) are the same as in the case of the sportsperson/employee.

---

207. *See* letter from the Chairman of the Supervisory Board of Ekstraklasa S.A. to the delegates to the PZPN Congress of 23 Feb. 2016, http://www.pilkanozna.pl/index.php/Wydarzenia/Ekstraklasa/775362-przed-zjazdem-statutowym-pzpn-wszystkie-koci-niezgody-kluby-okreliy-stanowisko.html, accessed on 8 Jun. 2016.

208. *See* A. Jabłoński, 'Ubezpieczenie społeczne sportowców', (in:) Księga dla naszych kolegów, Prace prawnicze poświęcone pamięci doktora Andrzeja Ciska, doktora Zygmunta Masternaka, doktora Marka Zagrosika, Prace Naukowe Wydziału Prawa, Administracji i Ekonomii Uniwersytetu Wrocławskiego, series of e-monographs, No. 36, Wrocław 2013, p. 162.

318. A frequent phenomenon in Polish sport clubs is that of sports grants granted to players. Grants may be awarded by sports clubs (Article 5 AoS) or local authority units (periodic grants for individuals for the sports results achieved – Article 31, paragraph 1 AoS). Grants may also be granted to coaches of players achieving outstanding sports results in international or national competitions (also paid by local authority units – Article 31, paragraph 2 AoS). The AoS also provides for periodic sports grants for sports results achieved in international competitions awarded by the minister responsible for physical culture to the members of a national team by way of an administrative decision (Article 32, paragraph 1 AoS). In particularly justified cases, it is possible to grant a higher amount of sports scholarship for members of the national team despite the lack of sports results (Article 32a, paragraph 1 AoS), as well as for young members of the national team (Article 32b, paragraph 1 AoS), players and coaches (Article 32c, paragraph 1 AoS).

319. Sportspeople/grantees are subject to compulsory pension, disability and accident insurance. However, they are not covered by sickness insurance, because the lawmakers acknowledged that there is no risk of a loss of income as a result of sickness or maternity because sports grants may also be paid at times of sickness or maternity.

320. It is common to combine a sports grant (most frequently awarded by the Club) with civil law contracts (often called contracts on representing the club). A grant is most frequently paid monthly, while the remuneration for the civil law contract is paid at the end of the season (or after specific competitions; namely it depends on the number of the appearances of the sportsperson in the club's colours).

321. In less popular sports that do not generate large revenues for the club, a frequent phenomenon is also the 'pushing' of the best sportspeople out for grants awarded by the minister or the local authority unit. In such a case, the sportsperson's basic remuneration is precisely the grant.

§7. Tax Law

322. Taxation with PIT is governed by the provisions of the Act on Personal Income Tax of 26 July 1991 (Act on PIT).

323. Sportspeople can conduct their activities:

(1) on the basis of an employment contract;
(2) in personally conducted business; and
(3) through self-employment.

324. In the case of an employment contract (1) income is taxable on a tax scale, according to which the tax is:

- for a tax base of up to PLN 120,00085,528: 12% minus tax reducing amount of PLN 3,60018% minus the tax-free amount;
- over PLN 120,00085,528: PLN 10,800 + 32% of excess amount over PLN 120,000PLN 15,395.04 + 32% of the excess over PLN 85,528 minus the tax-free amount.

However, the level of the costs of generating income is between PLN 4,500 1,335 and PLN 54,002,502.56 per year.

325. In the case of activities conducted personally, (2), the sportsperson's income is taxed according to the tax scale, whereas the deductible expenses are set at level of 20% of income minus any possible social security contributions.

326. In the case of self-employment (3), a flat rate of 19% can be applied, which applies regardless of the amount of the tax base, while all expenses on preserving or securing the source of revenue may be treated as expenses.

Part III. Doping and Sport

Chapter 1. General Issues

327. A key issue in modern sports is the battle against doping. Almost all sports have anti-doping rules prohibiting the use of doping substances.[209] Anti-doping policies have also been very largely harmonized at international level in recent years. Many countries have either already adopted new anti-doping rules in sports, or are just doing so. Although these are anti-doping rules, in the first place, the legal rules differ from each other. For example, only in certain countries, the mere use of doping is regarded as a crime in the meaning of criminal law, whereas other countries only treat the administration of doping to minors as a crime or this is not penalized at all under criminal law. However, likewise in the area of the anti-doping laws, increasingly more points of overlap and increasingly fewer differences can be seen between countries. Perhaps we shall shortly be able to say that what has failed for decades has just become fact – a uniform anti-doping system that is applicable around the world.

328. The WADA certainly has the ambition of creating such a uniform system. WADA was established in 1999 as WADA, an international organization operating as a foundation governed by Swiss law (Articles 80 et seq. Zivilgesetzbuch (Swiss Civil Code of 1907)); its headquarters is located in Montreal, Canada. WADA's mission is to combat doping, coordinate this activity throughout the world and make efforts to standardize the anti-doping rules. Since its establishment, WADA has been gradually gaining importance, becoming an absolutely essential player in the area of sport.[210]

329. It can also be mentioned at this point that the international sports federations most frequently have direct (based on membership) contractual control over

209. The vast majority of sports in this respect have implemented the rules of the *World Anti-Doping Code*, https://www.wada-ama.org/en/resources/the-code/world-anti-doping-code, accessed on 17 Jul. 2017.

210. On the sideline, it can be stated that the Polish Minister of Sport, Witold Bańka, was nominated representative of the Council of Europe in the Executive Committee of the World Anti-Doping Agency in the term of office of 2018–2019 and will represent forty-seven States of the Council of Europe during the WADA discussions, while a Polish city (Katowice) will organize a WADA Congress in 2019; Katowice defeated Geneva and Muscat. Therefore, decisions will be made in Poland a year before the Tokyo Olympics on the directions in which the battle against doping will go, and a new head of WADA will be elected.

their members (the NFs), but not on the members of those NFs – regional and local associations, sport clubs and sportspeople. Nevertheless, all these people and entities are subject to control by the international federations. The NFs are obliged to apply and require compliance with the rules, which are a direct reflection of the rules imposed by the international federations, by the mere fact that they are members of the international federations. However, disputes arise when a particular rule of an international federation is inconsistent with national law that is applicable in the country in which the given NF operates. Conflicts of this kind are most frequently publicized in those situations where the international federation is not satisfied with the decision made by the NF regarding a specific club or sportsperson. A classic example of this situation will be anti-doping cases, in which national associations may treat breaches of the rules by sportspeople under their jurisdictions more easily. World federations consistently defend their rights to change the decisions of NFs.

330. The legal regulations in force in Poland were preventing the use of pharmacological and other doping substances in sport long before the establishment of WADA. A formal ban has applied since 1984. Poland signed the Council of Europe's Anti-Doping Convention in 1989. This Convention was ratified in 1990. The Convention is a comprehensive international agreement, the aim of which is to combat the use of illicit means and methods by sportspeople. The signature and ratification of the Convention means that the Polish authorities have formally assumed responsibility for combating doping.

331. When the anti-doping system was being established in Poland, an Anti-Doping Commission was appointed in 1988, operating in 1991–1993 under the name of Council Against Doping in Sport, which was ultimately renamed in 1993 as the National Commission Against Doping in Sport.

332. The Polish Government adopted the National Programme for Combating Doping in Sport in December 1995. This programme, based on the Council of Europe's Anti-Doping Convention, the IOC Olympic Charter and Polish legislation, focused on education, conducting doping checks and monitoring the application of sanctions by the PSFs.

333. The AoQS mentioned above became effective in 2005, fundamentally amending the rules related to sports. This contributed to a change in the organizational structure of the National Commission Against Doping in Sport. The emergence of the UNESCO International Convention Against Doping in Sport, which was ratified in 2007, was a milestone in the world anti-doping programme. Under the Convention, the International Standard List of Prohibited Substances and Methods, as well as the International Standard for Therapeutic Use Exemptions, which are an integral part of the World Anti-Doping Code (WADC) adopted by WADA and constituting the fundamental act defining the battle against doping at international level, became the applicable law.[211]

334. The AoS entered into force in 2010, introducing changes in the definition of doping with regard to the individual and introduced penalization for the administration of prohibited substances to people preparing for or participating in sports competitions.

335. WADA's efforts also resulted in a significant change in the Polish regulations, which were made in 2017, while the National Commission Against Doping in Sport was transformed into the Polish Anti-Doping Agency.

336. The current anti-doping rules in sport are a part of the generally applicable provisions of the law. These are discussed in the next chapter.

211. The current version of the code is available at WADA's website: https://www.wada-ama.org/en/resources/the-code/world-anti-doping-code, accessed on 17 Jul. 2017.

Chapter 2. Public Regulation

§1. Current Rules Versus Previous Regulations

337. Currently (since July 2017), all legal issues related to combating doping are governed by a separate Act – the Act on Combating Doping in Sport of 21 April 2017.[212]

338. Before 2017, issues related to combating doping were dealt with in a legal act of a general nature, namely the AoS. The former regulation was limited to the definition of doping in sport, the specification of the tasks and partially to the organization of the entity responsible for combating doping in sport and the establishment of a mechanism of financing tasks related to the maintenance of accreditation of the WADA and purchasing equipment for conducting doping tests in the form of a special purpose grant.[213]

§2. The Scope of the New Act on Combating Doping

339. The new regulations of the Act on Combating Doping in Sport are comprehensive and encompass all aspects of combating doping in sport, including the organization and financial management of the Polish Anti-Doping Agency and the Agency's cooperation with such services as the police, the border guards and the customs service. After all, this was one of the reasons for adopting a separate regulation on this – most of the issues covered by the new rules cannot be classified into the principles of organizing and playing sport, namely the subject matter of the AoS.

340. According to the creators of the new regulation, the separation of the anti-doping regulations in sport into a new act was also supported by the nature of the obligations in this area, as well as international practice, including, in the first place, the recommendation of the Council of Europe within the framework of monitoring the Anti-Doping Convention. It was formulated, among others, in the report on the monitoring trip to Albania and Georgia.[214]

§3. Definition of Doping

341. The statutory definition of doping in sport which was applicable until 2017 (Article 43, paragraph 1 of the AoS, which is no longer in force) was modelled on the definition accepted in the WADC and then incorporated into the content of the International Convention Against Doping in Sport in Paris on 19 October 2005.[215]

212. Consolidated text: Journal of Laws of 202219, item 18721258, as amended.
213. E.J. Krześniak, *Prawo sportowe przyszłości* (in:) B. Hołyst (ed.), *Księga Pamiątkowa XX lecia Wydziału Prawa i Administracji. Przyszłość Prawa*, p. 465, Warsaw 2017.
214. *See* justification of the Act on Combatting Doping in Sport, p. 2.
215. Journal of Laws of 2007, No. 142, item 999, as amended.

The definition that was introduced in 2010 replaced the previous general (abstract) definition, which referred exclusively to the use or administration of substances and methods specified by the respective list (in Poland, this list was adopted in the form of a regulation). From that moment on the definition was based on an exhaustive list of behaviours considered to be doping in sport. This definition also took into account the so-called prohibited relationship (collaboration), when a player benefits from the assistance of a staff member – a doctor, a coach or a physiotherapist – who is punishable (e.g., with a disciplinary penalty) for doping activities. This change does not take into account the International Convention Against Doping in Sport, which is binding on Poland, although it was already included in the AoS in 2016.

342. In principle, the new Act repeats the definition of doping in sport in the wording in which it appeared in the AoS. This is replaced by the most current definition contained in the WADC.

343. Doping in sport consists of exhaustively listed behaviours:

(1) the presence of a prohibited substance or its metabolites or markers in an athlete's sample;
(2) the use or attempted use by an athlete of a prohibited substance or a prohibited method;
(3) evading, refusing or failing to submit to sample collection;
(4) whereabouts failures;
(5) tampering or attempted tampering with any part of doping control;
(6) possession of a prohibited substance or a prohibited method;
(7) trafficking or attempted trafficking in any prohibited substance or prohibited method;
(8) administration or attempted administration to any athlete in-competition of any prohibited substance or prohibited method, or administration or attempted administration to any athlete out-of-competition of any prohibited substance or any prohibited method that is prohibited out-of-competition;
(9) aiding, abetting or any other type of intentional complicity involving doping in sport or an attempt of such conduct or breaching the terms of disqualification by another person;
(10) association in a professional or sport-related capacity with any athlete support person who:
    (a) if subject to the authority of an anti-doping organization, is serving a period of ineligibility; or
    (b) if not subject to the authority of an anti-doping organization, has been convicted or found in a criminal, disciplinary or professional proceeding to have engaged in conduct which would have constituted a violation of anti-doping rules if code-compliant rules had been applicable to such a person. The disqualifying status of such person shall be in force for the longer of six years from the criminal, professional or disciplinary decision or the duration of the criminal, disciplinary or professional sanction imposed; or
    (c) is serving as a front or intermediary for an individual described in items (a) and (b):

(i) if the athlete or other person taking up the collaboration has previously been advised in writing by an anti-doping organization with jurisdiction over the athlete or other person, or by WADA, of the athlete support person's disqualifying status as referred to in item c, and the potential consequences of the prohibited association and if the athlete or other person can reasonably avoid the association. The anti-doping organization shall also use reasonable efforts to advise the athlete support person who is the subject of the notice to the athlete or other person that the athlete support person may, within fifteen days, come forward to the anti-doping organization to explain that the criteria described in items a and b do not apply to him or her.

(11) At the same time, some of the above behaviours (in particular, the presence of a prohibited substance or its metabolites or markers, and/or the use or attempted use, possession or administration or attempted administration of a prohibited substance or prohibited method) shall not be considered an anti-doping rule violation, if such behaviour is justified by therapeutic use and the athlete has received consent to use the given prohibited substance or prohibited method on the principles set out in Annex 2 of the International Convention Against Doping in Sport.

344. Prohibited substances and methods are defined in the Act, by reference to Annex 1 of the said Convention.

345. The Act also defines the terms 'out-of-competition' and 'in-competition', which are important to the course of the doping control. The need for the definitions arises from the fact that their statutory importance deviates from the general understanding of these terms. The 'in-competition' period does not commence at the time the competition starts, but twelve hours earlier. Likewise, doping control, and hence the process of taking an athlete's physiological sample does not need to end before the end of the competition for such control to be considered as having been conducted during the competition. This is because the term 'in-competition' includes not only the period of the competition up to its end but also the period of the related doping control.

§4. The Body Appointed for Combating Doping

346. The authority with the powers to combat doping in sport in Poland is a new organizational structure – the Polish Anti-Doping Agency,[216] which acts as a State

216. The name itself – the Polish Anti-Doping Agency – refers to the nomenclature accepted in the international environment for entities combatting doping in sport. It is sufficient to mention the World Anti-Doping Agency (WADA) or the United States Anti-Doping Agency, or the Australian Anti-Doping Agency.

legal person and therefore has a legal personality. It replaced two entities which operated to date – the National Commission Against Doping in Sport and the Commission's office.[217]

347. The Agency is supervised by the Minister of Sport. The internal organization of the Agency and its detailed scope of activities are specified by its statutes which are defined by the Minister of Sport.

348. The Agency's tasks include the following in particular by law:

(1) specifying the principles and the course of the doping control;
(2) laying down the disciplinary rules related to doping in sport;
(3) planning and conducting in-competition and out-of-competition doping controls;
(4) training and improving the qualifications of the doping controllers;
(5) granting therapeutic use exemptions, constituting consent to the use of a given prohibited substance or a prohibited method by an athlete, as referred to in Article 2, paragraph 2;
(6) promoting, developing and implementing educational, informational and training programmes in the battle against doping in sport;
(7) informing the athlete or other person taking up the collaboration, as referred to in Article 2, paragraph 1, item 10, if, within the professional or other sports-related duties, he is working with an athlete support person in preparing for sports competition, as referred to in Article 2, paragraph 1, item 10, points a–c;
(8) reviewing the bills and draft legislation in the battle against doping in sport;
(9) collaborating with the appropriate international entities for combating doping in sport;
(10) collaborating with the appropriate entities, in particular, public authorities and research institutes, in terms of scientific research supporting combating doping in sport.

349. The Agency's governing bodies are the Director of the Agency, who manages the Agency's activities and represents it externally (appointed and dismissed by the Minister of Sport), as well as the Agency's Council, which expresses opinions on many of the director's decisions. The director is selected on the basis of an open and competitive recruitment organized by the Minister of Sport. The Director of the Agency may only be a Polish citizen.

217. Given the certain uniqueness of Polish law, the discussion of which exceeds the scope of this monograph and would probably be of interest to nobody but the most hardcore researchers of the Polish legal order, the mere fact that the Commission had a separate office generated practical problems. For example, the Commission and not its office had the status of a national Anti-Doping Organization in the system of stakeholders of the World Anti-Doping Agency (WADA), but the funds for conducting the controls were provided from the State budget to the office of the Commission.

350. The membership of the Agency's Council includes the representatives of the minister responsible for internal affairs (in connection with the Agency's collaboration with the police), the minister responsible for health, the minister responsible for public finances (to ensure that the Agency appropriately collaborates with the customs service), as well as the POC and three people appointed for the term of office of the Council, which has been specified as four years, who work in the areas of medicine, sports, ethics, biology or law. All members of the Agency's Council are appointed and dismissed by the Minister of Sport.

351. The Act on Combating Doping in Sport regulates all personnel issues in detail – among other things, the Act regulates such details as the principles of holding examinations for the Agency's controllers and the validity of the certificate that the auditors must have to be able to conduct controls. The controllers themselves currently have the status of public officials, similar to those of, for example, police officers, which has significantly strengthened their position. The Act also regulates – albeit only generally – the principles of cooperation between the Agency and such services as the police, the customs service, the border guards, the military police and the prosecutors, *inter alia*, by allowing for the exchange of information between these entities and the Agency.

352. The Agency is financed by the State budget, although it can also perform profit-oriented activity and obtain grants. The budget is fairly modest – in 2017–2026 the State budget's maximum spending limit on the Agency's activity is PLN 3 million in the first year of operation (approx. USD 800,000) and, ultimately, PLN 6.7 million (approx. USD 1.7 million).

§5. Standards of Control

353. The Polish Anti-Doping Agency applies international WADA standards in its doping controls. In the case of the doping control process itself, all of its aspects have been discussed in the International Standard for Testing and Investigations, which is regularly updated. After all, for this reason, many aspects of doping control have not been described in the Act. The conditions and the circumstances of subjecting athletes to doping controls, including their rights, have yet to be specified in the principles and course of the doping controls accepted by the Agency, in compliance with the relevant provisions of the WADC. This matter is not created by the provisions of the applicable law, but by the provisions of the international sports movement that will apply regardless of the existence of any statutory regulations on this.

354. The Act imposes the obligation on athletes to undergo doping controls conducted by the Agency, both in-competition and out-of-competition (Article 9, paragraph 1). The provisions of the Act also provide for additional responsibilities of the athlete related to doping control. First of all, he is required to provide information on his whereabouts during the next three months, which has the objective of facilitating the Agency in conducting a possible out-of-competition doping control. The failure to provide this information alone constitutes doping in sport.

355. The athlete is also required to provide information during the doping control about medicines and dietary supplements taken, as well as blood transfusions performed.

356. PSFs are required to transfer the exclusive rights to lay down and implement Disciplinary Rules on doping in sport to the Polish Anti-Doping Agency. The Agency, and not the NGBs, is responsible for laying down the Disciplinary Rules on doping in sport. Every PSF has a statutory obligation to recognize and respect the rules laid down in this way (Article 13, paragraph 5 of the AoS).

§6. Determining Liability

357. In accordance with the rules of the WADC, the decision on liability for doping in sport rests with the Disciplinary Panel, a special authority operating at the Agency, but acting independently and impartially (Articles 35 et seq. of the Act on Combating Doping in Sport).

358. The proceedings are held in two instances, while a Panel rules both in the first and the second instances. The panel is made up of up to twenty members, of whom at least half should be lawyers.

359. The panel considers cases at a hearing (the rule) or behind closed doors (the exception). In principle, proceedings are open. The Agency's Director or an Agency employee nominated by him has the right to take part in the hearing.

360. The Disciplinary Panel was already operating in Poland before the current laws became effective. It was stated in the justification to the new Act that many PSFs welcome the idea of the functioning of such a body, and some of them decided in 2015–2016 to voluntarily transfer their powers to adjudicate on disciplinary matters for doping in sport precisely to the panel.[218] However, this idyllic picture should be supplemented. This matter was addressed several years ago at one of the annual general meetings of the Polish Golf Union, during a discussion, or rather a lack of discussion. The transfer of powers for settling matters related to doping to the Disciplinary Panel was, in fact, voluntary, but this transfer was certainly helped by the information that, in the event of the refusal, further funding of the Union with public funds may be withheld. Of course, this does not change the fact that the very idea of the Disciplinary Panel is absolutely correct.

218. *See* justification to the bill on combatting doping in sport, p. 13.

§7. Criminal Regulations and Summary

361. The Act on Combating Doping in Sport also contains a number of criminal regulations and the penalization of certain behaviours related to the administration of prohibited substances. The administration of a prohibited substance to a minor is punishable with imprisonment. In the case of an adult, the administration of a prohibited substance without his knowledge is punishable. Trafficking or storage for the purpose of trafficking of a specific prohibited substance is also punishable.

362. The planning and implementation of doping controls has become far more professional in Poland in recent years. A central authority has been appointed to deal with these issues – the Polish Anti-Doping Agency. The controls are conducted by qualified controllers, who are trained to perform this role by the Agency itself and who have the status of public officials (police officers, for instance, have a similar status). A Disciplinary Panel operates at the Agency, which makes decisions on disciplinary liability. The role of the NGBs has been reduced to a minimum – they are obliged by law to respect the exclusive powers of the Agency in the majority of cases related to investigating and preventing doping in sport.

363. Finally, it is worth mentioning the selection of the Polish Sports Minister, Witold Bańka, to be a member of the Executive Committee of WADA. This seems to suggest that the new regulations were appreciated in the environment of people involved in combating doping. The Polish regulations are currently fully consistent with the WADA regulations. It appears that the speed of implementation of the necessary changes to achieve this objective and the innovative ideas related, for example, to the establishment of the Polish Anti-Doping Agency have gained approval in Europe. Minister Bańka himself claims other countries, such as Azerbaijan and Ukraine, come to the Polish authorities for advice, while Japan due to its implementation solutions is similar to those in Poland.[219]

219. K. Rawa, *Antydoping po polsku*, Rzeczpospolita 4 Jun. 2017.

Chapter 3. Private Regulation

364. Until recently, entities conducting sports activities, in particular, the Polish NFs applied disciplinary liability for the use of doping in sport to the extent specified in their regulations. Consequently, the line of judgments of the PSFs in cases of a breach of the doping regulations was non-uniform. Disciplinary decisions were frequently issued, which were in conflict with the anti-doping regulations (e.g., ordering a penalty below the lower threshold of the threat). This resulted in a low overall assessment of the Polish system of disciplinary judgments in doping cases, which is manifested, among others, in a large number of cases in which WADA contested the decisions of the PSFs either before the POC Court of Arbitration, or before the counterpart of this court in Lausanne (CAS).[220]

365. The Polish Anti-Doping Agency mentioned above is currently responsible for laying down the Disciplinary Rules related to doping in sport. The NFs are responsible for the establishment and implementation of Disciplinary Rules to the remaining extent. Therefore, Polish law does not directly regulate these rules. Such a regulatory model arises from the concept of autonomy and uniqueness of sport, as mentioned above, which the Court of Justice of the EU also recognizes (*see* C-51/96 and C-191/97 – *Christelle Deliège v. Ligue francophone de judo et disciplines associées ASBL*, and C-176/96 *Lehtonen et al. v. Fédération royale belge des sociétés de basket-ball ASBL*). The specificity of sport is manifested, among other things, in the fact that disciplinary liability for doping in sport exists on the basis of the regulations of entities in the sports movement, regardless of whether or not it is regulated in the national legal order. These issues need to be regulated in an act to the necessary extent because of the international commitments that Poland has assumed as a party to the above international agreements. It enables the correct 'transposition' of international agreements that are binding on it into the national legal order, introduces uniform standards and, within the limits provided for in the above international regulations, assures uniform procedures for the parties to the proceedings on the use of doping in sport.[221]

---

220. Justification of the Act on Doping in Sport, p. 12.
221. *See* justification to the Act on the Polish Anti-Doping Agency, p. 11.

Part IV. Sport and Commerce

Chapter 1. General Issues

§1. Introduction

366. For some time, sport was treated as a branch of life which is outside the scope of the generally applicable provisions of the law. It was believed that sport can cope perfectly well without interference from the law and those regulations which are necessary in sport (if only the rules of sports disciplines), have been established by the interested parties – the sportspeople represented by sports federations or national sports organizations, such as sports associations.[222] To paraphrase Arthur Rowe's statement: 'Football's a simple game, it's the players who make it difficult';[223] it can be said that, according to a large proportion of the so-called world of sports 'sport is a simple thing, it's only the lawyers who make it difficult'.

367. Such an approach to the relationship between sport and the law, as presented above, is evident even today, sometimes in official documents. For instance, the Polish bill on sports contains a sentence saying that 'a significant part of the activity in the area of physical culture, including sport, takes place outside the sphere of legal regulation'. Such a conclusion is, of course, completely wrong. The law applies both on and off the field. Sport is fully subject to the legal order in force in the given country. However, this does not change the fact that sport largely governs itself.[224]

368. Sport, today, is a powerful business, with a turnover of huge amounts of money.[225] The commercialization and professionalization of sport, which took place

222. Such a view abroad has remained for many years among the group of so-called sports activists. *See* E. Grayson, *The Historical Development of Sport and Law*, in *Law and Sport in Contemporary Society*, 3 (S. Greenfield, & G. Osborn eds., London 2000). Likewise, the courts in the UK sometimes assumed a similar position.

223. *See* Haas, Martens, *Sportrecht*, p. 5.

224. In the justification to the AoS, the lawmakers certainly meant this, while the cited sentence is purely a lapsus.

225. Interesting data on the impact of sport on the development of the economies of the EU States is contained in the European Commission's study prepared with the participation of, *inter alia*, the Polish Ministry of Sport and Tourism – the *Study on the Contribution of Sport to Economic Growth*

in the last thirty years in Western countries, has also appeared in Poland. In conjunction with the continuous presence of sport in the media, commercialization has meant that both the legal relations and the conflicts to which these relationships give rise, increasingly frequently require reference to the legal regulations.

369. For many people involved in sport (sportspeople and trainers), as well as people involved in the organization of sports events, as well as the organization of the structure itself and the principles of playing sport (so-called activists), sport is no longer a hobby and pastime, but a way of life and an occupation. Many studies show that sport is an important element of the national economy of every developed country. For example, in the countries of the EU, 2% of GDP and approximately 7 million jobs (3.5% of all working people) are associated with sports in various ways.[226] Therefore, even the State has begun to materially regulate organizations and the methods of operation of sport in society. These standards are not always consistent with the norms laid down by the sports organizations.

370. Financing of sport in a country like Poland, which is constantly catching up with the countries of Western Europe, both in terms of per capita income and gross national product and, colloquially speaking, the broadly understood standard of living, is largely based on State financing. The tradition of private donors making large outlays on sport is not strong. Although the strongest leagues, namely football, volleyball and basketball, have a lot of sponsors, these leagues are rather the exception in Poland's bleak reality of sport (at least in terms of the financial aspect) and, furthermore, many of these sponsors are large companies controlled by the State. Colloquially speaking, poor children will always take priority – and rightly so – over a poor club or sports association.

371. Regardless of the above, both the clubs and the Polish NFs operate in a free market economy and their commercial activities should be considered with account taken of the rules of competition law.

§2. Polish Sports Federations and Sports Clubs and Competition Law

I. EU Rules

372. Business freedom is limited by the rules of competition. European integration has progressed since the beginning with account taken of the competition rules addressed to both businesses and the Member States.

---

and Employment in the EU. Study commissioned by the European Commission, Directorate-General Education and Culture. Final Report, November 2012, http://ec.europa.eu/sport/library/studies/study-contribution-spors-economic-growth-final-rpt.pdf, accessed on 20 Jul. 2016.

226. European Commission's data, http://europa.eu/rapid/press-release_MEMO-14-432_en.htm, accessed on 3 Jun. 2016.

373. Likewise sport is assessed from the point of view of compliance of the behaviour of market players with the competition rules. Even before the EU lawmakers decided to embrace sport directly with the Treaty regulation, in a number of important judgments, the ECJ clearly decided that 'the practice of sport is subject to community law only in so far as it constitutes an economic activity within the meaning of Article 2 of the Treaty' and is subject to the Treaty rules governing the free movement of workers and the free movement of services.[227] Therefore, the Court has taken the position since the beginning that, if playing sport is related to a business dimension, it is encompassed by the scope of EU rules, including the provisions of Community law governing the rules of competition. Successive judgments have confirmed this interpretation. The most groundbreaking judgments of the ECJ in the history of this body also include those related to sport. An example is the judgment in the famous *Bosman* case.[228]

374. Many practices related to issues, which are at the point of interconnect between sport and commerce, such as the broadcasting of sports events, ticket sales, and the organization of tournaments in a given sport by international sports federations and national sports associations, as well as the matter of ownership and trading of shares in sport clubs, have become a subject of proceedings before the European Commission, which have ended in either the issuance of a formal decision or the entry into a settlement.[229]

375. The addressees of the competition rules, including the rules prohibiting cartels, are primarily entrepreneurs, although the term 'entrepreneur' is treated broadly in European competition law (Articles 101–102 TFEU). The form in which business is conducted and whether or not it is profit-oriented is irrelevant. For this reason, international sports federations and national sports associations cannot rely on a non-economic objective of their business and, even if they do, this still does not release them from the regime of these regulations.

376. Therefore, it is currently already completely obvious and indisputable that the sports sector is subject to EU competition rules. Business involving playing sports and organizing sports matches, as well as the commercial use of its related rights, is a business activity and is subject to the laws governing the economic integration between EU Member States.[230]

377. At this point, a closer look can be taken at the status of sports clubs and associations as 'enterprises' in the meaning of the provisions of the Treaty. The

227. *See* the judgment in *Walrave*. I have given the quotation from B. Rischka-Słowik, *Konstytucja sportu w Unii Europejskiej*, pp. 362–363.
228. Cf. E.J. Krześniak, *Kluby i organizacje sportowe* (…), pp. 492–493.
229. *See* B. Rischka-Słowik, *Konstytucja sportu* … , pp. 364–365. *See also* M.K. Kolasiński, *Subsydiowanie ze źródeł publicznych inwestycji w infrastrukturę sportową w prawie Unii Europejskiej*, Studia Iuridica 2013, vol. 13, pp. 69–71.
230. *See* B. Rischka-Słowik, *Konstytucja sportu* … , p. 365.

notion of 'enterprise' was defined in Article 1 of Annex I to Commission Regulation (EC) No. 800/2008 of 6 August 2008 declaring certain categories of aid compatible with the common market in the application of Articles 87 and 88 of the Treaty 'General Regulation on Block Exemptions'. In accordance with the wording of this provision, an enterprise is considered to be any entity conducting business, irrespective of its legal form. Therefore, this includes self-employed people and businesses, as well as partnerships and associations regularly conducting business to their own account. The legal form, source of financing and even the element of the objective of generating a profit (or lack of profit) is irrelevant to the description of the given entity as an enterprise. In the vast majority of cases, sports clubs and associations operating in Poland will constitute enterprises in the meaning provided above.

378. Attention should also be drawn to the provision of Article 107(1) TFEU, which provides that 'any aid granted by a Member State or through State resources in any form whatsoever which distorts or threatens to distort competition by favouring certain undertakings or the production of certain goods shall, in so far as it affects trade between Member States, be incompatible with the internal market'. Therefore, the prohibition to grant State aid is not absolute, because the relevant footnotes distinguish both aid which is compatible with the internal market (Article 107(2) TFEU), and aid which may be considered compatible with the rules in force in that market (Article 107(3) TFEU). Sports clubs and associations should be treated as enterprises in the above meaning.

379. The European Commission presented a detailed methodology in Annex I to the so-called Staff Working Document that was attached to the White Paper on sport, showing how it will apply the rules of competition law in the sports sector. This methodology consists of four elements: (1) the establishment of whether a sports organization is to be considered an 'undertaking' or an 'association of undertakings', (2) the establishment of whether the rule in question, restricts competition or constitutes an abuse of a dominant position, (3) the determination of whether trade between Member States is affected and (4) the determination of whether the rule satisfies the conditions referred to in Article 102 TFEU.

380. Even if the sportspeople themselves are employed by sports clubs, they can also be treated as businesses if they conduct business independently of the club, for example, by signing promotional contracts.

381. There is also no doubt that sports clubs are enterprises in the meaning of Articles 101 and 102 TFEU, to the extent to which they conduct business activity. Merely selling tickets, selling television rights, signing sponsorship contracts or advertising contracts will be business activity. National sports associations may also be treated as enterprises in the meaning of Articles 101 and 102 TFEU or as associations of enterprises in the meaning of Article 101 TFEU. The mere fact that a national association associates both professional and amateur clubs does not mean that it cannot be treated as an association of enterprises. In this respect, of key significance is the judgment of 26 January 2005 in *Laurent Piau v. Commission of the*

European Communities. Therefore, the White Paper clearly shows that the European Commission takes the view that the EU rules of competition law can and should – in principle – apply to sports organizations.

II. Rules of Polish Law

382. It is even more important in Poland that PSFs hold positions of actual and legal monopolies in the area of sport.

383. Unfortunately, these matters have not given rise to any major interest to date in the Polish legal doctrine. There are essentially no major studies referring to this issue. Likewise, the analysis of the acquis of the Polish OCCP – the body that was established to combat cartels and protect fair competition, indicates that the subject of the activities of sports clubs, sports associations and PSFs has very occasionally found itself in the interests of the office. This can be surprising, given that the position of the PSFs is incomparably stronger in their area (matches in a given sport) than any other entrepreneur on any other market.

384. Some authors explicitly argue in favour of accepting the idea that the monopoly of PSFs is unnecessary and harmful. These authors suggest that there is no need for public law regulation in order to select organizations representing the country on the international arena, arguing that the large number of sports associations would not hinder the selection of national representatives for the individual sports, and claim that the suggestion contained in the justification to the bill on sport that the principle of 'one discipline – one association' is of a universal character is wrong.[231]

385. Similarly, speaking on behalf of the Parliamentary Free Market Group in the previous term of office of the Polish Parliament, M. Jaros, the author of the parliamentary member's interpellation to the Minister of Sport asked whether the Ministry of Sport and Tourism expects to introduce legal regulations into the AoS, which would allow for the operation of more than one association in a given area and simultaneously establish such legal solutions which would rule out the emergence of conflicts between competing associations. In the justification, M. Jaros, MP, stated that 'the changes we are proposing [by the said parliamentary group – added by E.J.K.] – enabling the operation of more than one sports association in a given area of sport – would require the establishment of such legal solutions that would rule out the emergence of conflicts between competing associations. The existence of one sports association, which acts as the representative in the international federation does not rule out the implementation of the changes we are proposing, which primarily have the objective of popularizing sport among young

231. P. Dobrowolski, *Ustawowy monopol w sądzie nie jest potrzebny*, Communication No. 16 of 16 Jul. 2012.

people – the more associations, the more sports schools and the greater the competition between the associations – Poland's representative would be the association, the members of which are achieving the best results'. The author of the interpellation simultaneously points out that the 'solutions we are proposing work successfully in such countries as the United Kingdom and the United States'[232] and even earlier argued that 'One of the proposals for improving Polish sport is the introduction of such rules into the Act on Sport which enable the demonopolization of Polish sports organizations. We are convinced that this revolutionary change over time would meaningfully translate into sports successes of our contestants.'[233]

386. The examples presented in this last statement should not be considered correct. The system of organization of sport in the United States differs fundamentally from the so-called European model of sport, while the use of solutions that have been implemented in that jurisdiction (or rather, several dozen State jurisdictions) into Polish realities would be very difficult. Likewise, the example of the United Kingdom is not altogether correct, because, despite the lack of legally guaranteed monopoly, national sports associations in the United Kingdom have an actual monopoly in most sports disciplines.

387. It is simultaneously worth taking this opportunity to mention a few groundbreaking judgments of the Polish courts and decisions of the regulatory body on sport with regard to competition law.

388. Among others, the Polish OCCP accused UEFA of breaching the collective interests of consumers and abusing the position of a monopolist. In the action against UEFA, the President of the OCCP[234] reported reservations about, *inter alia*, exclusions of liability for delays in the supply of tickets, the possibility of changing important terms and conditions of the contract in the event of the appearance of 'unforeseen circumstances' and forcing the consumer to change the purchased seat without giving a reason; doubts were also raised by the acceptance of the unbalanced principle of considering disputes – if the spectator files an action in a dispute, the court with jurisdiction is a court in Switzerland, whereas, if the claimant party is UEFA, it is able to refer the matter to the court with territorial jurisdiction over its headquarters or the court with jurisdiction over the consumer's place of residence.[235] The President of the OCCP contested a total of twenty-five contractual clauses. In its judgment of 22 June 2012, the court declared nineteen of them to be inadmissible.

---

232. Interpellation No. 8506 of 31 Aug. 2012, to the Minister of Sport and Tourism on the clarification of the objectives of the proposed amendments regarding the issue of demonopolizing Polish sports federations, SPS-023-8506/12.
233. Interpellation No. 6416 of 12 Jul. 2012 to the Minister of Sport and Tourism on the demonopolization of Polish sports federations.
234. Communication of the President of the OCCP on this matter, https://uokik.gov.pl/aktualnosci.php?news_id=3489, accessed on 4 Jun. 2016.
235. List of contested clauses, http://uokik.gov.pl/download.php?plik=11553, accessed on 4 Jun. 2016.

389. The whole procedure was criticized in the Polish legal doctrine, which was expressed in positions favouring UEFA. Even at the stage of the litigation itself, A. Wach's conclusions about the allegations in question were that 'at least some of them appear to be disputable'. The author simultaneously pointed out that the Polish bodies of public administration gave UEFA a guarantee on the sale and trading of entry tickets.[236]

390. It is also worth mentioning the case regarding the breach of consumer interests, which was pending against the Legia Warsaw. According to the President of the OCCP,[237] the club applied prohibited practices, including restricting the rights of fans to a refund for their tickets in the event of the closure of the stadium, the exclusion of the club's liability for changing the dates of matches, as well as imprecise provisions on the termination of the contract with customers buying passes in instalments. The club agreed to voluntarily change the model contracts it used, in accordance with the recommendations of the President of the OCCP. Consequently, in his decision, the President of the OCCP only ordered the implementation of these changes.[238]

391. The analysis of both the doctrine of competition law and the practice of the OCCP regarding issues related to the organization of sports matches, the position of the PSFs and the power that these organizations have in Polish sports, as well as the conduct of sports clubs clearly show that we are far behind the doctrine and practices of the countries of Western Europe in this respect. The doctrine almost completely ignores this subject. Suffice it to say that, even on such fundamental issues as the matter of the normative grounds for an actual monopoly of PSFs, no uniform views have been developed.

392. In turn, the analysis of the few decisions of the OCCP related to organized sport indicates that the OCCP is focusing on the sports club – spectator relationship or on issues regarding television broadcasting,[239] ignoring the essence of modern sport – the role of the PSF, the relationship between the PSFs and the international sports federations or a broad spectrum of issues related to the actual restriction of the right to a court hearing and compulsory arbitration (this latter issue will be discussed below).

---

236. A. Wach, *Odpowiedzialność osób naruszających reguły sportowe lub prawne w związku z UEFA Euro 2012, Warszawa 2012*, pp. 135–136.
237. Communication of the President of the OCCP, https://uokik.gov.pl/aktualnosci.php?news_id=10081, accessed on 4 Jun. 2016.
238. *See*, https://uokik.gov.pl/download.php?plik=12435, accessed on 4 Jun. 2016.
239. This is also addressed in the Polish doctrine, although, in my opinion, it is still not sufficiently detailed. Of the available materials, *see* the brief study by K. Kuik, *Transmisje z meczów piłkarskich – zagadnienia prawa konkurencji UE* (in:) A.J. Szwarc (ed.) *Prawne problemy sportu piłkarskiego, Warsaw 2013*, pp. 343–349.

393. It is true that some authors believe that, in the future, the most important legal disputes related to the functioning of sport in Poland will be settled on the basis of the antitrust law.[240]

394. It is impossible to agree with such an argument, as it appears to be wrong, in terms of both practice and legal justification.

395. As for the matter of applying the law, it can clearly be seen that the practice of this position has not been confirmed. The OCCP almost does not deal at all with the activities of PSFs and other sports organizations, even though a large proportion of them occupy a position in the market that would predestine them to assume the role of natural 'candidates' for proceedings related to an abuse of a dominant position.

396. The legal justification should also be considered wrong. This is because the author argues that the reasoning adopted by the EU courts should be transferred to Polish law and, from this, he argues the assumption that legal disputes related to sport in Poland will be settled on the basis of the antitrust law.[241] It is difficult to agree with such a position. Even if it were to be accepted that the method of reasoning of the EU courts should be transferred to Polish law with respect to sport, it certainly does not follow from this that sports-related disputes will be settled mainly on the basis of the antitrust criterion. Disputes related to sports at EU level were and are often settled on the basis of the provisions of competition law. This is almost certainly the source of the author's assumptions that it will be similar under Polish law. However, it must not be forgotten that competition law is a disproportionately large (compared with national legal orders) area of the *acquis communautaire*. Free competition is the basis of the functioning of the EU and, therefore, inherently disproportionately many (compared to the whole of the case law of the Polish courts) decisions made by the ECJ are based on the provisions of the broadly understood competition law. Conclusions cannot be drawn from this that it will be similar in Poland.[242]

240. M.K. Kolasiński, *Z orzecznictwa Trybunału Konstytucyjnego (sądowo-administracyjna kontrola orzeczeń polskiego związku sportowego w sprawie udzielania licencji na dany sezon rozgrywkowy). Glosa do wyroku z 19 X 2010, P 10/10, PiP 2011, z. 12*, p. 122.
241. M.K. Kolasiński, *Z orzecznictwa Trybunału Konstytucyjnego* ... , p. 122.
242. E.J. Krześniak, *Kluby i organizacje sportowe* (...), pp. 502–503.

Chapter 2. Public Regulation

§1. Media and Television Broadcasting Rights

397. The issue of rights to audiovisual broadcasts of a sports event has been fairly well written in the Polish legal doctrine.[243] However, in the Polish doctrine, as in many other countries, the subject of the discussion and controversy was a range of issues. In the first place, whether the organizer of the sports event should decide to record and broadcast the event and whether he should be able to reap the economic benefits from this was disputable. Discussions started in the doctrine from the introduction of a distinction between a sports meeting, a sports tournament and sports events. A sports meeting is a public act of sports rivalry in a particular sport, combined into a whole in terms of the place, time and result (e.g., a volleyball match or a mountain bike race). However, a sports tournament means an organizational and an economic project serving one or more acts of sporting rivalry, concentrated in time and combined with a result (as, for example, World Championships in handball or the Olympic Games). A sports event is a collective term referring to both sports meetings and individual sports shows and even parts of individual sports shows.[244]

398. In Polish law, there are no separate legal grounds on which the organizer's economic exclusivity to benefit from a sports meeting could be argued.[245] However, several directions of possible solutions are mentioned in this respect:

(1) A sports meeting treated as an intangible good (a work in the meaning of copyright law or an item of related rights in the meaning of copyright law).
(2) A sports tournament as a project, the result of which is a sports meeting constituting a specific product, which is an element of business trading.
(3) A sports meeting as a tournament, the framework of which is specified by appropriate agreements (e.g., a contract concluded between the organizer of the sports meeting and the purchaser of the ticket, in which the purchaser of the ticket may be required to behave in a certain way, for instance, refrain from filming the meeting, or otherwise recording it).

---

243. K. Wojciechowski, *Widowisko sportowe w telewizji i audiowizualna relacja z niego jako dobra chronione w świetle polskiego prawa prywatnego,* Warsaw 2005. *See also* K. Kuik, '*Transmisje z meczów piłkarskich* … , pp. 342–354 and M. Wojcieszak, '*Prawne problemy telewizyjnych przekazów meczów piłkarskich*' (in:) Prawne problemy sportu piłkarskiego … , ed. A.J. Szwarc, pp. 219–246. Of the earlier studies, which are partly still current, it is worth mentioning J. Bart, Markiewicz, '*Widowisko sportowe a prawo autorskie*' (in:) Sport i media – problemy prawne, ed. M. Kępiński, Poznań 1997, pp. 26–49 and M. Kępiński, '*Umowa o transmisję sportową*' (in:) Sport i media … , ed. M. Kępiński, pp. 50–66. *See also* A. Kijowski, '*Prawa i obowiązki sportowca związane z transmisjami sportowymi i przekazywaniem informacji sportowych*' (in:) Sport i media … , ed. M. Kępiński, pp. 130–138 and L. Wojtowicz, '*Program ochrony praw własności intelektualnej w związku z EUFA Euro 2012™*' (in:) Prawne problemy sportu piłkarskiego … , ed. A.J. Szwarc, pp. 310–313.
244. K. Wojciechowski, *Widowisko sportowe* … , pp. 21–25.
245. S. Fundowicz, *Prawo sportowe* … , p. 250.

(4) A sports event as an enterprise, or as a result of the activity of an enterprise, which constitutes a legal good that deserves effective protection from third parties.
(5) The primacy of the venue of the sports event (the sports facility) over the tournament itself.[246]

399. Some were discarded quite quickly from the above structure in the Polish legal doctrine. Neither the structure requiring the treatment of a sports tournament as a result of business activity of the enterprise nor the attempt to treat a sporting event as a meeting which is subject to copyright protection as, for example, a theatre play or a film, were accepted. A sports event is difficult to treat as a meeting in which an artistic performance takes place. Therefore, the interests of the event's organizer cannot be protected under copyright law. As a result, the protection of the rights of the organizer of the sports meeting is based on several different legal grounds, which coexist with each other. First, the purchaser of the ticket may be and actually is obliged to behave in a specific way, namely to either refrain from filming the meeting, or to record it only for his own purposes. Second, the television sports transmission, as part of the programme being broadcast is subject to legal protection, as a subject of broadcasting rights. As a result, the organizers of sporting events or the organizations authorized by them, including entities acting on behalf of the PSFs, enter into contracts with the television broadcasters for television sports broadcasting. Under such a contract, the organizer undertakes to hold a specific sports event consisting of specific sports meetings and allows the broadcaster to access and use the venue of these meetings and the equipment located there to record and disseminate the audiovisual broadcast of the meeting.[247]

400. The problem of so-called highlights from television broadcasts of matches should be mentioned as disputed issues. In accordance with Article 25, paragraph 1, item 1, point 2 of the Act on Copyright and Related Rights of 4 February 1994 (Journal of Laws of 2006 No. 90, item 631) reports and extracts from the reports and articles that may be distributed in the press, radio and television for information purposes. Therefore, as can be seen, this provision requires several conditions to be satisfied – the information objective, the currency of the event, the integrity of the normal use of the work, the lack of breach of the creator's legitimate interests and the presentation of the creator and the source. Therefore, it is possible to imagine that television broadcasters will take advantage of this provision and present highlights of sports events in the television programmes they broadcast. In trading practice on the Polish market, broadcasters not having the television broadcasting rights to the matches do not use highlights, but purely provide information on the sports result and the course of the match, illustrating it with still images from its course. After all, broadcasting rights to highlights are frequently one of the paid packages in the tenders for the television broadcasting rights.

---

246. M. Wojcieszak, *Legal Aspects of Football Match Broadcasting*, in *Conference Materials from the International Conference, Legal Problems of Football Sport* (Poznań, 10–13 May 2012). *See* S. Fundowicz, *Prawo sportowe,* Warsaw 2013, p. 250.
247. S. Fundowicz, *Prawo sportowe,* p. 253.

401. The provisions of EU law allow individual Member States to introduce restrictions securing against the organizers of specific events transferring the television broadcasting rights on those events to television broadcasters on the principle of exclusivity. This is about avoiding the situation in which certain events which are important from the public and political point of view would be broadcast in a manner which does not guarantee that the broadcast would reach the largest possible audience (e.g., by broadcasting them only via encoded channels or channels to which access is limited for other reasons). Article 3j(1) of Directive 89/552/EEC of the European Parliament and of the Council on the coordination of certain provisions laid down by law, regulation or administrative action in Member States concerning the pursuit of television broadcasting activities provides that Member States may, in accordance with European Community law, take steps to ensure that broadcasters under their jurisdiction do not have the exclusive right to broadcast events recognized by the Member States as being of major importance to the public in such a way as to deprive a significant proportion of the public of that Member State of the ability to watch these events in a live broadcast or rebroadcast in the generally available television channel. Member States should draw up a list of events, which they consider to be of particular importance to the public. This list should be prepared openly and transparently. The State should also specify whether these events should be available, in whole or in part, in a live broadcast or partially rebroadcast. The Polish Broadcasting Act lists events that are considered so important for society. Interestingly, it only contains sports events. These are the summer and the winter Olympic Games, the semi-finals and finals of the World Cup and the European championships in football, as well as all other matches in these events in which the Polish team is playing, including the qualifying matches and other matches played by the Polish national football team in official tournaments and matches involving Polish clubs in the UEFA Champions' League and the UEFA[248] (Article 20b, paragraph 2 of the Act on Broadcasting). Additionally, the National Broadcasting Council, the Polish audiovisual regulator may specify a list of other major sporting events by regulation; this list may include important volleyball matches in which the Polish national team is playing.[249]

402. A television broadcaster authorized to exclusively broadcast an event of high social interest is obliged to allow other television broadcasters to exercise the right to give a brief report (Article 20c, paragraph 1 of the Act). These obligations arise directly from the provisions of the European Convention on Transfrontier Television of 5 May 1989 (Journal of Laws of 1995, No. 32, item 160, as amended, *see* Articles 9 and 9a) and Directive 2010/13/EU of the European Parliament and of the Council of 10 March 2010 on the coordination of certain provisions laid down by law, regulation or administrative action in Member States concerning the provision

248. At this point this was about the UEFA Europa League, https://pl.wikipedia.org/wiki/Liga_Europy_UEFA_(2017/2018).
249. Regulation of the National Broadcasting Council of 17 Nov. 2014 on the list of important events.

of audiovisual media services (OJ L 2010, No. 95, p. 1; *see* Articles 14 and 15); which superseded Directive 89/552/EEC of 3 October 1989, the Television without Frontiers Directive.[250]

403. However, of the disputed issues, it is worth drawing attention to the fact that the common (including in Poland) practice of sports associations selling the rights to audiovisual broadcasting in packages, such as the rights to television broadcasting of the matches of all clubs in the top division played in the given sport could give rise to concerns from the point of view of compliance with competition law and is contested in the legal doctrine and the jurisprudence of certain countries. For example, the German jurisprudence and doctrine have not developed an unequivocal position in this respect. A part of the doctrine considers that the sale by the national sports association of the television broadcasting rights to matches organized by a sports club, instead of and with the exclusion of that club, is inadmissible, if that club is so recognizable in legal transactions that it can independently manage these rights on its own.[251] Although the sports association managing the football league in Germany obtained consent from the European Commission for selling the television broadcasting rights in one package in 2005,[252] this was only after it accepted certain obligations and restrictions (including the prohibition of exclusivity for an excessively long period and the prohibition to renew a contract on the basis of which the broadcasting rights were sold).[253] To this day, this understanding gives rise to doubts from the German Cartel Office (*Bundeskartellamt*), which formulates far-reaching concerns with respect to the sales of a package of Bundesliga matches.[254]

404. Likewise in the US judicature, (with regard to academic sport) the package sale of television broadcasting rights by the organizer of matches (in this case, it was the National Collegiate Athletic Association (NCAA)) was considered to be in breach of the provisions of competition law.[255] In particular, the provision which prohibited universities from selling television broadcasting rights to matches played on their campus, bypassing the rules imposed by the NCAA was found to be in breach of the law.[256]As a result of this judgment, television networks have the freedom to negotiate contracts for the sale of television rights with the most important US universities, which has led to the situation where matches currently played by some university teams are broadcast on one television station while matches played by other colleges are broadcast by another station.

---

250. Cf. *Leksykon prawa sportowego. 100 podstawowych pojęć.* M. Leciak (ed.), Warsaw 2017.
251. Haas, Martens, *Sportrecht*, pp. 96–97. For details on this, *see also* I. Hannamann, *Kartellverbot und Verhaltenskoordination im Sport, Berlin 2001*, pp. 257–261.
252. On the legal status on this area before the decision was issued by the European Commission, *see* T. Glinke, *§ 31 GWB – Notwendige Ausnahme zum Kartellverbot oder gesetzgeberische Gefälligkeit für den Deutschen Fußballbund?* Münster 2003, pp. 10–13.
253. N. Korff, *Sportrecht* … , p. 109.
254. This is described more extensively by N. Korff, *Sportrecht* … , pp. 108–110.
255. *NCAA v. Board of Regence*, 468 U.S. 85 (1984).
256. More on this subject – R.A. Garett & P.R. Hochberg, *Sports Broadcasting*, in *Law of Professional and Amateur Sports*, 20-50–20-55 (G.A. Uberstine ed., Joel C. Corry & J.K. Pressman assistant eds., Thomson Reuters).

405. Authors writing about sports law in Poland are currently bypassing these issues. A reasonably important fact, to which attention should be drawn in this context, is also being missed in the Polish literature. That is the different popularity of each sport in the countries of the EU and the impact of this fact on the legal conclusions. The fact that different sports have differing levels of popularity in individual European countries is no secret. This matter directly affects the interpretation of various types of action taken, especially by the national sports associations, regarding their compliance with competition law. For example, if an Italian television station concludes a ten-year contract giving it exclusive television rights to cricket matches, this will not have a major impact on competition on the Italian television market, because the number of people following cricket in Italy is limited to a handful of Britons working there. However, an identical agreement should be declared inadmissible in England, because this kind of reservation of exclusive rights for such a long period would probably breach the rules of competition law in force in that country – such a contract in England should be considered inadmissible by the competition authorities.[257]

406. In this context, the matter handled by the Polish OCCP against the television broadcaster, Canal+ and the PZPN should also be mentioned. The contested matter applied to the broadcasting of league matches. Television stations that wanted to screen matches from the first and second divisions of the time and the Polish Cup had to enter a tender organized by the PZPN. The tender for the most attractive broadcasts – live matches – was prepared in such a way that it favoured one of the entities (Canal+), which, according to the President of the OCCP, was anti-competitive. The privileged position of Canal+ in the tender for broadcasting in the seasons from 2005–2006 to 2007–2008 was guaranteed by the contract between PZPN and Canal+ of 2000. After the other participants of the tender submitted their proposals, PZPN was required to inform Canal+ of the competitive bids and, if Canal+ submitted a proposal that was just as attractive as the best of the others – it would receive the exclusive broadcasting right. This was a classic example of the right of first refusal, which is known from the common law system (which is structurally similar to the so-called Polish *prawo pierwokupu*). After the proceedings, the President of the OCCP[258] imposed a penalty of over PLN 7 million on Canal+ and more than PLN 400,000 on PZPN.[259]

407. The decision of the President of the OCCP was then challenged by PZPN, which went to the Competition and Consumer Protection Court. The Competition and Consumer Protection Court reduced the amount of the fine imposed on PZPN,

---

257. Example from B. Kennelly, T. Richards, *Applying the Competition Rules in the Sports Sector*, in *Sport: Law and Practice* Ch. F2, 1148 (Bloomsbury Professional, 2014).
258. Communication of the President of the OCCP, https://uokik.gov.pl/aktualnosci.php?news_id=165.
259. *See*, https://uokik.gov.pl/download.php?plik=9917, accessed on 4 Jun. 2016.

simultaneously confirming the breach of competition. The Court of Appeal held that the reduction in the fine is unreasonable and upheld the decision of the President of the OCCP.[260]

408. An important matter in the sports background which was handled by the OCCP was also that of the proceedings against Sportfive and eleven other businesses regarding the resale of the rights to broadcast Polish national matches in the pay-per-view system.[261] The matter did not actually apply to the contract between PZPN and Sportfive, but price collusion between Sportfive and the businesses purchasing the broadcasting rights. However, it received a relatively large amount of publicity in certain legal circles, so it is worth mentioning.

409. The matter applied to the broadcasting rights to football matches played by the Polish national team in the qualifying rounds for the World Cup in 2014: the meetings with Montenegro and Moldova. The matches were to be broadcast in the pay-per-view system, while Sportfive had the broadcasting rights.

410. Sportfive entered into contracts with eleven other businesses under which it awarded them a broadcasting licence. However, the OCCP's doubts were raised by the method of setting the prices for broadcasting – they were not to be less than PLN 20, which arose from the analysis of the correspondence between the businesses.

411. Antitrust proceedings were initiated in November 2012[262] and ended in August 2013.[263] During the proceedings, it was found that the uniform price was not a result of an independent decision of each of the businesses, but the collusion between them which is prohibited by antitrust law. The findings indicated that the initiative originated from Cyfrowy Polsat and therefore not from Sportfive, which had the rights. Penalties were imposed on all the companies, but Sportfive and Multimedia Polska benefited from the leniency programme, the result of which was the abolition of the penalty for the former and a 30% reduction of the penalty for the latter of these companies.

412. In conclusion, it is worth drawing attention to the fact that it was precisely the package sale of television broadcasting rights for sporting events which seem to be one of the reasons why PSFs introduce norms into their regulations requiring the pursuit by sports clubs of sound financial management and is a further argument – if it is admitted in principle – in favour of the admissibility of such restrictions. This is because Polish NFs are indirectly possessors of a range of rights with respect to sport, which they manage and conduct a kind of redistribution of income obtained from the sale of the rights. In the case of such package sales, the failure of one club

260. Communication on the judgment of the Court of Appeal, https://uokik.gov.pl/aktualnosci.php?news_id=2585, accessed on 4 Jun. 2016.
261. *See,* https://uokik.gov.pl/aktualnosci.php?news_id=10088, accessed on 4 Jun. 2016.
262. *See,* https://uokik.gov.pl/aktualnosci.php?news_id=10088, accessed on 4 Jun. 2016.
263. *See,* https://uokik.gov.pl/aktualnosci.php?news_id=10570, accessed on 4 Jun. 2016.

to perform a financial liability with respect to another not only breaches the general rule of the PCC requiring the settlement of liabilities, but also can potentially trigger a domino effect, when one club's debt to another can mean that this other club will default on the payment of its liabilities.[264]

§2. Sponsoring

413. One of the sources from which sports clubs, sports associations and PSFs obtain funding is sponsoring. The support comes from both the State and local authorities. The latter gained such a right upon the enactment of the AoS, which both directly introduced the grounds for the financing of sport (Article 27 AoS) and amended the Act on Municipal Management (Dz.U.2019.712), which was previously very restrictive in this respect. Each year, the Ministry of Sport itself has significant funding assigned directly to the co-financing of sport.[265] The funds are distributed among the PSFs and organizations supporting the organization of sports events. Support also comes from local authorities – it arises from some statistics that culture and sport constitute approximately 2% of the total spending of local authority units. One-time spending of this type does not normally exceed EUR 1 million per year,[266] although, obviously, local authorities and central government administration also indirectly support the development of sport in various ways, if only by financing the construction of sports facilities and, in this last case, the amounts can be significantly higher than provided above.

414. Clubs frequently need to pay for using sports facilities (as is the case, for example, in Kraków), but the support sometimes also assumes the form of an exemption from fees for the use of the local stadium (as, for example, in Szczecin). Sometimes, sports clubs receive loans with preferential interest rates from cities, as was the case in Chorzów where the football section of Ruch Chorzów received a loan of Polish Zloty (PLN) 18 million (approx. EUR 4 million) in 2016, which, after all, did not prevent Ruch from being relegated from the Ekstraklasa Division.

415. Local authorities are also sometimes shareholders of sports clubs and provide funding to them as a result (examples of this are Ruch Chorzów, Piast Gliwice and Sandecja Nowy Sącz – in the case of Ruch, the town is the majority shareholder, whereas, in the case of Sandecja, the town is the sole shareholder).

416. From the legal point of view, for some clubs, the receipt of sponsorship means the need to change their legal status. This is because sports clubs are divided

264. The issues described in this point are also discussed in E.J. Krześniak, *Kluby i organizacje sportowe* (…), pp. 496–501.
265. J. Pawłowski, *Finansowy doping nie zawsze trafiony*, Gazeta Prawna, 3 Aug. 2017, accessed online on 6 Aug. 2017.
266. For example, one of Poland's largest cities, Poznań, spent approximately EUR 1 million directly on the promotion of physical culture in 2016, while Gdynia spent approximately EUR 950,000. J. Pawłowski, *Finansowy doping nie zawsze trafiony*, Gazeta Prawna, 3 Aug. 2017, accessed online on 6 Aug. 2017.

into those which conduct business and those which do not conduct such business. Entities that supervise sports clubs periodically check whether those sports clubs, which declared that they do not conduct business, sometimes receive an income from sponsorship contracts. The inspection involves checking the documentation of the general meetings of clubs, including the management reports on the activities of the clubs. Until recently, the conclusion of sponsorship agreements by sports clubs, including those not conducting business was considered 'safe', while obtaining funds from this source for managing a sports business was not seen by the management boards of sports clubs as starting to conduct business. A sponsor is also frequently one of the members of the club or a related party, for which any receipt of valuables by the club is closer in nature to a donation, while a mutual performance by the club, as referred to in the sponsorship agreement – at least the inclusion of the sponsor's name or the name of the sponsor's related entity in the name of the cycle of tournaments organized by the club – is more of personal significance than financial (and this is also the case for the other members of the club who feel they are offering something in exchange for the sponsor's generosity). However, since 2015, the position of the supervisory authorities has been more restrictive, and the mere fact that a sponsorship agreement has been concluded is considered to be the start of business activity.

417. It appears irrational to treat the sponsorship of a local football tournament for a dozen or so people in the same way as multimillion sponsorship agreements concluded by the largest PSFs. Unfortunately, however, it is correct and in compliance with the law. The receipt of funding from sponsorship agreements by the association (sports club) is a business activity.[267] Conducting sports activities alone is not business activity, but can be associated with it. And precisely the conclusion of sponsorship and advertising agreements by sports clubs is an example of such sports-related business activity. The subject has been addressed on several occasions by the ECJ (e.g., in its judgment in *Motosykletistiki Omospondia Ellados NPID v. Elliniko Dimosio)*[268] and the European Commission (e.g., on the German Bundesliga).[269] Both sponsorship and advertising were considered as being of an economic nature, as they satisfy the needs of third parties through the provision of services for consideration, generating specific income for the entity performing this

267. For more on sponsorship in the Polish literature, *see* A. Sznajder, *Marketing sportu*, Warsaw 2015, pp. 232–289 and M. Czakon, '*Wpływ sponsoringu na rozwój dyscypliny sportowej na przykładzie skoków narciarskich w Polsce oraz Grupy Lotos S.A.*' (in:) Młodzi o sporcie 2015. Bohaterowie drugiego planu w sporcie, ed. K. Nessel, Kraków 2015, pp. 91–101; B. Czauderna, '*Rola sponsoringu w sporcie niszowym na przykładzie kajakarstwa freestylowego*' (in:) Młodzi o sporcie ..., ed. K. Nessel, pp. 102–114; A. Kruc, W. Szeląg, '*Wpływ sponsora na rozpoznawalność zawodnika na przykładzie umowy sponsorskiej firmy Milka z Andreasem Wellingerem*' (in:) Młodzi o sporcie ..., ed. K. Nessel, pp. 115–130 and M. Woźniakowski, '*Sponsoring sportu jako narzędzie public relations w komunikacji marketingowej*' (in:) Zarządzanie w sporcie ..., ed. P. Kuźbik, F. Moterski, pp. 37–48.
268. C 49/07, [2008] ECR I – 4863.
269. Commission decision of 19 Jan. 2005 on the German Bundesliga, CMOP/C-37.214, point 21.

activity (the sports club). The Polish regulations do not appear to have any distinctiveness in this respect which would justify a different interpretation than that adopted by the ECJ and the European Commission.[270]

418. At the same time, if it were to be accepted that such an interpretation is correct, numerous sports clubs that conduct business, which declare that they do not do so, are doing this in conflict with the law. This is because a sports club not conducting business is released from the obligation to register in the National Court Register. However, a club conducting business is subject to both the duty to register in the National Court Register (Article 49, paragraph 1 of the Act on the National Court Register) and in the register of entrepreneurs (Article 50 of Act on the National Court Register). In addition, conducting such actual business by the club breaches the provisions of the statutes, which do not provide for this.

419. Two solutions are applied in practice in this respect. The first is the amendment of the club's statutes by introducing the ability to conduct business and to register in the National Court Register. This remedies the situation for the future and brings about compliance of the legal situation with the actual situation, but it does not release the club from the risk of liability for breaching the provisions of the AoS and the provisions of the Act on the National Court Register in the past.

420. The second solution is for the clubs not intending to conduct business to conclude donation agreements instead of sponsorship agreements. The acceptance of a donation does not constitute a business activity. However, whether it can be considered as such depends on the content of these agreements (no counter performances from the club).

§3. Merchandising

421. Of the interesting issues related to merchandising, attention should be drawn to two important rights of Polish NFs, arising directly from the regulations.

422. First, the PSF (as well as the POC and the Polish Paralympic Committee) has the right to use items constituting a representation of the national team's kit (or the kit of the Olympic team and the kit of the Paralympic team) to the extent specified by the relevant provisions, for its own business purposes (Article 13 AoS).

423. Second, the obligations of the country's representatives have been correlated with the exclusive rights of the NFs. This is because a member of the national squad is obliged to provide his image in the kit of the Polish national team, on an exclusive basis, to the sports association, which is entitled to use this image for its

270. *See*, *inter alia*, G. Materna, *Stowarzyszenie sportowe jako przedsiębiorstwo z art. 82 and art. 86 TWE – glosa do wyroku ETS z 1.07.2008 r. w sprawie C-94/07 Motosykletistiki Omospondia Ellados NPID (MOTOE)*, EPS 2009, No. 12, p. 47.

business purposes to the extent specified by the rules of this association or the international sports organization operating in the given sport.[271] The AoS also introduces the principle that, before qualifying for the national squad or the Olympic team, the athlete agrees to the dissemination of his image in national kit in the meaning of the respective provisions of the Act on Copyright and Related Rights.

424. This kind of statutory entitlement is a specificity of Polish law.

425. For example, under German law, there are no rules that would attribute any benefits to anyone from advertising with the use of the sportsperson's image in a particular kit. The general provisions of German copyright law, which protect the rights of sportspeople (as well as everyone else) to enjoy the benefits from their own image or reputation, determine who is entitled to them. An important role is also played by the jurisprudence. According to the view adopted in the German case law, images of football teams primarily serve commercial and advertising purposes and therefore the provisions allowing for the (free) so-called admissible use do not apply. But, for example, the use of photographs of this kind on a wall calendar was considered acceptable. This is because it was accepted that calendars of this kind primarily have an informational and not an advertising function. This is also the case when using a photograph of a known tennis player on the cover of a tennis handbook. It was concluded in the jurisprudence that there is no need to receive consent from the sportsperson in this case.[272] This does not change the fact that German national sports associations frequently introduce the requirement to obtain the sportsperson's consent for the use of his image as a condition, for instance, of granting an appropriate licence. However, whether this will be admissible will be determined by the circumstances of the particular case and not by a blanket legal norm written directly into an Act.

426. The rule that, before qualifying for the national squad or Olympic team, the contestant agrees to the distribution of his image in the national team's kit, has already given rise to doubt under the previous legal regulations in Poland. It was prejudged by the Supreme Court in the precedent case involving the use of an image of the Polish national football team's player – M. Żurawski. The Supreme Court held that the player's mere willingness to be a part of the national squad (the term is broader than 'national team')[273] is equivalent to his consent to the use of his image to the extent specified in Article 33, paragraph 1 AoQS (this issue is currently regulated in Article 14, paragraph 1 AoS). The Supreme Court did not confine itself in this respect to the linguistic interpretation of the provision, but also

---

271. After all, the POC has similar rights – in accordance with Art. 14, para. 2 AoS, upon selection for the Olympic team, the Olympic team member shall make his image available in the Olympic kit in the national colours, on the principle of exclusivity, to the POC, which is entitled to use this image for its business purposes to the extent specified by its rules or the rules of the IOC.

272. However, the German court upheld Olivier Khan's action against an entity that produced a computer game using his image. The court took the stance that the use of the image of the German football team's goalkeeper without his permission breaches his rights. This case has been described in Haas, Martens, *Sportrecht*, pp. 213–214.

273. *See* M. Badura, H. Basiński, G. Kałużny, M. Wojcieszak, *Ustawa o sporcie ...*, pp. 227–228.

conducted a systemic interpretation. The Court held that the relevant provisions of the AoS (*lex specialis*) rule out the application of the copyright law (*lex generalis*). Although, in principle, the dissemination of an image requires the permission of the person presented on it (this is referred to in Article 81 of the Copyright Law), the use of the image of a member of the national team by the NFs is admissible if he satisfies the requirements of the AoS, without the need to obtain separate consent given in the procedure provided for in the Act on Copyright and Related Rights. However, the Supreme Court withdrew from unambiguously prejudging whether the provision of the AoQS (transferred, in principle, unchanged to the AoS) is in compliance with the Polish Constitution, indicating that the Constitutional Tribunal has the jurisdiction to consider whether an applicable provision is in conflict with the Polish Constitution and simultaneously stating that, in the case in question, there are 'serious doubts as to the compliance' of the respective provision of the AoQS with the Polish Constitution.[274]

427. After all, this issue gives rise to disputes in the doctrine to this day. Regardless of the above judgment of the Supreme Court regarding the respective regulations of the AoS, most serious allegations were raised, including the allegation of a breach of the Polish Constitution (specifically, Article 21, paragraph 2, expressing the principle of admissibility of expropriation only for public purposes and for due compensation, as well as Article 31, which expresses the principle of human freedom) by recognizing that such a regulation is actual expropriation and interference in the realm of 'a person's rights … his personal interests, namely his image, simultaneously depriving the addressee of the freedom to decide to grant permission for its use'.[275] In turn, other authors recognize that this regulation is fully valid, whereas there cannot be talk of any inconsistency with the Polish Constitution.[276] Finally, some take an intermediate position, accepting, in principle, the structure of the compulsory consent, simultaneously drawing attention to both the statutory shortcomings and not fully precise structure of the provision of Article 14 AoS,[277] as well as the doubts that can arise after reading the justification of the cited judgment of the Supreme Court, especially with regard to the assumption that was made that the

---

274. Judgment of the Supreme Court of 16 Dec. 2009, I CKN 160/09, OSNC 2010, Nos 7–8, item 114, p. 131.
275. *See* P. Podgórski, *Członek reprezentacji zrzeka się wizerunku*, Rzeczpospolita of 5 Aug. 2014 and R. Szczepaniak, *Problem prawa do wizerunku sportowca – reprezentanta kraju*, MoP 2007, No. 17, pp. 948–959.
276. *See, inter alia*, M. Świeca, *Konstytucja RP jako pospolita wymówka*, Rzeczpospolita of 22 Aug. 2014.
277. *See* W. Cajsel, *Ustawa o sporcie. Komentarz …* , pp. 119–120 and W. Cajsel, *Ustawa o sporcie kwalifikowanym. Komentarz, Warszawa 2006*, pp. 171–172; M. Badura, H. Basiński, G. Kałużny, M. Wojcieszak, *Ustawa o sporcie …* , pp. 230–231; J. Balcarczyk, '*Prawo do sportowego wizerunku w ujęciu prawa polskiego*' (in:) Współczesne problemy prawa prywatnego. Księga pamiątkowa ku czci profesora Edwarda Gniewka, ed. J. Gołaczyński, P. Machnikowski, Warszawa 2010, p. 5.

mere willingness to be selected for the national squad simultaneously means the consent of the interested party for using his image.[278]

§4. Ownership of Clubs

428. The Polish organizational model of sport is based on the principle of autonomy of sport and is included within the concept of the European model of sport.

429. Sports activities are conducted in the first place by sports associations and sports clubs. Sports clubs can operate in forms with legal personality (Article 3, paragraph 2 AoS). The most commonly encountered legal forms of sports clubs in Poland are joint-stock companies and limited liability companies, as well as associations. The advantage of this last form is the simple procedure of establishment and the lack of the need to contribute capital by the founders. Theoretically, sports clubs may also operate as cooperatives and foundations, although this is rather not encountered in practice. Sports activities can also be conducted in other legal forms – if only in the form of so-called sole proprietorships, but a sports club cannot be operated as a sole proprietorship, although it is not known why.

430. The rules do not fundamentally introduce ownership restrictions – therefore, the shareholders of sports clubs can be both individuals, companies and other legal persons, local authority units and churches. The only applicable restriction is the prohibition of a person or entity holding shares or stocks in one sports club from holding stocks or shares in another sports club, which is a member of a PSF participating in sports competitions in the same sport (Article 10 AoS).[279] The reason for this is to avoid the phenomenon that is known from other sectors of the economy, when the stronger competitor acquires weaker competitors, thereby increasing its own competitive advantage. This would not make sense in sport – competition is the essence of sport, while pure competition is only possible if the sports clubs participating in the rivalry are not controlled by the same owner.

431. The objectives of the owners of sports clubs in Poland obviously differ. The objective can be the sports result, financial gain (in Polish realities, there should rather be talk of a reduction of losses), support for the local community or prestige related to being the owner of a sports club.[280]

---

278. *See Ustawa o sporcie …* , ed. M. Gniatkowski, pp. 90–91. *See also* the carefully considered opinions of M. Wach, *Personality merchandising jako instytucja stosowana do wykorzystania wizerunku sportowca w celach promocyjnych i reklamowych*, PPH 2010, No. 10, pp. 22–29.

279. The prohibition also encompasses holding managerial and supervisory positions in such clubs.

280. M. Karwiński, *Wpływ systemu licencyjnego na zarządzanie klubami polskiej ekstraklasy piłkarskiej* [in:] Zarządzanie w sporcie. Organizacje. Ludzie. Marketing, Łódź 2015, pp. 129–140.

432. The amendments to the Polish AoS currently being planned will additionally increase these limitations with the introduction of a prohibition on the provision of services to PSFs by people holding managerial positions in these associations or by their relatives.

433. According to data from July 2019, almost 15,000 sports clubs were operating in Poland at the end of 2018.[281] These numbers may seem impressive, but only until they are compared with data from other countries. For example, Germany has more than 90,000 sports clubs.[282]

434. Poland has a much smaller number of sports clubs than in Germany. This primarily appears to be not only because of the generally lower interest in social activity than in Germany but also because of the lower level of interest in playing sport within organized structures.

435. The Polish AoS also, as far as I am concerned completely unnecessarily, introduces a special form of sports club, the so-called pupils' sports club. The only justification for separating this legal form of sports club is probably the assumption that the sports environment may have problems with registering the associations, so, in the case of school sports, a special, simplified subtype of the sports club needs to be established, which will not require registration.[283] In practice, the differences between pupils' sports clubs and other sport clubs boil down to precisely the different (simplified) procedure of registering the latter, including automatic registration, unless the authority to which the application has been addressed has meanwhile refused to make the register entry.

436. About 38% of all sports clubs in Poland are precisely pupils' clubs.[284]

437. The ownership structures of Polish clubs are subject to change, although they are relatively stable. In contrast, the spectacular transactions known even from the United States, involving the transfer of clubs with licences authorizing them to play in a professional league from one city to another, almost do not take place in Poland. Few (often unsuccessful) attempts to conduct such transactions are rather exceptions confirming the rule. The most famous case is the sale by a company controlled by Z. Drzymała, owner of Groclin, a football club playing in the first division, Ekstraklasa, of all the shares in Dyskobolia Grodzisk Wielkopolski (a football club) to the owner of a club with long traditions, but at that time, in a lower division – Polonia Warszawa. This actually enabled Polonia Warszawa to be pushed in 'through the back door' to the Ekstraklasa. This is because, as a result of the transaction, Groclin's club, Dyskobolia Grodzisk Wielkopolski changed its name to KSP Polonia Warszawa, while the 'old' Polonia was withdrawn from the league. On the

---

281. Central Statistical Office report of 31 Jul. 2019 'Physical education in Poland in 2018'.
282. *See* Haas, Martens, *Sportrecht*, p. 22.
283. M. Badura, H. Basiński, G. Kałużny and M. Wojcieszak refer to the former President of the POC, Stanisław Paszczyk, as the instigator of this organizational form. *See* M. Badura, H. Basiński, G. Kałużny, M. Wojcieszak, *Ustawa o sporcie* ..., pp. 42–43.
284. Central Statistical Office report of 2019 'Physical education in 2017 and 2018'.

sideline, it can be mentioned that, when the new owner of Polonia Warszawa wanted to conduct a similar move and sell Polonia (and, in fact, its licence) to the next candidate to Ekstraklasa – the owner of the club GKS Katowice, the transaction was blocked by the fans, who started mass protests.[285]

285. *See* M. Kurek, '*Jak ukształtować ograniczenia przekształceń struktury własnościowej polskiego klubu piłkarskiego?*' [in:] *Prawne aspekty funkcjonowania federacji sportowych. Podsumowanie ogólnopolskiej konferencji naukowej*. ed. M. Biliński, Kraków 2014, pp. 64–65.

Chapter 3. Private Regulation

§1. Introduction

438. Private and public regulations regarding sports and commercial matters intermingle in Polish realities. This is so because, in the first place, the general principles of creating professional leagues constitute a part of the generally applicable provisions, but the detailed principles are private, internal regulations of the NFs. There is also no doubt that it is precisely primarily in sport, in which professional leagues operate, that we deal with issues related to commerce – selling television broadcasting rights, selling the rights to the images of the players and sponsorship. Therefore, matters related to professional leagues will be discussed in this part of the monograph. Licensing systems also have a significant impact on the functioning of sports clubs in this system.[286]

439. Another specificity of Polish law should also be mentioned at this point – while equity restrictions related, for instance, to holding shares in more than one sports club are the subject of private regulation in countries with a so-called non-interventionist model of regulation, the respective rules have been included directly in the AoS.

§2. Professional Leagues

440. Polish law does not contain a statutory definition of a professional league. In the colloquial meaning of this term, it means sports matches played and managed professionally by an entity that has been organized for this purpose. Therefore, this meaning should be assigned to this term under the AoS.

441. In the case of non-Olympic sports, in which PSFs do not operate, everyone is entitled to this right, and it is a manifestation of the practical implementation of the principle of freedom of establishment.

442. In the case of sports in which PSFs operate, the right to establish a professional league by the PSF itself and the obligation of a company (joint-stock company or limited liability company) to take over the responsibilities of managing the professional league was additionally confirmed by the order to establish such a league, if more than half of the clubs playing league matches in the top division operate in the form of public limited liability companies. Only clubs operating as joint-stock companies can take part in professional league matches in team sports – in practice, the decided majority of professional leagues will operate precisely in team sports.

---

286. M. Karwiński, *Wpływ systemu licencyjnego* ..., pp. 129–140.

443. A professional league is managed by a legal entity in the form of a company (Article 15, paragraph 4 AoS), while the principles of functioning of the league are defined by an agreement between the management company and the given NF (Article 15, paragraph 5 AoS). The conclusion of the agreement depends on the minister responsible for physical culture granting his approval. The minister will refuse consent if the agreement is inconsistent with the provisions of the law. Consent is given or refused by way of an administrative decision (this regulation will be discussed below).

444. Of the examples of professional leagues in Poland, the football league (Ekstraklasa S.A.), the volleyball league (Profesjonalna Liga Piłki Siatkowej) and the basketball league (Polska Liga Koszykówki S.A.) can be mentioned. The method of organizing these leagues differs in the details. However, the main principles are the same – the leagues operate in the form of joint-stock companies, the shareholders of which are the sports clubs playing in them and the given NGB. Since the clubs playing in the top division in the league change each year, solutions are required that ensure the practical implementation of the principle that it is precisely those clubs that play in the league in the given year that are its shareholders. In the case of, for example, the football league, this was achieved by introducing extensive provisions into the Ekstraklasa S.A. statutes regarding the obligation to dispose of the shares. If a club loses the right for its team to take part in the Ekstraklasa matches, it is required to sell the shares it holds within thirty days, while only the club that has received the right to play in the Ekstraklasa league can be the purchaser. If the club fails to perform the obligation to dispose of the shares, the Management Board of Ekstraklasa S.A. is required to do so.

445. If the number of clubs eligible to play in Ekstraklasa declines, the share capital shall not be reduced despite the change in the number of shareholders. The number of shares assigned to the individual clubs is increased, however, with the observance of the principle that they are all equal.

446. The supervisory boards of the companies' managing professional leagues are selected with account taken of the parity giving an advantage in the membership of the supervisory board to the best teams of the previous season. Issues related to the functioning of the referees/umpires, observers and safety delegates, the principles of granting and withdrawing licences and termination of contracts between the clubs and the players or coaches are not a part of the responsibilities of the company managing the league – and are, therefore, still within the powers of the NGB.

§3. Licensing Systems

447. Licensing systems of various types are among the key instruments with which PSFs control the entities that are subject to their actual jurisdiction.[287] PSFs

287. We are not talking here about licences in the meaning of the Act on Copyright and Related Rights or the Industrial Property Law of 30 Jun. 2000 (consolidated text: Journal of Laws of 2021, item 324, as amended), but about licences understood as the right to participate in sports competitions.

are also not isolated in this respect. Various types of licences are commonly used in organized sport around the world. Licences may be awarded to sports clubs, sportspeople,[288] referees/umpires or even activists. Their legal grounds, the method of issue and the appeal procedure may differ. Meanwhile, one feature is common, namely the objective which they serve, which is the regulation of access to sports matches and other types of participation in organized sport, which is developed to a greater or lesser extent.

448. Before 2010, the requirement for the sports club to obtain a licence granted by the appropriate NF arose directly from the provisions of the law. The AoQS even specifies what should be attached to the application for such a licence (extract from the National Court Register or from another register, a copy of the statutes or articles of association, and a written undertaking of the sports club to comply with the statutes and regulations of the PSF and international sports organizations – Article 6, paragraph 2, AoQS). In practice, the authorities of the Polish associations were demanding additional information, including financial information, in addition to those explicitly mentioned in the Act. This is, for example, what the Club Licensing Commission for the PZPN did when requiring applicants to present their financial forecasts for the following season.[289] The other conditions and procedure of awarding and cancelling licences were specified in the rules of the respective PSF (Article 6, paragraph 3, AoQS). The club could be deprived of its licence if neither the sports club nor any of the players associated in this club takes part in a sports competition over a period of three successive years (Article 6, paragraph 6 AoQS).

449. Following the discussions in the doctrine, it was concluded that it is not necessary to include the requirement to obtain the licence in the applicable provisions of the law and that it would be better left to the discretion of the given NGB. Therefore, the AoS does not regulate the matter of licences at all.

450. However, PSFs apply various types of licensing systems. The licences currently issued by the PSFs, which are granted first to sports clubs, are certainly not of the nature of legal acts that are similar to administrative decisions or even – as some PSFs would like – directly administrative decisions. Such views were presented under the provisions in force before 2010. To this day, some of the PSFs have not adjusted their rules to the new provisions and still appear to recognize licences as being administrative decisions.[290] In the current legal situation, all licences are no doubt of a civil law nature.[291]

288. With regard to the legal nature of the so-called player's card, which can be considered the progenitor of the licence in the sense referred to in the preceding footnote, *see* W. Cajsel, *Charakter prawny karty zawodniczej (karty zgłoszenia)*, Sport Wyczynowy 2001, Nos 5–6, pp. 60–72.

289. *See* justification to the judgment of the Constitutional Tribunal of 19 Oct. 2010, P10/10, Journal of Laws of 2010, No. 202, item 1344.

290. The Polish Tennis Association is an example of an association, the rules of which are inconsistent with the current law.

291. *See*, *inter alia*, B. Wojnowicz, *Sport: licencja zawodnika jak umowa*, Rzeczpospolita of 11 Sep. 2014.

451. Obviously, agreements on sports 'licences' are not a Polish specificity. This issue is part of a greater whole – the issue of binding a sportsperson or a sports club with norms imposed by another entity. In the Polish legal system, we have clear rules about the rights of PSFs to set organizational rules in a given sport. In legal systems in which the lawmakers do not explicitly grant any entity rights to create sports, regulatory or other norms, the doctrine must cope differently. The model most frequently used is that in which sports clubs and sportspeople are bound by the norms imposed by the given NGB or the international sports federation by 'transferring' the norms imposed by the NGB downwards through successive organizational levels to the level of the club, of which the sportsperson is a member (bound by indirect membership).[292] This is the case in the German and Swiss systems, whereby, under Swiss law, the rules on the transfer of norms down from the association to the club, which may be located several levels below, are more liberal than under German law. An example would be the decision of the Swiss Supreme Court on the Brazilian player, Dodo, in which the Court held that the player is already bound by the norms laid down by FIFA, by the very fact of his membership of the Brazilian Football Association.[293]

452. Contracts, which introduce the obligation of sportspeople to comply with specific norms, are used relatively frequently in Switzerland, as well as in Germany. Such contracts are subject to the general rules of Swiss law regarding contracts. However, in contrast with German law, the view that such norms should constitute general terms and conditions is quite strongly represented in the Swiss doctrine.

453. Licensing systems used in Polish sport differ from each other in the details, but the basic principles are the same. The most commonly used licences are club, player and coach licences. A number of conditions imposed by the association's internal regulations must be met to obtain the licence. For example, a club applying for a licence must satisfy various criteria – sports, infrastructure, regarding personnel and administration, legal and financial. Licensing authorities operate within the NGBs; for instance, in the PZPN, this is the PZPN Commission for Club Licensing, which acts as the body of the first instance, as well as the Appeal Commission on Club Licences, acting as the appellate body.

454. The analysis of the regulations of selected PSFs regarding licensing procedures enables the formulation of certain general conclusions.

455. First, the developed 'licensing' systems are the norm rather than the exception. They are used by both the PSFs in team sports and the PSFs operating in individual sports. Licensing procedures are complicated, although the degree of this complication can vary – the most developed procedure is applied by the PZPN.

---

292. On the basis of the German doctrine, *see*, among others, Haas, Martens, *Sportrecht*, pp. 76–77.
293. *See* E.J. Krześniak, *Prawne mechanizmy zabezpieczenia* ... , p. 18.

456. However, it is hardly surprising that the detailed criteria and infrastructure requirements (regarding the stadium and the related infrastructure) are being introduced by those PSFs in which strong professional leagues operate.

457. The PSF will always be presumed to have the right to issue licences, although the actual right will sometimes be delegated to the voivodship sports associations, the organizers of matches or the sports clubs.

458. As a rule, the licensing procedure takes place in two instances. The most common intra-association regulations provide that the decision of the appellate body is final. Some also allow for the possibility of appeal to the voivodship administrative courts, which is clearly in conflict with the current laws. It is simultaneously clear that the latter provisions from 2010 can no longer incite legal consequences.

459. There is no uniformity regarding the term of validity of the licence – some associations award them indefinitely, while others issue them for a year or two. In certain cases (including the coach licence of the Polish Athletic Association and the coach licence of the Polish Volleyball Federation), the award of the licence depends only on meeting some simple and formal conditions, which are not subject to an in-depth inspection, while meticulous inspections are conducted in others (the PZPN club licence).

460. Meanwhile, as for the technical method of regulating licensing procedures, the form of rules or attachments to resolutions of PSF management boards dominates. In some associations (including the Polish Skiing Association), the rules on licences are comprehensive, while other provisions are brief and rudimentary. Some sets of rules are fundamentally identical, although they apply to different sports (as in the case of the competition rules of the Polish Ice Hockey Association and the PZKosz).[294]

294. Licensing systems are described extensively in E.J. Krześniak, *Kluby i organizacje sportowe* (…), pp. 451–471.

Chapter 4. COVID-19 and Its Impact on National Sports

461. The COVID-19 pandemic has had a significant bearing on the possibilities of playing sports and holding sporting events in Poland. On 8 March 2020, the Chief Sanitary Inspector recommended calling off all mass-audience events of more than 1,000 spectators which were to be organized indoors, including at sports arenas. On 10 March 2020, the Government Crisis Management Team decided to cancel all mass events (as provided for in Article 3(1) of the Act of 20 March 2009 on Mass Events Safety, i.e., O.J. 2019.2171). On 14 March 2020, the nationwide state of epidemic hazard was announced in connection with the spread of SARS-CoV-2 infections (O.J. 2020.433). While on 20 March 2020, the state of epidemic was announced – until further notice – in connection with the spread of SARS-CoV-2 infections (O.J. 2020.491).

462. Announcing the state of epidemic has directly affected the course of sports tournaments in Poland at every level. As of 20 March 2020, a number of temporary restrictions have been enacted on the business operations of individuals organizing sporting events and on those otherwise involved in sports.

463. The original far-reaching prohibitions of March 2020, which in fact put on hold many sporting events in Poland and significantly restricted amateur and recreational sporting activity (part of second quarter of 2020 in Poland saw, among others, a ban on entering forests, while mobility other than for bare necessities was discouraged), were being gradually lifted as of May 2020; however, since March 2020 until the day of this writing, sports and sporting events in Poland have not fully returned to normal.

464. As of early May 2020, sporting activity was partially restored. Among others, the following have been allowed: (1) sporting activity at open-field facilities – up to six participants– for instance at stadiums, playing fields or tennis courts; (2) activities at the Olympic Preparation Centre in Spała; (3) individual practice of professional athletes.

465. The second quarter of 2020 also saw the resumption of Football Major League and Speedway Major League.

466. The shorter season and significantly reduced takings, among others due to complete or partial spectator ban, have adversely affected the financial standing of both clubs and Polish sports associations. The latter have made up for the losses owing to a much greater interest in obtaining a licence in a given discipline. For a long time in 2020 and 2021, the possibility of using sports facilities was – pursuant to the government resolution – restricted to players only, them being defined as individuals holding player licences issued by Polish sports associations. Consequently, many of over seventy Polish sports associations were stormed by potential members. For instance, the number of licence requests placed with the Polish Tug-of-War Association rose from approx. 1,000 per annum to more than 2,000, but per week (in total, in 2020 the association welcomed at least 25,000 new members and affiliated more than 300 new clubs). The number of professional badminton players, skiers (Polish Skiing Association licence holders) and figure skaters (licensed by the Polish Figure Skating Association) at least doubled.

467. In early October 2020, mass-audience events were banned again and fitness centres operations were restricted.

468. This somewhat of a tug-of-war between the government and the Polish sports associations sometimes bore unexpected fruit. At the turn of 2020 and 2021, the government enacted further restrictions on playing sports. As of 28 December 2020, only professional athletes, Polish national team players and children and youths training at clubs affiliated with sports associations could practice and participate in competitions. The Polish Triathlon Association and the Polish Swimming Association retorted by calling up all of its licence holders to the national team (more than 20,000 in swimming alone).

469. Further restrictions seem to be even more far-reaching. For instance, the Council of Ministers regulation on semi-lockdown between 20 March 2021 and 9 April 2021 provides for sports facilities functioning only for professional athletic activity with no spectators. All other stadiums, playing fields, swimming pools, fitness halls, gymnasiums, aqua parks, etc. are to remain closed. In the interest of making a concession to the sports world, the quarantine requirement was lifted for Polish sports associations' national team members, coaching staff, physicians, physical therapists and referees returning to Poland from overseas training camps and international tournaments.

470. The enacted legal solutions relating to sports and mass-audience events, meant to contain the COVID-19 pandemic, have come under much criticism from legal profession circles in Poland. Their arguments include unreasonable favouritism of cultural events over sporting events. Inasmuch as in the second half of 2020 it was possible to hold cultural events (concerts, plays) with audiences, sporting events were to be organized without spectators. The government side partially understood these arguments, yet it indicated that empty bleachers during sports events do not directly affect the course of the game, while cultural events without any audience (albeit reduced) may not be held.

471. The COVID-19 pandemic also means that most countries, Poland included, have stopped anti-doping screening.

472. The pandemic and the related restrictions have not automatically affected the legal relations between clubs and players. Initiative in that regard has been taken both by international federations and by certain Polish sports associations and professional leagues. For instance, the Football Major League, at the behest of all the clubs, has adopted a resolution authorizing the clubs to reduce the players' salaries by 50%. The pay cuts were supposed to be in effect from 14 March 2020 until the end of the 2019–2020 season.

473. Additionally, the Polish legal framework has two institutions which allow for the contractual terms to be modified in the wake of extraordinary events: first, force majeure (Article 475 and 495 of the Civil Code), second, *rebus sic stantibus* clause (Article 357(1) of the Civil Code). The former applies when performance under a contract is impossible. The latter takes effect if performance may be possible, though due to an extraordinary change of circumstances, such performance would entail excessive difficulty for or threaten serious losses incurred by one of the parties, which the parties could not have anticipated upon executing the contract – that being the case, the court may, having considered the parties' interests, with the principles of community life in mind, determine the manner in which to fulfil the contractual obligation, the value of the performance thereunder or, even, rule on terminating the contract. Terminating the contract, the court may also determine the parties' financial settlements.

474. A number of entrepreneurs, including those operating in the realm of sports, have availed themselves of several government assistance instruments throughout the pandemic. The basic instruments of the sort include cash benefits for employers in connection with employee furlough or reduced working time (for sports clubs), so-called stoppage benefits (for athletes), partial subsidies of employee salaries, preferential and sometimes non-refundable (subject to conditions) loans and social insurance relief. The period in which sport scholarships are paid has also been extended (Article 15zzo of the Act on Particular Solutions Related to Preventing, Counteracting and Combating COVID-19, Certain Other Infectious Diseases and the Consequent Crises).

Selected Bibliography

Badura, M., Basiński H., Kałużny G. & Wojcieszak M., *Ustawa o sporcie. Komentarz*, Warszawa 2011.

Balcarczyk, J., Prawo do sportowego wizerunku w ujęciu prawa polskiego (in:) J. Gołaczyński, P. Machnikowski (ed.), Współczesne problemy prawa prywatnego. Księga pamiątkowa ku czci profesora Edwarda Gniewka, Warszawa 2010.

Barta, J. & Markiewicz R., *Widowisko sportowe a prawo autorskie* (in:) *Sport i media – problemy prawne*, M. Kępiński (ed.), Poznań 1997.

Baza Piłkarzy, Nasz wywiad: Okiem agenta piłkarskiego, https://bazapilkarzy.pl/wywiad-okiem-agenta-pilkarskiego/ of 29 November 2016.

Bąba, M., Zapis na sąd polubowny w sporach z zakresu prawa pracy, ADR. Arbitraż i Mediacja 2009, No. 4.

Beloff, M., Kerr T., Demetriou M. & Beloff R., *Sports Law*, London 2012.

Bidziński, M., Kontrola i nadzór nad polskimi związkami sportowymi (in:) T. Gardocka, D. Jagiełło (ed.), Problemy prawne na styku sportu i medycyny, Warszawa 2015.

Borges, M.F.P., Verbandsgerichtsbarkeit Und Schiedsgerichtsbarkeit Im Internationalen Berufsfussball: Unter Berücksichtigung Der Verbandsinternen FIFA-Rechtsprechung In Bezug Auf Die Lex Sportiva, Frankfurt am Main 2009.

Brodecki, Z. & Rischka-Słowik B., *Jaki świat, takie igrzyska*, Gdańskie Studia Prawnicze, vol. XXVI, 2011.

Cajsel, W., Charakter prawny karty zawodniczej (karty zgłoszenia), Sport Wyczynowy 2001, No. 5–6.

Cajsel, W., Ustawa o sporcie. Komentarz, Warsaw 2011.

Cajsel, W., Zasady zatrudniania obcokrajowców w polskich klubach (na przykładzie koszykówki), Sport Wyczynowy 2004, No. 11–12.

Cajsel, W., Ustawa o sporcie kwalifikowanym. Komentarz, Warszawa 2006.

Chełmecki, B., *Rola menadżera w polskim związku sportowym a jego przygotowanie zawodowe*, doctorate thesis submitted in 2015 at the Józef Piłsudski University of Physical Education in Warsaw, Faculty of Physical Education (unpublished).

Cyrol, T., Mediacja sportowa w Polsce, Kwartalnik ADR Nr 4, 201.

Czakon, M., Wpływ sponsoringu na rozwój dyscypliny sportowej na przykładzie skoków narciarskich w Polsce oraz Grupy Lotos S.A. (in:) K. Nessel (ed.), Młodzi o sporcie 2015. Bohaterowie drugiego planu w sporcie, Kraków 2015.

Selected Bibliography

Czauderna, B., Rola sponsoringu w sporcie niszowym na przykładzie kajakarstwa freestylowego (in:) K. Nessel (ed.), Młodzi o sporcie 2015. Bohaterowie drugiego planu w sporcie, Kraków 2015.

Dajczak, W., Kodeks zobowiązań jako lekcja metody prawnoporównawczej, KPP 2014, z. 4.

Deutsch, E., Das 'sonstige Recht' des Sportlers aus der Vereinsmitgliedschaft (in:) E. Deutsch (ed.), Teilnahme am Sport als Rechtsproblem. Verbands-, vereins- und deliktsrechtlichen Probleme, Heidelberg 1993.

Dobrowolski, P., *Ustawowy monopol w sporcie nie jest potrzebny*, communication No. 16 of 6 July 2012, http://bit.ly/1RMOi4X.

Doliński, Ł., *W jaki sposób Agent Sportowy może pomoc w rozwoju Twojej kariery?*, http://www.virtualsportagent.pl/articles/54/n/11.

Dróżdż, M., Odpowiedzialność deliktowa oraz kontraktowa organizatora imprezy masowej, PS 2002, No. 10.

Dróżdż, M., Glosa do wyroku Sądu Najwyższego z dnia 19 października 2012 r., IV CSK 439/11, Ius Novum 2013, No. 2.

Dróżdż, M., Potrzeba zmian ustawy o bezpieczeństwie imprez masowych. Praktyczne problemy z jej zastosowaniem – wybrane zagadnienia. Ius Novum 2014, No. 3.

Flejszar, R., *Ugodowe rozwiązywanie sporów z zakresu prawa pracy*, Studia z zakresu prawa pracy i polityki społecznej 2010, No. 1.

Foster, K. 'Lex Sportiva and Lex Ludica: The Court of Arbitration for Sport's Jurisprudence'. *Entertainment and Sports Law Journal* no. 3 (2004).

Fundowicz, S., *Prawo sportowe*, Warsaw 2013.

Gábriš, T., *International Encyclopaedia of Law. Sports Law. Slovakia.* Alphen aan den Rijn: Kluwer Law International, 2015.

Gardocka, T. & Jagiełło D., (ed.), *Problemy prawne na styku sportu i medycyny*, Warsaw 2015.

Garett, R.A. & Hochberg, P.R., 'Sports Broadcasting'. In *Law of Professional and Amateur Sports*, edited by G.A. Uberstine, assisted by Joel C. Corry & J.K. Pressman. Minneapolis-Saint Paul: Thomson Reuters, 2014.

Giersz, A., *Cele i założenia ustawy o sporcie* (in:) A.J. Szwarc (ed.), *Ustawa o sporcie*, Poznań 2011.

Giezek, J., Sportowe sankcje dyscyplinarne (in:) Odpowiedzialność dyscyplinarna w sporcie, A.J. Szwarc (ed.), Poznań 2001.

Glinke, T., § 31 GWB – Notwendige Ausnahme zum Kartellverbot oder gesetzgeberische Gefälligkeit für den Deutschen Fußballbund? Münster 2003.

Gniatkowski, M. (ed.), *Ustawa o sporcie. Komentarz*, Wrocław 2011.

Gniatkowski, M., *Zawieranie kontraktów przez agentów sportowców*, http://gniatkowski.com/zawieranie-kontraktow-przez-agentow-sportowcow/, entry of 21 December 2017.

Golat, R., Specyfika polubownego rozstrzygania sporów w stosunkach pracowniczych, Służba Pracownicza 2006, No. 9.

Grayson, E. 'The Historical Development of Sport and Law'. In *Law and Sport in Contemporary Society*, edited by S. Greenfield & G. Osborn. London 2000.

Greenfield, S. & Osborn, G. 'Introduction: Locating Law and Sport'. In *Law and Sport in Contemporary Society*, edited by S. Greenfield & G. Osborn. London, 2000.

Gulak-Lipka, P., *Rola menedżera sportowego w dwutorowej karierze sportowca [Role of an Manager in a Dual Career of Athletes]*, Journal of Education, Health and Sport. 2016; 6 (9):117–132, http://dx.doi.org/10.5281/zenodo.159174, http://www.ojs.ukw.edu.pl/index.php/johs/article/view/3822, and https://pbn.nauka.gov.pl/sedno-webapp/works/750400.

Gulan, U., *Uwarunkowania tworzenia profesji menedżerów sportowych w Polsce*, Doctorate thesis, University of Warsaw, Faculty of Management, June 2012; https://depotuw.ceon.pl/bitstream/handle/item/315/pracadoktorska.pdf?sequence=10.

Hannamann, I., Kartellverbot und Verhaltenskoordination im Sport, Berlin 2001.

Haslinger, B., Die Rechtsprechung der CAS zur Haftung bei Zuschauerausschreitungen vir dem Hintergrund statuarischer Regelungen internationaler Verbände (in:) Verantwortlichkeiten und Haftung im Sport, Baden-Baden 2012.

Haas U. & Martens D.-R., Sportrecht – eine Einführung in die Praxis, Zürich 2011.

Hauser, R., Aspekty administracyjnoprawne w ustawie o sporcie (in:) A.J. Szwarc (ed.), Ustawa o sporcie.

Hilpert, H., Sportrecht und Sportrechtsprechung im In- und Ausland, Berlin 2007.

Jabłońska-Bonca, J., Istotna spójności regulacji prawnych oraz niesprzeczności regulacji pozaprawnych z regulacjami prawnymi (in:) A.J. Szwarc (ed.), Kompatybilność pozaprawnych regulacji sportowych z regulacjami sportowymi, Poznań 2014.

Jabłoński, A., Ubezpieczenie społeczne sportowców (in:) Księga dla naszych kolegów, Prace prawnicze poświęcone pamięci doktora Andrzeja Ciska, doktora Zygmunta Masternaka, doktora Marka Zagrosika, Prace Naukowe Wydziału Prawa, Administracji i Ekonomii Uniwersytetu Wrocławskiego, series of e-Monographs, No. 36, Wrocław 2013.

Jagiełło, D., Ramy odpowiedzialności i postępowanie dowodowe w związku z podejrzeniem stosowania dopingu w sporcie (in:) T. Gardocka, D. Jagiełło (ed.), Problemy prawne na styku sportu i medycyny, Warszawa 2015.

Jaros, R.L., Status prawny sportowców zagranicznych w Stanach Zjednoczonych (in:) A. Kijowski (ed.), Status prawny sportowców, Poznań 2001.

Jędruch, S., Odpowiedzialność za szkody wyrządzone w związku z uprawianiem sportu, Warszawa 1972.

Jóźwiak, P., Odpowiedzialność dyscyplinarna w sporcie, Poznań 2014.

Kaliszuk, M., *Oto najwięksi gracze na rynku menedżerskim w Polsce*, http://www.przegladsportowy.pl/pilka-nozna,oto-najwieksi-pilkarscy-agenci-w-polsce,artykul,556781,1,279.html, published 4 April 2015.

Karski K., Problematyka funkcjonowania polskich związków sportowych – zagadnienia wybrane (in:) K. Nessel (ed.), Bohaterowie drugiego planu w sporcie, Kraków 2015.

Karwiński, M., *Wpływ systemu licencyjnego na zarządzanie klubami polskiej ekstraklasy piłkarskiej* (in:) Zarządzanie w sporcie. Organizacje. Ludzie. Marketing, Łódź 2015, pp. 129–140.

Kępiński, M., Umowa o transmisję sportową (in:) Sport i media – problemy prawne, M. Kępiński (ed.), Poznań 1997.

Kijowski, A., Transfer w piłce nożnej w świetle polskiego prawa cywilnego i prawa pracy (in:) A.J. Szwarc (ed.), Prawne problemy transferu w piłce nożnej w Polsce i Republice Federalnej Niemiec, Poznań 1991.

Kijowski, A., Prawa i obowiązki sportowca związane z transmisjami sportowymi i przekazywaniem informacji sportowych (in:) Sport i media – problemy prawne, M. Kępiński (ed.), Poznań 1997.

Kijowski, A. (ed.), *Prawne problemy sportu zawodowego*, Poznań 1995.

Kijowski, A., Status prawny sportowca zawodowego (in:) A. Kijowski (ed.), Problemy prawne sportu zawodowego, Poznań 1995.

Kijowski, A., Stosunki prawne sportowców z klubami sportowymi (in:) A. Kijowski (ed.), Status prawny sportowców, Poznań 2001.

Kirschenhofer, M., Die Verbreitung von Programmen und Territorialitätzprinzip am Beispiel von Film, Fernseh und Sportprogrammen – Rechtsfragen im Bereich Sport, Zeitschrift für Urheber- und Medienrecht 2006.

Kolasiński, M.K., Subsydiowanie ze źródeł publicznych inwestycji w infrastrukture sportową w prawie Unii europejskiej, Studia Iuridica Toruniensia 2013, volume XIII.

Kolasiński, M.K., Z orzecznictwa Trybunału Konstytucyjnego (sądowo -administracyjna kontrola orzeczeń polskiego związku sportowego w sprawie udzielania licencji na dany sezon rozgrywkowy). Glosa do wyroku z 19 X 2010, P 10/10, PiP 2011, book 12.

Koncewicz, T.T. & Rischka B., *Autonomia związków sportowych: europejski ideał, polska karykatura*, Rzeczpospolita of 4 October 2008.

Korff, N., *Sportrecht*, Stuttgart 2014.

Kornobis-Romanowska, D. (ed.), Sport w prawie europejskim. Współczesne wyzwania dla teorii i praktyki, Warsaw 2014.

Kruc, A., Szeląg W., Wpływ sponsora na rozpoznawalność zawodnika na przykładzie umowy sponsorskiej firmy Milka z Andreasem Wellingerem (in:) K. Nessel (ed.), Młodzi o sporcie 2015. Bohaterowie drugiego planu w sporcie, Kraków 2015.

Krześniak, E.J., Prawne mechanizmy zabezpieczenia realizacji zasady autonomii sportu na przykładzie struktury i sposobu funkcjonowania Międzynarodowej Federacji Piłki Nożnej (FIFA), PPH 2016, No. 2.

Krześniak, E.J., Wybrane elementy z problematyki rozstrzygania sporów w obszarze sportu na drodze arbitrażu (in:) B. Jelonek-Jarco, R. Kos, J. Zawadzka (ed.), Usus magister est optimus. Rozprawy prawnicze ofiarowane profesorowi Andrzejowi Kubasowi, Warsaw 2016.

Krześniak, E.J., Uwagi na temat niezależności i bezstronności arbitra na tle zasad organizacyjnych w arbitrażu sportowym i arbitrażu handlowym, PPH 2017, No. 3.

Krześniak, E.J., Specyfikacja arbitrażu sportowego i przydatność stosowanych w nim reguł przy konstruowaniu regulaminów innych sądów polubownych, PPH 2017, No. 7.

Krześniak, E.J. 'The Court of Arbitration for Sport at the Polish Olympic Committee v The Court of Arbitration for Sport (CAS) – Background, Powers and Authority'. *Young Arbitration* No. 24, April 2016.
Krześniak, E.J., Kluby i organizacje sportowe w prawie polskim na tle rozwiązań zagranicznych, Warsaw 2016.
Krześniak, E.J., Prawo sportowe przyszłości (in:) B. Hołyst (ed.), Księga Pami ątkowa XX lecia Wydziału Prawa i Administracji. Przyszłość Prawa, pp. 457–472, Warsaw 2017.
Kuik, K., Transmisje z meczów piłkarskich – zagadnienia prawa konkurencji UE (in:) A.J. Szwarc (ed.), Prawne problemy sportu piłkarskiego, Warsaw 2013.
Kummer, M., Spielregel und Rechtsregel, Bern 1973.
Kurek, M., Jak ukształtować ograniczenia przekształceń struktury własnościowej polskiego klubu piłkarskiego? (in:) Prawne aspekty funkcjonowania federacji sportowych. Podsumowanie ogólnopolskiej konferencji naukowej. Ed. M. Biliński, Kraków 2014, pp. 64–65.
Kurlantzick, L., An International Dimension: Player Movement, the NBA-FIBA Agreement, and Foreign League.
Leciak, M., *Agent sportowy* (in:) Leksykon prawa sportowego. 100 podstawowych pojęć, ed. M. Leciak, C.H. Beck, Warsaw 2017, pp. 1–3.
Leniarski, R., *Igrzyska olimpijskie 2016. Czym polecą Polacy? PKOl ma problem*, Rzeczpospolita of 19 October 2015, http://www.sport.pl/rio2016/1,130063,1904 9778,igrzyska-olimpijskie-2016-czy-leci-z-nimi-pilot.html.
Leoński, Z., *Odpowiedzialność dyscyplinarna słuchaczy państwowych szkół wyższych w prawie polskim*, Zeszyty Naukowe Uniwersytetu im. Adama Mickiewicza. Prawo 1955, book 1.
Lewis, A. & J. Taylor eds. *Sport: Law and Practice*. Haywards Heath: Bloomsbury Professional, 2014.
Łebek, P., *Autonomia organizacji sportowych*, Problemy Współczesnego Prawa Mi ędzynarodowego Europejskiego i Porównawczego 2011, No. 9.
Łochowski, P., Uwagi o stosowaniu metody prawnoporównawczej w nauce prawa prywatnego na marginesie transmisji spadku w prawie polskim, Palestra 2016, No. 1–2.
Manssen, G., Buchbesprechung von: Klaus Vieweg, Normsetzung und -anwendung deutscher und internationaler Verbände – Eine rechtstatsächliche und rechtliche Untersuchung unter besonderer Berücksichtigung der Sportverbände, http://epub.uni-regensburg.de/9349/1/ubr04075_ocr.pdf.
Masiota, J., *Kontrakty sportowe czytać uważnie*, http://www.akademiasiatkowki.com.pl/b/kontrakty-sportowe-czytac-uwaznie/0 of 19 September 2017).
Materna, G., Stowarzyszenie sportowe jako przedsiębiorstwo z art. 82 i art. 86 TWE – glosa do wyroku ETS z 1.07.2008 r. w sprawie C-94/07 Motosykletistiki Omospondia Ellados NPID (MOTOE), EPS 2009, No. 12.
Mielnik, B., Międzynarodowy Komitet Olimpijski (in:) D. Kornobis-Romanowska (ed.), Sport w prawie europejskim, współczesne wyzwania dla teorii i praktyki, Warsaw 2014.
Morek, R. (in:) *Kodeks postępowania cywilnego. Komentarz*, ed. E. Marszałkowska-Krześ, Legalis/el.

Nowakowski, A., Propozycje zmian modelu organizacyjnego kultury fizycznej w Polsce z 1981 roku. Kartka z najnowszych dziejów kultury fizycznej, Prace Naukowe Wyższej Szkoły Pedagogicznej w Częstochowie. Kultura Fizyczna 2000, book 3.

Onet Sport, *Agenci to rak toczący kluby*, https://sport.onet.pl/pilka-nozna/liga-wloska/agenci-to-rak-toczacy-kluby/gx1zds published 5 October 2016.

Pawlak, Z. & Smoleń A., *Etyczne problemy działania agentów zawodników w piłce nożnej* (in:) 'Annales. Etyka w życiu gospodarczym', Archidiecezjalne Wydawnictwo Łódzkie 2012.

Pawłowski, J., '*Finansowy doping nie zawsze trafiony*', Gazeta Prawna, 3 August 2017, online access 6 August 2017.

Piechota, R., Prawa do transmisji widowisk sportowych – zarys problemu, Sport Wyczynowy 2006, No. 5–6.

Podgórski, P., *Członek reprezentacji zrzeka się wizerunku*, Rzeczpospolita of 5 August 2014.

Powałowski, A. (ed.), *Prawo gospodarcze publiczne*, Warsaw 2011.

Prawo Sportowe, *Agent czy menedżer?*, http://prawosportowe.pl/p,276,agent-czy-menedzer.html of 19 September 2017.

Prawo Sportowe, *Licencjonowanie agentów sportowych*, http://prawosportowe.pl/p,347,licencjonowanie-agentow-sportowych.html of 19 September 2017.

Prawo Sportowe, *Pełnomocnicy w sporcie*, (źródło: http://prawosportowe.pl/p,400,pelnomocnicy-w-sporcie.html of 19 September 2017.

Prawo Sportowe, *Rola menagera w spor*cie, http://sportngo.pl/rola-menagera-w-sporcie/ published 13 January 2014.

Radke, H., Sport i prawo – jakie regulacje, jaki zakres?, Sport Wyczynowy 2007, nr 7–8.

Rawa, K., *Antydoping po polsku*, Rzeczpospolita 4 June 2017.

Report of the Central Statistical Office of 24 July 2017 '*Kultura fizyczna w Polsce w 2016 r.*' [Physical Education in Poland in 2016].

Rischka-Słowik, B., Konstytucja sportu w Unii Europejskiej, Warsaw 2014.

Rymkevich, O. International Encyclopaedia of Law. Sports Law. Russia. Kluwer Law International, 2021.

Sanetra, W., Zmiana klubu sportowego przez sportowca w świetle polskiego prawa.

Sawicki, W., Ustawa o kulturze fizycznej z komentarzem, Kraków 1996.

Schneider, M., Sponsoring von Hochleistungssportlern unter rechtshistorischen und ZX Gesichtspunkten, Frankfurt am Main 1998.

Sławicki, P., Odpowiedzialność dyscyplinarna w sporcie w świetle nowej ustawy, Państwo i Prawo 2012, No. 4.

Smith, A.C.T. & Stewart B., *The Special Features of Sport: A Critical Revisit*, Sport Management Review, 2010, pp. 1–13 available at http://econpapers.repec.org/article/eeespomar/v_3a13_3ay_3a2010_3ai_3a1_3ap_3a1-13.htm.

Sondel, K., Prawo o stowarzyszeniach i związkach sportowych w Drugiej Rzeczpospolitej, Czasopismo Prawno-Historyczne 2004, No. 2.

Sponsoring Sport, *Agencji w piłce ręcznej muszą przyzwyczaić się do zmian*, http://sponsoringsport.pl/aktualnosci/agencji-pilce-recznej-musza-przyzwyczaic-sie-zmian/ of 19 September 2017.

Srogosz, K., *Najlepsi polscy menedżerowie ostatniego okienka transferowego*, https://sport.onet.pl/pilka-nozna/i-liga/najlepsi-polscy-menedzerowie-ostatniego-okienka-transferowego/0t7ep published 06 September 2013.

Starakiewicz, U. & Kubów M., Przejawy przedsiębiorczości w sporcie w kontekście uwarunkowań kulturowych i organizacyjnych rozwoju branży, Problemy Zarządzania 2014, No. 3.

Study on the Contribution of Sport to Economic Growth and Employment in the EU. Study commissioned by the European Commission, Directorate-General Education and Culture. Final Report, November 2012, pp. 1–203, available at http://ec.europa.eu/sport/library/studies/study-contribution-spors-economic-growth-final-rpt.pdf.

Suski, P., *Stowarzyszenia i fundacje*, Warsaw 2008.

Sznajder, A., *Marketing sportu*, Warsaw 2015.

Szumański, A., Prawne instrumenty reagowania na niedopuszczalną niekompatybilność pozaprawnych regulacji sportowych z regulacjami prawnymi w systemie rozstrzygania sporów sportowych na drodze arbitrażu (in:) Kompatybilność pozaprawnych regulacji sportowych z regulacjami prawnymi (ed. A.J. Szwarc), Poznań 2014.

Szwarc, A.J., Sport a prawo karne. Wprowadzenie do problematyki karnoprawnej oceny tzw. naruszeń sportowych, Poznań 1971.

Szwarc, A.J., 'Karny' charakter odpowiedzialności dyscyplinarnej w sporcie (in:) A.J. Szwarc (ed.) Rozważania o prawie karnym. Księga pamiątkowa z okazji siedemdziesięciolecia urodzin Profesora Aleksandra Ratajczaka, Poznań 1999.

Szwarc, A.J. (ed.), Prawne problemy sportu piłkarskiego, Poznań 2011.

Szwarc, A.J. (ed.), *Prawne problemy sportu zawodowego*, Poznań 1995.

Szwarc, A.J. (ed.), Prawne problemy sportu piłkarskiego, Poznań 2013.

Szwarc, A.J., Znaczenie i problemy odpowiedzialności dyscyplinarnej w sporcie (in:) Odpowiedzialność dyscyplinarna w sporcie, A.J. Szwarc (ed.), Poznań 2001.

Świeca, M., *Konstytucja RP jako pospolita wymówka*, Rzeczpospolita z dnia 22 sierpnia 2014 r.

Vieweg, K., Teilnahmerechte und –pflichten der Vereine und Verbände (in:) E. Deutsch (ed.), Teilnahme am Sport als Rechtsproblem. Verbands-, vereins- und deliktsrechtlichen Probleme, Heidelberg 1993.

Vieweg, K., *Faszination Sportrecht*, http://www.irut.de/Forschung/Veroeffentlichungen/OnlineVersionFaszinationSportrecht/FaszinationSportrecht.pdf.

Wach, A., Transfer piłkarski w Polsce i jego regulacje w przepisach sportowych (in:) A.J. Szwarc (ed.), Prawne problemy transferu w piłce nożnej w Polsce i Republice Federalnej Niemiec, Poznań 1991.

Wach, A., *Jaki arbitraż w sporcie*, Rzeczpospolita z dnia 1 października 2013 r.

Wach, A., Wach M., *Spór o spory sądowe*, Rzeczpospolita z dnia 9 czerwca 2010 r.

Wach, A., Odpowiedzialność osób naruszających reguły sportowe lub prawne w związku z UEFA Euro 2012, Warszawa 2012.

Wach, M., Personality merchandising jako instytucja stosowana do wykorzystania wizerunku sportowca w celach promocyjnych i reklamowych, PPH 2010, No. 10.

Wasylkowska, M., *Rola menedżera sportowego w zarządzaniu klubami sportowymi*, Zeszyty Naukowe Wydziału Nauk Ekonomicznych i Zarządzania Uniwersytet Szczeciński, Finanse, Rynki Finansowe, Ubezpieczenia No. 46/2011, pp. 283–293.

Wesołowicz, P., *Rzut za osiem punktów*, Rzeczpospolita of 3 March 2016.

Węglarski, J. & Klenczon, Ł. Agencja Managerska New Sport Star, *Agent piłkarski, czyli zło futbolu. Jaki nie powinien być 'opiekun' piłkarza?*, http://juniorfutbol.pl /agent-pilkarski-czyli-zlo-futbolu-jaki-nie-powinien-byc-opiekun-pilkarza,artykul.html?material_id=55155ef6e1e17ddb7f9e9459 published 27 March 2015.

Wojciechowski, K., Widowisko sportowe w telewizji i audiowizualna relacja z niego jako dobra chronione w świetle polskiego prawa prywatnego, Warsaw 2005.

Wojcieszak M., Prawne problemy telewizyjnych przekazów meczów piłkarskich (in:) A.J. Szwarc (ed.), Prawne problemy sportu piłkarskiego, Warszawa 2013.

Wojcieszak, M. 'Legal Aspects of Football Match Broadcasting'. In *Conference Materials from the International Conference, Legal Problems of Football Sport*. Poznań, 10–13 May 2012.

Wojnowicz, B., *Sport: licencja zawodnika jak umowa*, Rzeczpospolita of 11 September 2014.

Wojtowicz, L., Program ochrony praw własności intelektualnej w związku z EUFA Euro 2012™ (in:) A.J. Szwarc (ed.), Prawne problemy sportu piłkarskiego, Warsaw 2013.

Woźniakowski M., Sponsoring sportu jako narzędzie public relations w komunikacji marketingowej (in:) P. Kuźbik, F. Moterski (ed.) Zarządzanie w sporcie. Organizacje. Ludzie. Marketing, Łódź 2015.

Zedler, F., *Postępowanie polubowne w sporcie* (in:) A.J. Szwarc (ed.), *Ustawa o sporcie*, Poznań 2011.

Zieliński, A., Flaga-Gieruszyńska K. (ed.), *Kodeks postępowania cywilnego. Komentarz*, Legalis/el.

Żyśko, J., Zmiany we współczesnych systemach zarządzania sportem wyczynowym w wybranych krajach europejskich, Warsaw 2008.

Table of Cases

Polish Rulings

International Rulings

Awards of the CAS

Rulings of the ECJ

Table of Cases

Judgment of the ECJ of 11 April 2000 in *Christelle Deliège v. Ligue Francophone de Judo et Disciplines Associées ASBL,* Ligue Belge de Judo ASBL, Union Européenne de Judo (C-51/96) and François Pacquée, C-191/97, ECR 2000, p. I-02549, 58, 365

Judgment of the ECJ of 13 April 2000 in Jyri Lehtonen and Castors Canada Dry Namur-*Braine ASBL v. Federation Royale Belge des Societes de Basket-Ball ASBL,* C-176/96, ECR 2000, p. I-02681, 58

Judgment of the ECJ of 12 April 2005 in *Igor Simutenkov v. Ministerio de Educación y Cultura and Real Federación Española de Fútbol,* C-265/03, ECR 2005, p. I-02579, 58

Index

The numbers here refer to paragraph numbers.

www.ingramcontent.com/pod-product-compliance
Lightning Source LLC
Chambersburg PA
CBHW071448230926
51846CB00001B/381
9789403506371